Policy Making in a Three Party System

POLICY MAKING IN A THREE PARTY SYSTEM

Committees, Coalitions and Parliament

IAN MARSH

METHUEN
London and New York

First published in 1986 by
Methuen & Co. Ltd
11 New Fetter Lane, London EC4P 4EE

Published in the USA by
Methuen & Co.
in association with Methuen, Inc.
29 West 35th Street, New York, NY 10001

© 1986 Ian Marsh

Typeset by Scarborough Typesetting Services
and printed in Great Britain at the
University Press, Cambridge

British Library Cataloguing in Publication Data

Marsh, Ian
Policy making in a three party system: committees, coalitions and
Parliament.
1. Great Britain – Politics and government – 1979–
2. Great Britain. *Parliament. House of Commons*
Committees
I. Title
354.4107′2   JN679

ISBN 0–416–92090–X

Library of Congress Cataloging in Publication Data
Marsh, Ian.
Policy making in a three party system.
Bibliography: p.
1. Great Britain.   Parliament.   House of Commons –
Committees.   2. Pressure groups – Great Britain.
3. Political parties – Great Britain.   I. Title.
JN679.M37 1986   328.41′0765   86–5311
ISBN 0–416–92090–X

Contents

List of tables

Acknowledgements

I owe a considerable intellectual debt to Professor Samuel Beer. Its magnitude will be clear in the following chapters. I also thank Hugh Heclo for advice and criticism. The manuscript owes its present orientation and thrust to Bernard Crick's stimulating assessment of an earlier draft. Distance has magnified my need for the encouragement which all these people have provided. None is of course responsible for my conclusions.

A number of friends have been patient and supportive. I thank Bill and Pat Crowley, Mary Spillane, Roger Luscombe, Chris Cunneen, Van Hodgkinson, Bill Lasser and John Edwards.

Financial support for research came from the Australian Graduate School of Management and the Committee for Economic Development of Australia. I thank Professor Jeremy Davis and Mr Peter Grey. Mary Spillane made possible my survey of interest groups. I thank her for time generously given. Peeyush Gupta and Laurence Hibbert computed the results. Bob Wood's counsel was essential in this task. I thank him for advice and help. My manuscript has been patiently typed and retyped under the direction of Maria Pernetta. I thank her, Pam Rodgers, Monica Bray and Eryl Brady. The tables were expertly prepared by Michael Kockemann. I am grateful to Janet Tyrrell for her suggestions and patient attention. The NSW Parliamentary Library gave me access to their collection of House of Commons Papers. I am indebted to Dr Cope and Mr Greg Tillotson. Staff of the House of Commons Committees were generous in providing papers and in answering my questions. I also appreciate the assistance of members and officials of interest groups who were willing to meet with me. The Australian Studies Centre gave me a congenial 'home' in London. I thank John Warhurst and Professor Geoffrey Bolton.

I am grateful to Her Majesty's Stationery Office for permission to quote Hansard and House of Commons Papers and to the Institute for Fiscal Studies and the Harvard Law Review Association for permission to quote from their journals. Although not directly connected with this study, I owe a particular personal and intellectual debt to Professor Edward Banfield. My most heartfelt debt is to Lorine. Her support was essential and has been unfailing.

Introduction

A House of Commons in which no single party commands a majority of members can no longer be considered fanciful.[1] How would effective government be constructed in a hung parliament? Perhaps two minority parties might join in coalition. Perhaps an executive might be constituted from one minority party with the expectation of support from another.[2] For reasons that will be developed later, it is hard to imagine either method producing effective – even stable – government by itself. Such an outcome would 'break the mould' of the two-party system only in the most superficial sense. A 'strong' executive would be maintained – at least in intention. The power of political initiative would remain wholly concentrated in the hands of ministers. Policy making would continue to be the (largely private) preserve of ministers and departments. Interest groups would remain distanced from the political process. Backbench MPs would continue primarily as 'lobby fodder'.

Arrangements that maintain the central features of the two-party system do not exhaust the possibilities. The outline of an alternative design for government can be discerned in developments that have taken place in the legislature since 1979. This configuration – largely unrecognized by existing political protagonists[3] and barely remarked by commentators – involves restoring a deliberative role in the Commons. This would 'break the mould' of the two-party system in the most fundamental sense. The traditional concern for a strong executive would be modified by the liberal priority to extend political participation and to qualify concentrated power.[4] Parliamentary select committees would share the powers of political initiative now concentrated in the hands of ministers. Backbench MPs would acquire an independent role in the political process. Policy making would become more public and visible. Interest groups would be engaged directly in the political process. The elected executive would be required to win authority for its proposed actions on the floor of the Commons. Policy making would be mediated by the work of backbench select committees as well as by ministers and departments.

Evidence for the style, shape and potential effectiveness of such a policy-making structure is available from the work of the select committees established by the first Thatcher government in 1979. These committees were established for the duration of parliament. Each shadows a major department of state. Each committee has considerable powers to call witnesses and to require the tabling of papers. Each has independent funds to hire research support and to travel beyond Westminster, indeed beyond the UK. Since their establishment, these committees have conducted over 300 inquiries. They have taken evidence from ministers, officials, individual experts, and a host of interest groups. They have been assisted by numerous expert special advisers. In pursuit of their inquiries they have travelled beyond Westminster, throughout the UK, and to EEC countries, the US, Asia and Japan. Published reports place on public record all written and oral evidence. They include extensive information about the workings of government, the attitudes of ministers and about specific policy issues. Much of this information has not hitherto been available. Yet few of these reports have been debated in the House of Commons. Few have had a discernible immediate impact on the issue at hand.

In evaluating the work of these committees, most observers have accepted the terms espoused by the parliamentary reformers.[5] They have adopted criteria which draw upon concern about the balance of power between parliament and the executive. They look to a strengthened capacity within the parliament to scrutinize the work of the executive and to hold it to account. On this view, the new select committees are to be conceived on the model of the Public Accounts Committee. They represent a much extended capacity for parliamentary scrutiny and review.

I propose a different perspective in assessing the potential of these committees. I propose to evaluate their performance not primarily from the perspective of past essays in parliamentary reform. I want rather to approach the committees from the perspective of the dissolution of the two-party system. The chapters that follow evaluate the work of the committees in the context of their ability to create a deliberative role for the legislature. On the basis of the evidence gathered in these chapters, we can attempt answers to some fundamental questions: in a hung parliament, might parliamentary committees with independent powers of political initiative provide an essential buttress to effective government? Are there, indeed, political tasks for committees separate from, but a necessary complement to, the political tasks of the executive?

The grounds for weighing the potential contribution of the committees arise in the first instance from the prospect of a hung parliament. Committees could develop backbench understanding of policy issues and in the process provide opportunities for the executive to gauge likely parliamentary responses to its proposals. Committees might make a further contribution to policy making. In the process of gathering backbench support for the executive might they also provide a context for mobilizing interest group consent?

Recent studies demonstrate that recalcitrant interest groups are the principal cause of policy failure.[6] The durable power and widening political role of interest groups is evident, for example, in Mrs Thatcher's failure to contract the welfare state or to reduce public expenditure. Do select committees provide a context for the integration of interest groups in a way that will protect the public interest? Do they, in other words, offer a remedy to that drift and immobilism that now characterizes policy making?

A role for parliament in the politics of policy making is central to the liberal tradition in British politics.[7] Writing in 1867, Bagehot identifies a number of deliberative functions for the House of Commons. These extend well beyond 'watching and checking ministers of the Crown'. First, Bagehot conceives parliament to have an 'expressive' function.

> All opinions extensively entertained, all sentiments widely diffused, should be stated publicly before the nation. We must take care to bring before [the] . . . legislature, the sentiments, the interests, the opinions, the prejudices, the wants, of all classes of the nation.[8]

Bagehot also conceives parliament performing a 'teaching' function.

> A great and open Council of considerable men cannot be placed in the middle of society without altering that society. It ought to alter it for the better. It ought to teach that nation what it does not know.[9]

Third, Bagehot envisages an 'informing' role for parliament:

> The House of Commons has what may be called an informing function. . . . The English nation only comprehends what is familiar to it . . . a great debate in Parliament does bring home something of this feeling. Any notion, any creed, any feeling, any grievance which can get a decent number of English members to stand up for it, is felt by almost all Englishmen to be perhaps a false and pernicious opinion, but at any rate possible − an opinion within the intellectual sphere, an opinion to be reckoned with.[10]

Most relevant for our purposes, Bagehot attributes to the House of Commons what he terms an 'elective' function.

> Our House of Commons is a real choosing body; it elects the people it likes. And it dismisses whom it likes too. . . . Doubtless in such cases there is a tacit reference to probable public opinion; but certainly also there is much free will in the judgement of the Commons. The house only goes where it thinks in the end the nation will follow; but it takes its chance of the nation following or not following; it assumes the initiative, and acts upon its discretion or its caprice. . . . Because the House of Commons has the power of dismissal in addition to the power of election, its relations to the Premier are incessant. They guide him, and he leads them. He is to them what they are to the nation. He only goes where he believes they will go after him. But

he has to take the lead; he must choose his direction, and begin the journey.[11]

An analysis of committee performance in the context of their potential to equip the legislature to play an effective deliberative role requires evidence of successful committee work in the policy systems that are now (formally) the private province of ministers and departments. In appraising the work of the committees in these 'policy systems' the conventional functional divisions between policy areas – Treasury, Health and Social Security, Education, and so on – are not appropriate. This serves to focus attention on substantive policy issues, not on the process of policy making itself. Rather I propose to examine the work of the select committees as it bears upon those phases of policy making to which the legislature must be introduced if it is to form an independent judgement of policy-making exigencies: first, budget strategy and estimates reviews; second, current government policies and proposals; and third, strategic assessment of existing or proposed programmes.

The role select committees have been crafting in these three phases of policy making will be assessed through a study of all the inquiries originating in the 1981–2 parliamentary session, the reports debated in the Commons in that period, all the reports on major economic issues during Mrs Thatcher's first term, and selected inquiries from other sessions of special interest. This amounts to some ninety-three reports – approximately a third of all the inquiries conducted by committees between 1979 and 1983. In the course of these inquiries, evidence was taken from some 450 interest groups as well as from ministers, departments and various official advisory commissions, statutory authorities and nationalized industries.

The first chapter reviews the development of the principles which buttress the reform movement. How did concern about the role of parliament emerge? What forces within the political system sustained this concern? What principles unite the reformers? What has been achieved under their rubric? Are these principles powerful enough to underwrite the development of an independent role in policy making for select committees?

Chapter 2 reviews committee performance in the context of the budget system. Here parliament's bid for a role in policy making is most elaborated. Because the budget process goes to the heart of the distribution of power in policy making, this is also the most important of the arenas in which committees are seeking a role. Here we shall see if the Treasury Committee displays the capacity for formulating independent judgements on medium-term economic issues and on the government's annual cycle of economic announcements. Can it transmit its judgements to other departmental committees and to the House? Have individual departmental committees displayed the capacity to identify wasteful departmental spending? Are they willing to challenge this spending? Do the results of inquiries suggest departmental committees are prepared to place fundamental economic considerations ahead of sectoral concerns?

Chapter 3 explores how far committees have gone in developing a new role in linking the government, departments and interest groups in reviewing current issues in particular policy areas. In the majority of these cases the issues considered arise from the government's pursuit of privatization and lessened regulation, expenditure control and the reduction of trade-union power. These are the basic themes which the Thatcher government has attempted to incorporate in current policy. In a more plural system, the task of parliamentary committees would be to review, perhaps reformulate, government proposals. They would do so in framing a prudential judgement about the justice and efficacy of the executive's stated plans. Chapter 3 considers whether the inquiries conducted by the various departmental committees point towards this capacity. Have committees been willing to tackle vexed issues? What are the phases of policy making in which they have intervened? Have they sought to engage interest groups in their inquiries? Have committees adopted a sufficiently comprehensive approach? Have they reached conclusions contrary to those of the government? Has partisan allegiance influenced the judgements or constrained the action of committee members?

Chapter 4 considers how far the select committees have gone in developing a wholly new capacity within the public choice system: the capacity to focus interest group, party, and departmental debate on strategic questions – that is, fundamental review both of established programmes and of what might be termed 'emerging' issues. If the political system is to successfully adapt to the variety of pressures to which it is exposed, it needs to be able to reappraise major programmes and to identify emerging areas of concern.[12] The policy system needs the capacity to create a dialogue between participants in a context that produces decisions that can be implemented and that serve the public interest. It needs to be able to deal with issues on their own terms, irrespective of the current distribution of responsibilities between departments or programmes. Ideally committees, in widening access to debate about the public interest, would be creating the framework for a prudent and moderate reconciliation between the protagonists that is consistent with this value. Chapter 4 explores how far committees have gone down this path. Have committees recognized a gap in the present machinery of policy making? Do inquiries demonstrate their competence to tackle these issues? Have the committees reached bipartisan conclusions? Have they recognized that evaluation of such questions requires extensive outreach to interest groups? Have inquiries provided a focus for departmental policy-making activity? Have they contributed to the 'social learning' of interest groups, departments and ministers?

Chapter 5 reviews the impact of these select committee inquiries on participating interest groups. The ability of interest groups to thwart policy making or to produce outcomes inimical to the public interest has been well documented. Their claim to a place in policy making derives both legitimacy and necessity from the political power they can deploy. The need to enlist their support if current and emerging issues are to be managed successfully has been widely recognized. This chapter first reviews current methods for integrating interest groups. Do these strengthen or weaken the attachment of interest groups to their sectional aspirations? It then assesses the contribution of the committees to the integration of interest groups in policy making. It reports the results of a survey of all the interest groups giving evidence to the committees in the 1981–2 session. Is there evidence that select committee inquiries bring essential information about interest group attitudes and arguments to the attention of ministers and departments? Have they been the catalyst for directing interest group attention to policy issues? Is there evidence that they provide a level of access and influence for interest groups that holds in prospect their reconciliation to policy outcomes that are consistent with the public interest? Is there evidence that inquiries provide a more effective medium for interest groups to influence departments and ministers, and ministers to influence interest groups?

A final chapter assesses the outlook for reconstruction of the policy-making system. It first reviews the proposals for further development of the role of select committees advanced by recent procedures inquiries. A two-stage budget process has been suggested.[13] The implications of this proposal for the structure of policy making are explored. What conventions and practices would need to be modified if this procedure is introduced? What are the alternatives in the development of the policy-making system? The chapter concludes with a review of the risks associated with such a development, a summary assessment of the evidence concerning the potential of committees to contribute to effective government, and an estimate of the political conditions required for the realization of what would be historic constitutional development.

We begin with an assessment of the scope and force of the intellectual base of the current parliamentary reform movement and an account of the changes that have taken place since 1979.

Chapter 1

Development of
the select committee system

The 1979 Tory manifesto proclaimed that party's concern for the erosion of the role of parliament. It seemed to foreshadow radical remedial action:

> The traditional role of the legislature has suffered badly from the growth of government over the last quarter of a century. . . . [We] will see that parliament and no other body stands at the centre of the nation's life and decisions. . . . We will seek to make it effective in its job of controlling the executive.[1]

The Leader of the House, Norman St John Stevas, introduced the ensuing Commons debate in the following terms:

> Today is . . . a crucial day in the life of the House of Commons. After years of discussion and debate we are embarking upon a series of changes that could constitute the most important parliamentary reform of the century. . . . The proposals that the government are placing before the House are intended to redress the balance of power between parliament and the executive, to enable the House of Commons to do more effectively the job it has been elected to do.[2]

The changes to which Norman St John Stevas refers involved the establishment of twelve new select committees to shadow each major department of state. Whether these departmental committees represent as decisive a step as St John Stevas implies will be considered in subsequent chapters. Here I want to trace the development of the climate of opinion which contributed to their establishment. Through this process, concerns about the balance of power between parliament and the executive, and the role of parliament in the scrutiny of expenditure, entered the political agenda. These concerns provided the rationale for the extension of parliament's powers that occurred during the first Thatcher government. They continue to be influential in shaping the approach of committee members to their task. Two questions remain however: do these concerns have sufficient intellectual weight to propel extension of the select committee system? In particular, can they mobilize the political coalition necessary to achieve fundamental change?

CRITIQUES OF PARLIAMENT'S ROLE

Criticism of the diminished role of parliament and of the dominance of the executive has recurred throughout the collectivist period. Notable Tory and Labour commentators have favoured reform. For example Sydney and Beatrice Webb's *Constitution for the Socialist Commonwealth*[3] and Harold Laski's *A Grammar of Politics*[4] include proposals that, however different in detail, would strengthen parliament's powers at the expense of the executive and the civil service. These works were published in the 1920s. Sir Winston Churchill's Romanes lectures[5] in 1931 and Leo Amery's *Thoughts on the Constitution*[6], first published in 1951, explore the implications for parliament of a society in which the major producer groups (unions and employers) acquire a political role. None of these reflections had any immediate practical impact. The basic framework of the two-party 'collectivist' system has remained unchanged.

The contemporary movement for reform emerged in the 1960s. It has been led by individuals beyond and within parliament. Beyond parliament, the Study of Parliament Group has been the catalyst for change. Within parliament, individual parliamentarians from all parties have championed reform. The catalyst amongst parliamentarians has been a series of procedure inquiries as a result of which the arguments for reform have become more focused, support for reform has spread amongst members, and parliament's bid for an enlarged role has taken a specific form.

The conventional starting point of the contemporary reform movement is 1964. The year of Sir Harold Wilson's first election victory also saw the publication of two influential books on parliamentary reform. The first, *Reform of Parliament* by Bernard Crick,[7] reflected the views of some Labour members and their academic supporters – including Professors Hanson and Wiseman and MPs such as John Mackintosh and Richard Crossman. Bernard Crick advocated a system of pre-legislation committees. He envisaged parliamentary committees as the bridge between informed opinion, interest groups, and the executive. But he did not envisage a challenge to the government:

> Control means influence, not direct power; advice not command; criticism not obstruction; scrutiny not initiation; and publicity not secrecy. . . . The only means of parliamentary control worth considering and worth the House spending any time on, are those which do not threaten the parliamentary defeat of a government, but which help to keep it responsive to the underlying currents and the more important drifts of public opinion.[8]

Crick maintained this view in a further essay in 1970. Reflecting on then current proposals for new committee arrangements, he was adamant that an extended role for committees did not mean a parliamentary challenge to the executive. 'Parliament should not and does not threaten the ability of the government to govern.'[9] Labour members and sympathizers who initiated the first phase of parliamentary reform generally held to this view.

Tory interest in parliamentary reform has been stimulated by a somewhat different set of concerns. One powerful and continuing theme is parliament's diminished role in public expenditure. This line of argument can perhaps be traced to a second book published in 1964. This was by pseudonymous clerks of the House, Hill and Whichelow. They concentrated on the decline of parliament's traditional responsibility for public expenditure: 'The historic roots of parliament lie very simply in money . . . the control of the nation's money is at the heart of our parliamentary system.'[10] They traced the development of parliament's powers through the series of struggles first with the King and later with the Lords to ensure the Commons held ultimate control of revenue and expenditure. These struggles culminated in the conflict between Lords and Commons over the 1911 budget. The Commons were victorious. But this 'victory' was short-lived. It was overtaken by the emergence of the two-party system. Hill and Whichelow point out that there have been only two occasions since World War I when the House has rejected an estimate – one in 1919 concerned a second bedroom in the Lord Chancellor's residence; the other in 1921 concerned members' travelling allowances.

Thus the themes of the first phase of the parliamentary reform movement were restoration of parliament's historic role in scrutiny of public expenditure and enhanced public involvement in legislation and policy making, but in a context which would not threaten the executive. Those sponsoring reform believed an enlarged role for parliament could be reconciled with unchanged executive prerogatives. Various committee experiments (to be described later) were introduced under the aegis of these principles.

In a pessimistic appraisal of these developments, written in 1976, Professor Stuart Walkland concluded that enhanced scrutiny and unchanged executive prerogatives were incompatible. He judged effective committee work would be thwarted without the power to challenge the executive. He argued that successful committees

> would entail a distancing of the House of Commons from the Executive and a diminution of the powers of ministers and party leaders which could only ensue from important alterations in the political structure of parliament and consequent changes in the conventions which govern its relations with the executive.[11]

The Callaghan government appointed a further comprehensive procedure inquiry in 1977. The Study of Parliament Group's submission reflects the contrary currents abroad amongst its members at the time:

> There are now two main schools of thought. The one that has been dominant this century, perhaps even since 1868, accepts that the power of

Government, derived from the authority it gains from the sanction of a popular franchise and exercised through the party majority in the House, has effectively deprived the House of any direct power of decision making it may ever have had. The Government (Ministers plus civil service) governs, and the Government controls the House not vice versa in any meaningful sense. . . .

There is now emerging a second school of thought which . . . argues that without some measure of power the House of Commons can have no authority; that any power the House has possessed has been so sapped and eroded by Government that it is now meaningless to talk of parliamentary government in Britain. There are . . . still doubts amongst some members of the Study of Parliament Group as to whether the largely adversary party situation in the present House of Commons is not basically hostile to an expansion of Select Committee work and whether a different political structure is not needed to allow Select Committees to realise the potential they undoubtedly have.[12]

Less cautiously *The Economist* editorialized about the decline of parliament in a lengthy article in 1977. Its attitude was clear in the caption: 'Blowing up a tyranny'. These issues remain relevant to current debates:

These pages are concerned . . . with the undignified, inefficient, undemocratic and above all, unparliamentary government that is Britain's lot today. Britain's very stability, the beguiling flummery attending its institutions hold most of its citizens in a trance of acceptance. Britain's apparent democracy is dignified by the golden cloak of its efficient constitutional monarchy whose usefulness as a guarantor of stability in a time of change, its politicians abuse by changing nothing. . . . As Britain's executive has done more, as its involvement in economic life has grown and its impact on citizens' powers and freedoms has widened, the capacity of the House of Commons to investigate its activities has diminished. Students of parliamentary institutions all over the world accept that this kind of scrutiny for keeping officials alert and accountable is as effective as its system of regular committees.[13]

After reviewing various executive devices for maintaining its dominance and their deficiencies and consequences, *The Economist* turned to proposals for reform:

The blue print for a new British democracy on the day after the bang is not hard to sketch, though much harder to design in complementary detail. The central parliament in that British state would . . . distance itself from the executive. Such a legislative parliament would take on much of the power over the executive enjoyed by America's Congress. . . . That such a parliament's deliberation would be respected, its speakers admired, its investigative committees heard, would be ensured by the ancient weapon of the power of the purse and the modern one of televising, in full or edited versions, its sessions both on the floor and in committee.[14]

In a further work sponsored by the Study of Parliament Group in 1980 the editors, S. A. Walkland and Michael Ryle, appraised the development of this debate. Contrast the problematic judgement Walkland had expressed in 1976 with their assessment here: 'There have emerged significant differences about the very purpose and functions of parliament. . . . At the beginning of the 1980s a consensus on the current state and likely future of parliamentary government in Britain is not possible.'[15]

The debate beyond parliament has thus come to focus on the incompatibility between an effective committee system and unchanged executive prerogatives. It has emphasized the desirability of renewing parliament's powers of scrutiny and review – in other words of holding the executive accountable. It has not, however, linked the work of parliamentary committees to the requirements of successful policy making. It has not cast the case for an enlarged role for select committees in the context of the need to accommodate policy making to the rise of interest group power or in the context of the conduct of government if no one party were to control the House of Commons.

Tory and Labour reformers

This debate beyond parliament has been reflected within the Chamber itself. Amongst members one notes first a diffuse concern at the growth and powers of the government. This has gradually resolved, at least amongst key protagonists, into a determination to seek to recover parliament's historic role in controlling expenditure. This movement of opinion embraces neo-liberals in the Tory Party and social democrats in the Labour Party. A complementary movement of opinion, albeit at a more philosophic level, has occurred amongst Liberal and SDP leaders. The latter have been concerned to define the ideological base of their new party. Widened citizen participation has been espoused as a major theme. They have envisaged parliamentary committees as a device for extending participation. But survival has focused the Alliance on plural voting. Its leaders have not emphasized their commitment to more plural policy-making structures. They have not indicated how they would envisage such a development taking shape.

The first group of parliamentary reformers, embracing individuals such as Richard Crossman, Roy Jenkins and Lord Hailsham, was united by concern about the excessive growth of executive powers. In 1976, the Conservative, Lord Hailsham minted the terse phrase 'elective dictatorship' to describe contemporary British government.[16] In language no less sweeping than that of *The Economist* he wrote:

Our Constitution has one advantage of priceless value: its immemorial antiquity which, with its powers of continuous growth, gives it a prestige and mystique not shared by any other nation in the world. . . . I think the time has come . . . to recognise how this nation . . . has moved towards totalitarianism which can only be altered by a systematic and radical overhaul of our Constitution. . . . Of the two pillars of our Constitution, the rule of law and the sovereignty of Parliament, it is the sovereignty of Parliament which is paramount in every case. . . . We live under an elective dictatorship, absolute in theory, if hitherto thought tolerable in practice.

Lord Hailsham reviewed in detail how power had become progressively more concentrated in the executive:

A good deal of water has flowed under Westminster Bridge since the sovereignty of Parliament was first established. And almost every drop of it has flowed in one direction: enhancement of the actual use of its powers. There has been a continuous enlargement of the scale and range of Government itself. The checks and balances, which in practice used to prevent abuse, have now disappeared. . . . Until comparatively recently Parliament consisted of two effective Chambers. Now for most practical purposes, it consists of one. Until recently, the power of the Government within Parliament was largely controlled either by the Opposition or by its own Backbenchers. It is now largely in the hands of the Government machine. Until recently, debate and argument dominated the Parliamentary scene. Now, it is the whips and the Party Caucus. . . . Debate is becoming a ritual dance, sometimes interspersed with catcalls.

He concluded not with a specific agenda, but with a call to reform that continues to inspire many Tories:

I have reached the conclusion that our Constitution is wearing out. Its central defects are gradually coming to outweigh its merits and its central defect consists in the absolute powers we confer on our Sovereign Body, and the concentration of those powers in an executive Government formed out of one Party which does not always fairly represent the popular will.

Lord Hailsham's criticism of executive power has proved influential within the Tory Party. Amongst centrists in the Labour Party in the 1970s, Roy Jenkins has been an important intellectual influence. In a lecture to the Royal Institution in 1977, Jenkins expressed concern about the lack of flexibility and adaptability of the two-party system.[17] He points to the dominance of the struggle for office over the management of issues, the lack of bureaucratic accountability, and the way unions and employers are integrated in policy making, as the root deficiencies in present political arrangements:

I do not believe that we can make our way in the rough world of the late twentieth century unless we can make our society more adaptable, and I do not believe that we can make our society more adaptable unless we can change the political habits which at present hinder adaptation. . . . Parliament is sovereign only in a highly technical sense which has little in common with the normal connotation of the world. Its capacity to scrutinise and control the civil service and to influence policy at the formative stage, is inadequate. . . . Parliamentary sovereignty really means Party sovereignty: and a Party that wins a bare majority of seats in the House of Commons enjoys the full fruits of sovereignty, even if it has won the votes of well under half the electorate. . . .

The great bureaucracies of Whitehall are unadventurous, inflexible and ill-adapted to the task of managing a society with little but its wits to live on. . . . The net result is that British Governments find it all too easy to carry through harmful changes, and extraordinarily difficult to carry through beneficial ones. . . .

This is buttressed by far from satisfactory relationships between Government and the great producer groups – organised labour on one hand and the organised employers on the other. . . . By definition the great producer groups are highly conservative. They derive their power from their weight in the economy as it is, and they therefore have a natural tendency to want the economy to stay as it is. . . . They do not want the disturbance without which growth is impossible.

The left wing of the Labour Party has not placed such emphasis on parliamentary reform. Its ideological roots in Marxism predispose the left towards measures which build from class as the key political grouping. Nevertheless it has been willing to support parliamentary reform partly as a corrective to what is perceived to be excessive bureaucratic power and partly as a step towards its ultimate goal of more direct (but party based) participation. Tony Benn, speaking in a debate on procedural reform, welcomed the establishment of the select committee without seeing in this development any prospect for fundamental change:

I do not entirely disagree with what the Right Hon. Member for Taunton [Mr du Cann] said . . . [but] I do not accept that detailed parliamentary scrutiny of expenditure offers as much to the House as the Right Hon. Gentleman believes.[18]

Development of reform proposals

Within parliament itself the catalyst for reform has been a series of procedure inquiries which began in 1964. In that year a Select Committee on Procedure was established on a continuing basis. Between 1918 and 1964 there had been only three procedure reports – in 1932, 1946 and 1959. Now a systematic review of all important aspects of procedures was proposed. The Crossman reform of select committees in 1966 maintained the spirit, but not the specific recommendations, of these procedure inquiries.[19] In 1968–9 the Report on

Parliamentary Control of Public Expenditure recommended the creation of an Expenditure Committee in place of the long-established Estimates Committees.[20] The Heath Government implemented this proposal after its election in 1971.

Commentators at this time saw in the Expenditure Committee a parliamentary structure to match the reforms in the machinery of government foreshadowed by the Plowden and Fulton Reports. In reflecting on this judgement, the Study of Parliament Group later commented:

> The Procedure Committee had exaggerated the extent to which new techniques of expenditure planning and management were being introduced to British Government. Anxious to produce a new conceptualised model of how Parliament could scrutinise expenditure, it overstated the progress being made in techniques of output budgeting, programme review and accountable management. Careful reading of Treasury and Civil Service Department memoranda to the 1968/69 Procedure Committee, would have shown that, apart from a well developed scheme in the Ministry of Defence, output budgeting was limited to feasibility studies of its application in three or four major Departments.[21]

The Expenditure Committee itself had a checkered existence. The General Sub-Committee gained attention when its adviser Wyn Godley unearthed five billion pounds of 'missing' public expenditure.[22] Deficiencies in the expenditure process that were revealed contributed to a deepened determination amongst parliamentarians to build their role in expenditure control, and to a deeper analysis of the political requirements for achieving this objective. The Expenditure Committee nourished scepticism amongst parliamentarians about the limitations of control techniques, pioneered in business, in a political context. The Expenditure Committee may not have had much direct impact on government. However it performed the invaluable service of introducing to a number of parliamentarians the issue of the size and control of public spending. It created a body of backbench MPs from both major parties who were concerned about public spending. These individuals united in seeking ways to restore parliament's role in assessing and controlling the government's spending bids.[23]

In the wake of the economic vicissitudes which beset Britain in the 1970s, and with the advent of minority government in 1976, the Callaghan administration agreed to establish a further review of select committee arrangements. This procedure inquiry reported in 1978. It recommended the creation of select committees to shadow each major department. It recommended that these committees be empowered to review policy and expenditure. It also suggested a further more comprehensive review of financial procedures. This report represented the first parliamentary acknowledgement that effective reform is linked to diminution of executive prerogatives. It concluded:

> The essence of the problem is that the balance of advantage between Parliament and Government in the day to day working of the Constitution is now

weighted in favour of the Government to a degree which arouses wide spread anxiety and is inimical to the proper working of our parliamentary democracy. . . . It is clear to us that the present financial procedures of the House are inadequate for exercising control over public expenditure and ensuring that money is effectively spent. The House as a whole has long since ceased to exercise detailed control over public expenditure in any but the formal sense of voting the annual estimates and approving the Consolidated Fund and Appropriation Bills.[24]

Following backbench pressure and some shrewd manoeuvring by Norman St John Stevas, the Tory manifesto committed Mrs Thatcher to an early Commons debate of these proposals.[25] This debate was followed by implementation of many of the 1979 Procedure Committee proposals. The departmental select committees were established. A new procedure inquiry into the estimates process was launched.

The development of members' attitudes, and their narrowing focus onto expenditure control issues, can be traced through the evidence given before these procedure inquiries and in the ensuing debates in the Commons. Members have protested (in terms similar to the Study of Parliament Group) that present arrangements subvert their historic role. They have argued that parliament's traditional authority over expenditure needs to be restored. Members from differing political traditions have made common cause of this issue. In his evidence to the 1980 Procedure Committee, St John Stevas defined the basis of this bipartisan approach:

The power of the purse – the authority to grant and withhold supply – has been regarded by most historians as the key to Parliamentary supremacy, first over the Crown and then over the Executive. . . . Struggles between Crown and Commons were the key events between the 16th and 18th centuries which shaped the growth of parliamentary powers. There was no stronger protest against the power of the Executive than Dunning's famous motion of 1780 which stated that the 'power of the Crown is increasing and ought to be diminished!'[26]

St John Stevas went on to trace the transformation of parliament's role in expenditure control from a substantive to a formal function which occurred in the nineteenth century. With the democratization of the House 'the condition of the people' question came to the fore. Supply days were gradually given over to criticism of existing policies and programmes. This development was confirmed by the emergence of the two-party system. The opposition used supply debates to project its alternative approach and to attack the government. Post-war economic growth left this system unchallenged. But the collapse of economic growth in the 1970s restored questions of expenditure control and government efficiency to the political agenda.

Enoch Powell has criticized existing arrangements for their encouragement of irresponsibility in public spending. His concern is the separation of revenue from expenditure. He holds that this prevents the House holding the executive to account. The split between the treatment of supply (expenditure) and tax (ways and means), reflects past parliamentary victories over the Crown. In his judgement maintenance of this separation now encourages financial irresponsibility. These procedures were conceived when there was a real separation of powers. The monarch planned state expenditure which he sought to fund through revenues voted by the Commons. The Commons sought to make the Crown more accountable. 'In retrospect we can watch with sympathy Henry III's Barons and John of Gaunt struggling vainly with the theorem which Edward Hyde and Robert Walpole were to find soluble.' That conundrum was resolved in 'that supreme stroke of political genius of the English people – the combination of Ministerial responsibility for the Crown's actions with the choice of Ministers from amongst those who could command compliance on the part of the Assembly'.[27]

With the development of the two-party system, Powell surmises, the House might have been expected to develop new procedures to check public spending. The possibilities for extending public expenditure were implicit in the preservation of a distinction that the development of party government rendered otiose. With the emergence of a mass electorate, Powell holds, political leaders found it convenient to maintain the fiction that services could be provided to citizens without the associated costs. His solution is to change procedures to ensure the House considers the revenue requirements of government as it considers its bids for expenditure. At the same time, since modern government generates funds by borrowing and by printing money as well as by taxation, parliament needs to widen its scrutiny to cover all the funding sources for public expenditure.

The principal protagonist for reform amongst backbench Tories has been Edward du Cann. His position as chairman of the 1922 Committee gave him powerful leverage. Until the current parliament, du Cann had also been chairman of the key departmental committee – the Treasury Select Committee. Edward du Cann has been amongst the most persistent, articulate, and politically skilful advocates of reform. One can trace through his evidence to procedure inquiries, the development of his views about the best structure of committees. But he has not deviated from principles first expressed to the procedure inquiry of 1977:

> My view basically is a very simple one. It is that the Chamber of the House of Commons . . . is not really a proper forum for detailed scrutiny by Members of Parliament of the activities of government. . . . Broadly speaking government expenditure is not within parliamentary control.

His solution is to create select committees with

> a very clear remit from the House of Commons to do this detailed work of examination of policy alternatives, comparison of out turn with forecasting, and the continual surveillance of Government Departments. . . . It

would then be for the House to decide whether or not it agreed with the Committees.[28]

Three years later at the 1980 procedure inquiry into the estimates Edward du Cann developed the argument for giving committees the power to challenge the executive and, where ministers reject their proposals, to oblige ministers to defend their decisions openly on the floor of parliament.

> What I have argued for a long time is this: for all the great uses of debate and, as a debating chamber, ours is unique in the world, drawing up two sides in phalanxes facing one another is no adequate method of surveying spending programmes in detail . . . you have to establish some other forum. . . . We are now using our old instrument, the Select Committees. . . . I think we could make much greater use of the Select Committee System. This could be most effectively done if they were given authority to propose changes in expenditures within the Budget which is proposed to be spent, or alternatively, reductions. . . . I would hope that Ministers would be required on the floor of the House to defend what their proposals are. I think if the Select Committees came out with a clear recommendation it might be very difficult for Ministers to carry the day with the House as a whole unless their arguments were wholly convincing. . . . There will then be a real chance to change proposals.[29]

Edward du Cann's views have been echoed by other members in debates on procedure over the last few years.[30] On the Labour side strong supporters of placing powers of initiative with the legislature include Michael English, Joel Barnett (both of whom have since left the Commons) and Dr Jeremy Bray. Amongst the Liberals, Richard Wainwright has been an active protagonist.

While most attention has been paid to expansion of the committee system, there has also been discussion of how parliamentary control can be increased on the floor of the House. Terence Higgins (a Conservative backbencher, a former Financial Secretary to the Treasury, later Chairman of the Inquiry into Finance Procedure and currently Chairman of the Treasury Select Committee), argued in 1978, 'The work of Select Committees cannot be as effective as it should be unless adequate time is available for the whole House to debate the Select Committees Reports.' Apart from one estimates day debate, only three committee reports were directly debated over the period of the first Thatcher government. Lack of access to debating time has been a major obstacle to committee impact. The government has conceded three days to committees to review estimates. Otherwise it has rejected extension of committee powers.[31]

Current Tory and Labour attitudes

There are some indications of growing member interest in the parliamentary control of public spending and in procedure matters generally. Since 1979 there have been at least five debates in the Commons on procedure.[32] These debates are judged to have been well attended.[33] Three hundred members were willing to sign a motion supporting transfer of authority over the Auditor General to the Public Accounts Committee in 1982.[34]

The strongest evidence of member attitudes to committees is provided by a detailed survey conducted by Michael O'Higgins of Bath University.[35] This covered 100 MPs in the 1979–83 parliament. Respondents included 14 Tory ministers and 40 backbenchers and 12 Labour shadow ministers and 33 backbenchers. Some 80 per cent of MPs polled thought the new select committee system was a 'much needed reform'. Members placed select committees at much the same level as party committees and letters to ministers as devices for scrutinizing the machinery of government. 91 per cent of respondents said the new system had increased the flow of information to members. 70 per cent judged the new committees had been successful in increasing parliament's ability to hold ministers accountable. Only 30 per cent considered the new select committees had strengthened parliament's ability to control the executive. 88 per cent of respondents (including 67 per cent of ministerial respondents) judged it important to have increased committee scrutiny at the pre-legislative stage. 74 per cent of respondents (including 40 per cent of participating Tory ministers) favoured an enlarged role for committees in the policy formulation stages. 76 per cent of respondents (including 53 per cent of ministerial participants) favoured more committee control over expenditure priorities and allocation. These results indicate quite high levels of member support for committees at the end of the last parliament. Of course the turnover of members and the change in the relative balance of the parties means these results need to be treated with caution in assessing the attitude of the present House. At the least the high proportion of favourable responses amongst the Tory back and front benches suggests members' support for committees will be maintained during the current Thatcher government. These committees will be working in an environment sympathetic to proposals for an extension of their powers.

The most persistent and articulate opponent of the development of select committee powers has been Michael Foot. His arguments deserve attention because such views continue to exercise a powerful influence, albeit for different reasons, over backbenchers and frontbenchers. Michael Foot correctly places the challenge to the prevailing theory of representation at the centre of the argument about the development of select committee powers:

> I am suspicious of Select Committees, because they work on a non-partisan basis, and the basis of the House of Commons is a party argument, and the basis of our democratic politics in this country is based with that in my judgement. . . . What I am saying . . . is that Members of Parliament are sent to this place to represent the people who elect them, and therefore the clash of Parties is absolutely essential to the whole operation. That is what

democracy is about. If you drain that away in too many non-partisan activities then you will destroy party democracy in this country. . . . The bulk of the activities in this place should be on the basis of the party clash which is the democratic clash in this country.[36]

The notion that political parties might become less ideological and might lose their encompassing social bases is not congenial to this view. Equally, the notion that citizens might mobilize for political purposes through political parties as well as interest groups is, on this view, unacceptable. Michael Foot's views have been echoed by Gerald Kaufmann. Speaking in a 1979 Commons debate on procedure Kaufmann argued:

It is not . . . the role of this Chamber to place itself in direct contention with the Executive as some form of alternative government. This House of Commons is not the government and it is not its job to try to be a government. . . . Select Committees in direct contention with the government departments that they are designed to shadow [would] be very dangerous for this country and for the way it is governed on the basis of parties, with an Opposition legitimately seeking to replace the government. . . . These Committees will obviously evolve their own policies. . . . The coalition policies thus evolved will carry great weight, because the newspaper headline 'All Party Committee proposes this or that' is a very great and potent pressure on any government and any party. . . . The policies that they propose . . . will buttress either the government or the Opposition by giving to one side or another a non-partisan seal of approval. Whichever way they go, they will seriously damage the party system which we have in this country and which is a valuable part of our Parliament.[37]

The Labour Party's attitudes to further select committee reform is unclear. The front bench includes two members who have been active on the Treasury Committee. But the leadership might be expected to be strongly influenced by the party's historic role as the political champion of the trade unions and of the working class generally. These traditions may be expected to continue to exercise strong influence despite the evident disintegration of working-class voting solidarity.[38] If further reform required diminution of executive prerogatives Labour would probably be hostile. More radical groups in the Labour Party have emphasized reform proposals which strengthen the role of the party against ministers. Tony Benn has supported the development of select committee powers. But his support for this development is ancillary to other proposals to make ministers subordinate to the party and to widen participation at this level. The proposals for radical reform sponsored by the Campaign Group of the Labour Party will be reviewed in the last chapter. The left could be expected to oppose any extension of select committee powers that threaten the exclusive representational role of the parties.

Conservative ministers have so far not taken a public stand on the general principle of further reform. Their reaction, perhaps not unexpectedly, has been cautious support for reforms that coincide with what they take to be their own purposes. Thus Treasury ministers have been willing to encourage provision of more information to the House in the belief that this would aid expenditure control. Similar sentiments led them to support the adoption of procedures to give select committees new opportunities to scrutinize the estimates. They have, however, drawn back from any proposals which threaten to trespass directly on established ministerial prerogatives.[39] In rejecting proposals for more power for committees, the government has argued that present procedures need to be assimilated before further reforms can be considered. It has not rejected out of hand the possibility of further concessions. That said, a number of parliamentarians have expressed the view that the reforming impulses of the Thatcher government were spent in its first term.[40]

The Alliance and parliamentary reform

Argument within parliament has concentrated on restoring parliament's historic role over appropriations and taxation. Here the reform movement has been spearheaded by Tories. Beyond parliament, the Alliance has taken a strong stand on the general principle of parliamentary reform. The Liberal Party has sponsored decentralist and participative approaches. But these go well beyond the parliamentary arena.[41] The new Social Democratic Party has given most emphasis to parliamentary reform. Its proposals are diffuse and unfocused. But its arguments draw on the view that a more plural structure of policy making would accord better with a more fragmented political environment. It looks to a greater use of parliamentary committees as a source of more flexible and adaptable policies. Dr David Owen offers the most extensive programme in his book: *Face the Future*.[42] Owen's remedies seek to extend participation without embracing the values of radical democracy. He unites a sympathy for the Guild Socialism represented by G. D. H. Cole with a concern for effective central power which marked the Webbs. Dr Owen writes: 'The task now . . . is to build up through democratic involvement a sense of community in order to rediscover a responsibility from the individual to the State.'[43] He argues the real message of the Crossman Diaries is that:

> Ministers confront an appallingly detailed workload and an amazing range of activity, and the extent of Ministerial discretion is matched only by the irrelevance of most of the supposed parliamentary controls of the executive. . . . It is the relationship between politicians in government and civil servants which is crucial for understanding the nature of modern government . . . parliamentary scrutiny and public scrutiny should focus on the specific minister responsible for a decision and named civil servants responsible for decisions that are not referred to the Minister.[44]

Dr Owen places select committees at the forefront of his proposals to reform the policy-making system. He sees them easing a number of the problems associated with the present structure of policy making – for example ministerial overload, the privileged access of sectional interests, excessive civil service caution, and an inadequately informed public opinion:

The practice of blurring accountability by Ministers retreating behind Cabinet decisions, or civil servants behind Committee decisions should be challenged through their accountability to select committees. . . . The more Parliament and the public hear and see all these private arguments fully exposed before decisions have to be made, the more likely it is that ministerial decisions will reflect the wider debate. . . . In Britain there is a danger that there is no productive tension between the Executive and Parliament, within the Executive, or between Ministers and civil servants. . . . An important task of the Select Committee is to lead and inform public discussion about what government is about to do, or has failed to do or ought to be doing. . . . If the vested interests can be mobilised to put pressure on decision making, why cannot public opinion be mobilised as well. . . . The way a Minister interacts with Parliament and Parliament with a Minister will determine whether or not Parliamentary democracy can be revived in Britain. The role and place of Select Committees within the Parliamentary system will probably be the decisive factor. . . . Select Committees have the potential to provide the varied stimulus which is needed in many areas of Parliamentary government. . . . Movements towards Select Committee reform has over the past fifteen years been the most successful area of parliamentary reform.[45]

In a subsequent article Dr Owen repeats his argument for an enlarged role for committees.[46] He joins this suggestion to a long list of proposed changes in the structure and management of the civil service. It seems clear that whilst generally disposed towards an enlarged role for parliament and whilst conceiving a more plural policy-making structure as a remedy for present political vicissitudes, Dr Owen has a miscellany of changes in mind. Translating his loose agenda into a more precise programme will strengthen not only the credibility of his proposals but also their prospects of being implemented were his party to gain pivotal influence in parliament.

The SDP President, Mrs Shirley Williams, has written in favour of a pre-legislative role for select committees:

Select Committees are excellent instruments for exploring the policy making of departments and the relations between departments and interest groups. . . . I would advocate no legislation should be presented to Parliament in future without first being discussed in draft form with the appropriate Select Committee.[47]

EXTENSION OF COMMITTEE POWERS: 1979–83

Further development of parliament's powers occurred during the first Thatcher government. This covered the role of select committees in the estimates process, the form and scope of the financial information supplied to parliament, the control and powers of the Auditor General and the use of select committee procedures in reviewing proposed legislation. These developments are reviewed in turn.

The estimates process

The 1979 Procedure Report included a recommendation to establish a further review of financial procedures. Norman St John Stevas gained endorsement from Cabinet for this proposal.[48]

A procedure inquiry under the chairmanship of Terence Higgins was set up in 1979. Its charter involved evaluation of the appropriations process. This committee reported in the 1980–1 session.[49] The government accepted key recommendations[50] which were first embodied in procedures in the 1982–3 session.[51] Under the new procedure, departmental select committees can propose reductions in departmental estimates. Three days (currently used by the Opposition as supply days) have been set aside for these debates. Parliament can, if it chooses, vote on recommendations from its committees under an amendable motion. The first such debate in January 1983 did not go beyond a 'take note' motion. The 1983 election foreclosed further development of this procedure. Thus the House has still to explore the implications of its new powers.

The new procedure does not go as far as the Estimates Report recommended. On the important issue of the amount of time to be available for debate, the Procedure Committee recommended eight days. The government conceded only three days.

The report reflects the current of opinion abroad amongst reform-minded parliamentarians:

> Fundamental to any scheme must be that it is the right of the House of Commons to authorise or refuse supply expenditure. Subject to this basic principle any changes must seek to ensure the House can both scrutinise and control expenditure.[52]

The report considers whether select committees should themselves be authorized to amend the estimates downwards – which could then be reversed by the House – or to propose changes to the House. It opts for the latter, more cautious, path. The advocates for a more trenchant role for committees included two leading Tories (Edward du Cann and Norman St John Stevas) and one former senior Labour Minister (Joel Barnett).

The select committees were not slow to respond to this development. As we shall see in the next chapter, several departmental committees approached scrutiny of the 1981–2 estimates with these recommendations in mind. The Energy Committee indicated its dissatisfaction with particular estimates. It foreshadowed its intention to propose changes. The Foreign Affairs Committee expressed its opposition to some items in the overseas aid vote. The Treasury Committee indicated it would have invited the House to vote on an EEC item in the Summer Supplementary Estimates.

The first debates under the new procedure occupied a half day of sittings. Three items were considered – spending by the Overseas Development Agency on airport development in the Turks and Caicos Islands (proposed by the Foreign Affairs Committee) and two votes of the Stationery Office (proposed by the Treasury Committee). How the committees make use of this new procedure in the current parliament will presumably be one important influence on their further development. This will be considered in the final chapter.

Financial information

The availability of financial information was first taken up by the Expenditure Committee in a report in the 1977–8 session.[53] Subsequently both the Public Accounts Committee and the Treasury commented on its suggestions.[54] The decision to review financial procedure gave new impetus to the issue. The Procedure Committee (Supply) invited the Treasury Committee to recommend an improved format for the estimates.

Dr Jeremy Bray outlined the continuing problems arising from present arrangements in a speech to the House in 1982:

> To be effective, the votes in the House will have to be matched by changes in the structure of the Votes. There was no single vote that covered Concorde expenditure. There were constant scandals about the odd 100 million pounds tucked away here and there in Votes, which were being put towards Concorde on the sly by Ministry of Aviation officials.
>
> This question arose in the Treasury Select Committee this year. I asked the deputy secretary in the Ministry of Defence about coverage of the Trident Programme in the Defence Estimates. Mr. Bryars told us that within the Department, decisions on resources allocation were taken on a basis which takes account of expenditure relevant to a particular project on which ever vote it will eventually fall. In other words, the Votes do not do a thing in regard to the way that particular programmes do and the way that particular decisions are taken in Departments.[55]

The Treasury Committee concluded its review of the presentation of information to the House with the judgement that significant changes would be needed if select committees were to play an adequate role. The report declares the Committee's allegiance to parliamentarism in the opening paragraph:

> The form of the estimates is determined by Treasury. The primary and essential purpose of the estimates should be to provide the House of Commons with the information it needs in the most convenient form to carry out its duty of assessing the justification for, or withholding approval from, government requests for supply. The estimates, we believe, should also be comprehensible to those outside government and parliament who take an interest in these matters.[56]

Later the report remarks:

> The House should be in a position to select for detailed examination and further enquiry from the government any areas of expenditure it wishes. . . . In their present form, the estimates do not provide enough information for the House (or its committees) to make a selection.

The Committee's proposals were accepted in part by the government. The 1983–4 Supply Estimates included comparisons with spending in previous years, extra information on staff numbers and capital projects and a summary statement of the aims and scope of programmes. However, the Committee on Procedure (Finance) commented on the continuing inadequacy of the information supplied to parliament.[57] It complained of the lack of information on the level of services or on targets and outputs. It drew attention to the variations between and within votes. The Committee also commented on deficiencies in the Public Expenditure White Paper. The Treasury Committee has also sought information on programme objectives – where possible precise targets – and resources used or proposed. Some changes were made to the 1983 White Paper. But the statements of objectives that were included were vague (e.g., 'to ensure a fair standard of living for the agricultural community'; 'to provide an income for those who are not earning').

In its response to a Treasury Committee report on civil service effectiveness the government announced what it termed the Financial Management Initiative.[58] Under this proposal departments are to break down their activities into cost or responsibility centres and to devise output measures to enable performance to be evaluated. In evidence, the Treasury suggested that reconstruction of the Public Expenditure White Paper could be expected to follow the introduction of this approach. The government has also agreed to identify and provide more information about long-term capital projects. To maintain pressure on the government and the Treasury, the Treasury and Public Accounts Committees have undertaken further inquiries into the format, structure and content of the financial information provided to the House during the current parliament.[59]

Control of the Auditor General

A third area in which parliament's powers were extended during the first Thatcher government involved the Auditor General. The Auditor General provides an independent check on the efficiency of departmental spending. His inquiries ensure that the purposes of public policy have been achieved as intended by parliament and without undue waste. The Audit Office consists of some 800 staff. Prior to 1984, formal control was shared between the Treasury and the Public Accounts Committee. These arrangements had barely changed since the establishment of the Public Accounts Committee in 1861. The government published a Green Paper on the role of the Controller and Auditor General in March 1980. The Public Accounts Committee reviewed the proposals. Its report does not disguise its disappointment:

> We share with many of those who have given evidence to us a sense of disappointment that the Green Paper included the assumption that the main provisions of the 1866 and 1921 (Exchequer and Audit Department) Acts remain valid . . . . the Green Paper does not tackle the fundamental questions about the need for satisfactory accountability to parliament for public expenditure.[60]

The report includes a sweeping indictment of the ability of ministers to hold departments accountable:

> The present position is that a minister often does not have the information he reasonably needs in order to control the public expenditure for which he is responsible. This means that the form of public expenditure is often not sufficiently tested to see whether the same result can be obtained for less money or indeed better results for the same money. It means in many cases it is not possible to assess accurately in advance what a change in policy is actually going to cost, nor the difference in cost in doing the same thing one way rather than another, nor, even after the event, what a particular change has cost. Nor is there any clear or satisfactory way of establishing a cost or value of the resources being employed on a continuing basis in a particular official programme.[61]

The inquiry took evidence from, amongst others, Treasury (four times), the Auditor General, the Consultative Committee of Accountancy bodies, the British National Oil Corporation, the Nationalized Industries Chairmen's Group and local authority associations. It received fifty-eight written submissions including ten from individual MPs, eleven from local government associations and eleven from individual nationalized industries and private interest groups.

The Committee concludes that the functions of the Controller should be taken over and expanded into a new National Audit Office. The relevant legislation should also be amended to cover value-for-money investigations that now make up an increasing proportion of inquiries. The National Audit Office should be solely responsible to parliament. It should be financed independently of Treasury. The Auditor General would be empowered to scrutinize the expenditure of public funds wherever they go. Local government, nationalized industries and private groups should all fall within his purview.

These proposals were rejected by the government. The Nationalized Industries Chairmen's Group expressed concern about their implications for managerial autonomy. The issue was debated in the Commons in November 1982. A Commons motion calling for implementation of the Public Accounts Committee's recommendations was signed by over 300 members from all parties. The motion was jointly sponsored by Edward du Cann (Chairman of the Treasury Select Committee) and Joel Barnett (Chairman of the Public Accounts Committee).

Subsequently Norman St John Stevas introduced a Private Member's Bill whose terms implemented the Public Accounts Committee's proposals. This was first debated in the Commons in January 1983. While the bill journeyed through standing committee, negotiations between the government and its backbench sponsors produced a compromise. In the event, the government conceded full control of the Auditor General to parliament. It agreed to amend his terms of reference to cover 'effectiveness audits'. It would not, however, agree to allow him access to the nationalized industries. This Act took effect from January 1984.[62]

Special standing committees

To widen parliament's role in legislation the 1978 Procedure Committee recommended that standing committees on bills should be able to sit for up to three days in select committee form — that is, to take evidence from interest groups. Mrs Thatcher's Leader of the House, Norman St John Stevas, could only persuade his colleagues to accept this proposal on an experimental basis. Under his influence three bills were handled under this procedure in the 1980–1 session.

Bruce George and Barbara Evans conducted a survey covering 87 per cent of members who participated in these committees. They found a positive reaction:

> 22 out of 37 respondents said they would like to see all committees use an investigatory phase and a further 10 said they would like it employed for bills which did not involve too much party conflict. When asked for a judgement on the utility of the experiment 28 said it had been 'very worth-while', 8 said it was 'fairly worthwhile' and only one said it 'made no difference'.[63]

The role of the Leader of the House in advancing this development is critical. After St John Stevas's departure from that office, the pressure for reform has relaxed. Only one bill was so handled in the 1981–2 session. No bills were handled in this fashion in the 1982–3 session. Only one has been treated thus in the new parliament. So long as the government continues to regard this proposal as experimental, it retains control of the initiative.

THEORY AND PRACTICE

The ideas underwriting these procedural reforms have achieved widespread support amongst Tory, Labour and Alliance parliamentarians. These ideas originated in debate in a specialized community beyond parliament. This debate concerned the balance of power between parliament and the executive. Protagonists include eminent former ministers from the Tory and Labour parties. The outcome was agreement that the 'scrutiny and review' powers of the House of Commons should be reasserted. Several earlier experiments with committees suggested not only the need for congressional-style coverage of departments but also for independent power to challenge the executive. The former aspiration was translated into practice partly through Mrs Thatcher's desire to lead a government of reform and partly through the personal commitment of her first Leader of the House, Norman St John Stevas.

St John Stevas, in the words quoted at the beginning of this chapter, interprets the creation of the select committee system as 'the most important parliamentary reform of the century'. For this claim to be vindicated, it would be necessary for committees to acquire independent powers of initiative on policy issues. Only a few protagonists accept unequivocally the need to give this power to committees. This view is still confined to a few backbench reformers. They base their case on the need to reassert the 'scrutiny and review' role of the Commons. The 'scrutiny and review' argument underwrote the establishment of the departmental committees. It was deployed to gain endorsement of the further procedure reforms in the 1979–83 period. Apart from its dubious basis in constitutional history, it remains to be seen whether this argument is sufficiently powerful to legitimize further reform.

Independent powers of initiative for committees have been suggested most recently by the procedure inquiry on the financial process. Indeed, the committee concerned has proposed a specific structure – a two-stage budget process – within which such a development could be achieved. The implications of this proposal will be considered in detail in chapter 6. It is clear, however, that this would alter decisively the structure of policy making. It would lead to the replacement of the two-party system by a more plural structure with the Commons acquiring an independent deliberative role. Constitutional change on this scale presumably requires justification of a very high order. Efficient spending seems too arid and prosaic to overturn the theory of representation that is the ultimate buttress of existing conventions. Efficient spending does not seem capable of mobilizing that broadly based multi-party coalition which would be necessary to sustain major constitutional change.

A multi-party parliament with a minority executive would provide the opportunity for the two-stage budget proposal to be revived. But the conceptual buttress of the reformers will surely be critical for their success. Their ability to mobilize support, to argue with conviction, and to build a broadly based coalition for change depends on their conceptual foundations. Thus far they have stayed within the boundaries of the 'scrutiny and review' argument. Within this boundary they have formulated proposals for an enlarged role for parliament in policy making.

The scope of the constitutional transformation that is envisaged would seem to require more. What is ultimately at issue is the foundation of executive power. The contention that a deliberative role for parliament might provide a necessary buttress for an effective executive requires examination. A second ground might be derived from recent studies of policy failure. Successive empirical studies have pointed to the power of interest groups to thwart unwanted policy changes. Change in the structure of policy making could thus be justified if it could be shown that select committees could play a decisive role not merely in permitting parliamentary consideration of executive proposals but also in mobilizing the consent of interest groups. The object of the following four chapters is to establish if the evidence sustains these propositions.

Chapter 2

Economic policy making and the budget cycle

The budget process encompasses the first area of policy making to which MPs need to be introduced if the House is to have an independent deliberative role. Major interest groups too need access to current economic data and to Treasury judgements of opportunities and constraints if they are to formulate more realistic, less wishful, policy agendas.

The budget cycle within government is both an economic and a political process. As an economic process, it produces judgements about the medium-term economic outlook and the scope for government action to influence this outlook. Desirable revenue and expenditure targets are determined. As a result of increasing international and domestic economic interdependence, policy is settled in the context of a growing number of variables (e.g. public sector borrowing requirement, exchange rate range, interest rates, money supply, average level of wage settlements, etc.). Through the budget process these determinations are reconciled with other independently determined, independently legitimized, judgements about desirable levels of government expenditure in particular policy sectors (e.g. transport, health, local government, education, industry) or in pursuit of particular (trans-sectoral) social objectives (e.g. the employment–education mix for sixteen- to eighteen-year-olds). The budget, in other words, creates and manipulates resources in the context of the government's sectoral, economic and social assessments.[1]

Budget assessments blend technical expertise and political judgement. They involve an annual appraisal of the community's general economic interests. Only those authorized by the electoral process – that is members of the executive – make the ultimate budget judgements. Others may be legitimate protagonists for sectional points of view. For example, the CBI usually urges government to constrain spending and to improve taxation incentives. The TUC usually urges attention to employment and welfare. Welfare, education, local government and other interest groups annually offer public advice to the Chancellor and his cabinet colleagues as they make crucial expenditure and revenue decisions. But the information required to determine general interests is confined to a very few. The claims of external groups are, and are seen to be, special pleading.[2]

This results from the political process through which budget judgements are made. As a political process the budget cycle is composed of a set of institutions and conventions. These determine who participates in budget assessments, the timing and significance of their participation, and the access of participants to relevant information. Current arrangements are a function of the two-party system. The most significant consequence of this system is its concentration of formal power. The two-party system confines participation in key economic determinations to a very few people. Decisions are taken at the end of a private policy process. Information bearing upon critical revenue and expenditure decisions is private. The Cabinet as a whole, some twenty-three people, make the ultimate judgements about expenditure. The Prime Minister and Chancellor and only those ministers they choose to involve, make the ultimate judgements about revenue. This power gives these individuals a decisive formal influence over all key budget judgements. Whether this formal control can be translated into effective power is one of the central problems which currently bedevil governments.[3]

Under present arrangements ministers are the principal agents for reconciling sectoral and general objectives. On the one hand they are defenders of their departments' interests and of the various sectoral objectives symbolized by current and proposed programmes. This frequently involves them in individual bargaining sessions with the Financial Secretary after aggregate expenditure limits are established.[4] In practice, their concern about their own programmes diminishes their attention to overall strategy. Despite this, formally they are members of the government and thus committed to its overall priorities, if such exist.

Apart from the Prime Minister, Chancellor and the principal Secretaries of State, the group with greatest influence in budget deliberations is the Treasury. Its role is assured by access, expertise and control of information. Treasury concentrates on building the understanding of the Prime Minister, Treasury Ministers and, to a lesser extent, Cabinet, of relevant budgetary issues, tactics and strategies. Treasury concentrates its intensive economic exposition on this very small group.[5]

These arrangements are deliberately designed to limit participation in key decisions on the presumption that the government's authority will be sufficient to elicit public and interest group compliance.[6] This authority is derived exclusively from the most recent general election. If the political power mobilized at that election proved to be enduring, these arrangements would indeed underwrite effective and flexible policy making.

The presumption that the government's authority should be relatively unfettered dictates the role of the Opposition and of backbenchers. The Opposition, whose job is to hold the government accountable, does so generally not by contesting particular decisions. The Opposition typically challenges the government's overall strategy. This is the most politically expedient course. It permits vivid distinctions, trenchant criticism, and the projection of enticing hopes. Backbenchers are not usually significant actors in this process. Both government and Opposition backbenchers are usually too disorganized to play any significant role, except occasionally on single controversial issues.[7]

Interest groups beyond government (trade unions, local government bodies, vice-chancellors, hospital administrators, employer groups) are even further distanced from the process. They may participate in various ways in formulating individual departmental expenditure bids. In their role as claimants on public expenditure or as groups whose co-operation is essential to achieving desired outcomes, or both, governments have been increasingly obliged to take account of interest group views. But these groups are deliberately distanced from decisive budgetary information. They take part in budget discussions by invitation of the government. Their discussions with officials or ministers are usually private. Interest groups are invited to make proposals only from their sectional point of view. The consultation process is not designed to encourage either government or interest groups to moderate or adapt their initial positions.[8]

This is a summary of the formal structure within which budget making now takes place. The relationship between this formal structure and interest groups will be considered further in chapter 5. This is the system into which the select committees have been inserted. Their formal remit gives them powers of scrutiny and review. My purpose will be to assess whether their use of this power provides evidence of the capacity of committees to revive a deliberative role for the House.

In making this judgement we will consider five aspects of the committees' work. First, what coverage of the budget cycle has been achieved? Second, have significant topics been chosen for inquiry? Third, has the conduct of inquiries been adequate? Fourth, have committees produced clear, bipartisan findings? Finally, have they transmitted these findings to each other, to the House, the media, Treasury and relevant interest groups?

COVERAGE OF THE BUDGET CYCLE

For policy purposes, the budget cycle can be conceived as consisting of four major elements. The first element is the medium-term strategy. In formulating this, empirical and theoretical evidence concerning future trends and appropriate policy responses needs to be weighed. Complex technical relationships are invoked at both theoretical and empirical levels. Economists of different schools contest each other's forecasts as well as the theory that determines what relationships count. Their recommendations are grounded in these disputes. The government is introduced to their disputes by its professional advisers in the Treasury. It weighs their recommendations in reaching a political judgement about the 'right' medium-term strategy.

The medium-term strategy flows into current policy in the determination of the annual budget. This is the second element of the budget cycle. The government determines revenue and expenditure targets annually. It does this privately through a regular pattern of Cabinet and Cabinet Committee meetings. This process generally begins in May or June. An aggregate expenditure target is set by Cabinet. Over the summer individual spending bids are settled bilaterally between ministers and the Financial Secretary, with the support of the appropriate Cabinet Committee. These totals are confirmed by Cabinet in October. Disputed expenditure bids are also determined by Cabinet around this time. Revenue proposals are finalized just prior to the budget. These decisions are announced in March to parliament according to a well-established process.

The third element of the budget cycle involves spending by individual departments. New and on-going programmes determine annual expenditure bids. This process occurs independently of developments at the macro-economic level. Departments initiate new programmes with planning lead times of perhaps three to five years. Expenditure in any particular year will usually reflect the decisions of past years (e.g. hospital or educational construction programmes, defence equipment). Some new programmes usually enter the expenditure process each year. Some programmes vary because of demographic change or some other change in the underlying circumstances. These developments are monitored by Treasury and subject to private negotiation between it and the relevant department both when the programme is conceived and at key points in its evolution.[9] This process culminates in an annual allocation of funds to departments.

The final element of the budget cycle arises from the activity of nationalized industries and advisory authorities. These bodies function like departments as independent claimants of public resources. But their relative independence dictates their separate treatment. They deal first with their sponsoring departments and only indirectly with Treasury. The factors determining nationalized industry needs for capital or operating funds are quite different from those bearing upon departmental budgets. In addition to the nationalized industries an array of tripartite bodies has been established, some with executive responsibilities in particular areas (e.g. Manpower Services Commission, Commission for Racial Equality). These bodies too lay independent claim to public resources.

Our first task is to establish how comprehensively the select committee inquiries have covered these four elements of the budget cycle. Evidence comes from the twenty-one inquiries reviewed in tables 2.1 to 2.4. These inquiries involve four of the five reviews carried out by the Treasury Committee in its first five years into aspects of the medium-term financial strategy, plus the seventeen inquiries carried out by this committee and other departmental committees into economic assessments and current estimates in the 1981–2 parliamentary session. In this session, seven of the fourteen departmental committees scrutinized their department's estimates. In addition, two committees conducted short reviews – of the performance of individual nationalized industries and of the corporate plan of a major independent advisory commission.

Table 2.1 Treasury Committee reports on the medium-term economic issues

Session	Inquiry	Scope/Approach	Size	Witnesses		Recommendations
				Oral	Written	
1979/80–1980/1	Monetary Control (H.C. 713, 720 1979/80; H.C. 163 1980/1)	* Relationship between money supply, PSBR, inflation and growth. * Duration 8 months. * Advisers Dr Alan Budd; Prof. D. Hendry; Prof. W. Buiter; Prof. M. Miller; Dr P. Neild; Prof. H. Rose; T. Ward.	* Report 116 pages * Evidence and appendices 800 pages	* Chancellor, Treasury – Bank of England – 3 experts – Deutsche Bundes-bank	* 9 Central Banks * 14 Experts (Friedman, Kaldor etc.) * CBI, TUC, NIESR	* Questions direct link between monetary control and inflationary expectations. * Lack of government control of exchange rate threatens efficacy of monetary control. * Bipartisan report.
1980/1	Financing the Nationalized Industries (H.C. 348, 1980/1)	* Philosophy of counting all nationalized industry investment in PSBR. * Mechanisms for limiting nationalized industry investment. * Contrasts UK with French and German practice. * Duration 2 months.	* 400 pages	* Nat. Inds Chairmen's Group * Treasury * 4 Nat. Inds * Bank of Eng.	* 8 Nat. Inds * Treasury * 2 experts * 1 union	* Gov. restrictions inhibited up to £500 m. worthwhile investment (= between 3.5% and 7% of state industries £7,100 m. capital requirement). * Rejects argument that nat. industry investment 'crowds out' private sector. * Bipartisan report.

(continued)

33

Table 2.1—*continued*

Session	Inquiry	Scope/Approach	Size	Witnesses		Recommendations
				Oral	Written	
1982/3 (Debated in context 2nd Brandt Report – 18.4.83)	International Monetary Arrangements (H.C. 403, 1981/2; H.C. 21, 385, 1982/3)	* Duration 14 months. * Special advisers: Profs W. Buiter, Brian Tew, John Williamson, plus 3 commissioned studies. * First Report concerns international lending by commercial banks. * Second Report concerns exchange rates, monetary policy, reserves, international co-ordination of economic policy. Draft published without full Cttee approval because of dissolution and Williamsburg Summit. * Annex surveys recent developments in relevant economic theory.	* 1,000 pages approx.	* 12 experts * Labour Party Economic Policy Group * Ford, Unilever	* 10 academics * 3 central banks	* Failure of global recovery represents principal risk. * Strengthen supervision by private banks of loans to NIC's and other countries. * Proposes joint money supply/exchange rate policy regime. * Recommends approach for British Government to Williamsburg Summit.

(continued)

34

Table 2.1—*continued*

Session	Inquiry	Scope/Approach	Size	Witnesses		Recommendations
				Oral	*Written*	
1982/3	Structure of Personal Income Taxation and Income Support (H.C. 386, 1982/3; Evidence, H.C. 20 i, ii, 1982/3)	* Covers 25% of expenditure on pensions, UB and supplementary benefit. * Special advisers: John Kay (IFS), Mrs H. Parker (CPS), Prof. T. Atkinson. * Reviews UK and int. theoretical research. Contrasts practices in France, Germany and US and various schemes for eliminating poverty trap. * Report published without Cttee endorsement because of dissolution. Separate report by Ralph Howell also published – a variation of CPS proposed Basic Income Guarantee Scheme.		* CPAG, Family Forum, CBI, TUC, etc. (9 representative groups)	19 interest groups	* DHSS needs opportunity to comment on proposed tax changes. Joint Treasury/DHSS planning of medium-term future of benefits system required. * Recommends abolition married man's allowance plus increase in child benefit, or graduated tax structure plus former 2 steps.

Table 2.2 1981–2 Treasury Committee review of economic statements

Government announcement	Timing of Treasury Committee hearings	Advisers	Duration	Evidence	Conclusions
Autumn review (H.C. 28)	Evidence taken prior to Chancellor's statement to parliament. (Evidence 16.11 and 23.11 – Statement 2.12).	* Dr Paul Neild Paul Ormerod Dr Bill Robinson Terry Ward	* 3 weeks (evidence to report)	* Chancellor (twice) * Treasury Officers (once)	* Changes in projected expenditure are not disclosed – only total figures. * No comparability between budget proposals and Public Expenditure White Paper proposals. * Autumn statement discloses only 'planning total' forecast for public expenditure. Not enough for parliament's needs. * Discussion of economic strategy requires that information on revenue proposals be available with expenditure forecasts.

(continued)

Table 2.2—*continued*

Government announcement	Timing of Treasury Committee hearings	Advisers	Duration	Evidence	Conclusions
1982 Budget (H.C. 270)	Evidence 17.3, 24.3 and 29.3; Report 31.3; 2nd reading Finance Bill Debate commenced 6.4.	* As above	* 2 weeks	* Chancellor * Treasury Officers * Bank of Eng. * Written evidence: – Brit. Road Fed. – TUC – CBI etc. * Report contrasts Treasury forecasts with EIU, London Business School, Phillips & Drew and NIESR	* M3 no longer sole target. 'What is not clear is what policy changes can be expected if the aggregates move in different directions.' * Cttee welcomes more attention to exchange rates. Notes gov. has moved focus of medium-term strategy from preoccupation with expectations. * Gov. has not achieved its aim of reducing significantly role of public sector (as measured by PSBR % of GDP). * Foreshadows further inquiry on impact of index-linked gov. securities on fin. markets. * 'Treasury consultations with outside interests were of a limited nature.' * Concern at no prospect of easing of employment situation.

(continued)

37

Table 2.2—*continued*

Government announcement	Timing of Treasury Committee hearings	Advisers	Duration	Evidence	Conclusions
Gov. Expenditure Plans 1982/3 to 1984/5 (H.C. 316)	Evidence 17.3 and 31.3. (Exp. and Budget Reports separated in 1981/2 because of new form of Public Expenditure White Paper).	* Terry Ward	* 2 weeks		* Criticizes exclusive presentation in cash terms. Members and the public entitled to know volume implications. Volume and cost data also should be published. * Criticizes excess burden carried by public investment for reduction in public expenditure, particularly nationalized inds and housing. * Draws attention to uncertainty surrounding EEC rebates despite importance to budget calculations.
Review of Summer Supplementary Estimates (H.C. 448)	Evidence taken on presentation of the estimates				* Singles out £7 m. EEC supplementary vote. 'The Gov. would have been better advised to put the question of payment of public money to judgement of House before disbursement.'

The Treasury Committee conducted four major inquiries in the 1979–83 period concerned with aspects of the medium-term financial strategy, and they are summarized in table 2.1. These inquiries concerned the practicability of monetarist doctrine as a basis for the government's medium-term financial strategy, the financing of nationalized industries, international monetary arrangements, and the relationship between income tax and social security benefits.

The Treasury Committee has also evolved a routine in reviewing government announcements during the unfolding of the budget cycle. The inquiries are summarized in table 2.2. Reflecting the private activity within government concerning budgetary strategy, the Chancellor now makes a parliamentary statement in the autumn about economic developments since the previous budget and about the future outlook. Just before, or in conjunction with the March budget, he releases an updated Public Expenditure White Paper. In the 1981–2 parliamentary session, the Treasury Committee conducted four inquiries. One coincided with the autumn review and two with the budget and public expenditure papers released in March. The fourth inquiry concerned the Summer Supplementary Estimates.

The inquiries conducted by the various departmental committees into estimates and expenditure plans in the 1981–2 parliamentary session are summarized in table 2.3. In all, seven committees staged inquiries. Their hearings cover the major spending departments – Defence, Health and Social Security, Transport, Education and Energy. The Scottish Affairs Committee also conducted hearings on the role of its departments. These inquiries took place before the new procedure for estimates review (discussed in chapter 1) was adopted. Under this procedure, select committees are assigned three days of parliamentary time each session for debate of their findings. However, the report of the Select Committee on Procedure was under consideration during the 1981–2 session. Hence several of the committees approached their task with its recommendations in mind. Four committees undertook no estimates inquiries. The Industry and Trade Committee concentrated on nationalized industries. Various reasons were offered by the three other committees for omitting these inquiries. One committee chairman expressed the view that it would involve committees entering an area which was the government's exclusive prerogative. Other committee members have commented that estimates reviews occur too late to be effective. Major policies will have been endorsed two or three years before. Current estimates simply reflect the unfolding of the logic of these earlier decisions. Estimates are not, on this view, the right area in which to press for an enlarged committee role in policy making. As we shall see later the evidence does not sustain these reservations.

The fourth category of inquiry involves review of nationalized industries and advisory authorities. Nationalized industries fall within the responsibility of three committees. The Transport Committee covers the National Bus Company and other transport authorities. The Energy Committee covers the

Table 2.3 1981–2 reviews of departmental estimates and expenditure plans

Committee	Expenditure estimate	Approximate % of total expenditure 1979/80–1982/3	Approach	Recommendations
Defence (Defence White Paper) (H.C. 428)	£14,000 m.	10.9	* Evidence session from Sec. of State. Follows Falklands. Reviews gov. re-equipment plans, including decisions taken and pending.	* No recommendations because of special post-Falklands circumstances.
Foreign Affairs (O'Seas Dev. Sub-Ctee) (H.C. 330)	£1,605 m.	2.8	* Oral evidence ODA and Dept of Trade. * Written evidence ODA, Trade, Centre for World Education Development, British Volunteer Programme, Oxfam. * Research assistance: Dr Mosley – Bath Univ.; Mrs C. Geldart – Univ. of London; Mr Bridger.	* Specific proposals to improve presentation. * Increase grant to British Volunteers Programme £500,000. * Specific proposals for review management of Aid/Trade programme.
Transport (Roads programme and transport aspects of Public Exp. White Paper) (H.C. 334)	EEC progs = £320 m. Local authority roads = £469 m. Motorways, trunk routes = £500 m. NBC loss = £17.5 m. £1,306.5 m.	4.4	* Evidence from Sec. of State and Dept officers.	* Warns against dependence on EEC programmes for future public expenditure. * Cash presentation inhibits evaluation. * Refers to BR claim that rail under-investment £200 m. plus £50 m. for electrification.
Scottish Affairs (H.C. 413)	£6,063 m.	6	* Analysis of impact by special adviser David Heald. * Comprehensive explanatory memos from Scottish Office. * Evidence: Sec. of State plus 4 officials.	* Special adviser criticizes lack of volume information. Makes review of impact difficult. * Examination of witnesses only.

(continued)

Table 2.3—*continued*

Committee	Expenditure estimate	Approximate % of total expenditure 1979/80–1982/3	Approach	Recommendations
Education and Science Expenditure Plans (H.C. 90)	£8,600 m.	13.9	* Evidence from Minister and officials re. – School meals – ILEA – Libraries – Inspectorate evaluation of schools – Village school closures – Feasibility block grants	* No formal report submitted. * Exchange of correspondence between Minister and Chairman concerning possibility of block grant.
Energy (H.C. 231)	£764.7 m.		* Sec. of State gives Cttee estimates before budget. * Evidence from Permanent Under-Secretary of State.	* Disputes £231 m. to NCB for uneconomic pits (1983/4 deficit grant £410 m.). * Criticizes lack of conservation spending. * Proposes to challenge specific estimates. * Bipartisan Report.
Social Services (H.C. 306)	£40,000 m.	37.5	* Advisers Prof. R. Klein } Bath M. O'Higgins * Evidence from Dept, Sec. of State, Assoc. of Dtrs of Social Services.	* Refers spending on animal research to PAC. * Identifies issues being examined by Policy Strategy Unit. * Endorses Treasury Cttee call for publication volume data. * 39 specific recs. * Cttee welcomes Dept scrutiny of NHS after earlier cttee criticism.

Table 2.4 Nationalized industries and advisory commissions

Committee	Industry/Agency	Net Budgetary Position 1981/2	Approach	Recommendations
1981/2 Industry and Trade	The Post Office (H.C. 343)	* Net Assets £530 m. Revenue £2,280 m. Employment 185,000	* Evidence from PO, Dept of Industry, Minister, unions and users committees, competitive services. * Duration 2 months.	* Covers Dept surveillance, External Finance Limits, use of accumulated reserves, productivity etc.
Industry and Trade	British Leyland (H.C. 194, 160)	–£990 m.	* Follows Hearing April 1981.	* Endorses gov. advance. * Notes report 'provides most comprehensive public explanation of BL's current situation'.
Industry and Trade	British Steel Corp. (H.C. 308)	–£315 m. External Finance Limit £730 m.	* Evidence from Ian McGregor – 25/11/81, Sec. of State 9/12/81. * Builds on inquiry in spring. * BSC delegation includes chairman, deputy, 3 functional managing directors.	* Expresses concern at US actions against EEC steel exports. Also impact of high UK energy prices.
Industry and Trade	British Shipbuilders (H.C. 192)	–£41 m.	* Evidence BS, Dept of Ind., shipbuilding unions, TUC etc. * Inquiry 3 months. * Adviser J. Cockerill – Manchester Institute of Science and Tech.	* More co-operation from MoD on naval shipping to ensure export potential realized. * Supports industry case for further preferential arrangements.

(continued)

42

Table 2.4—*continued*

Committee	Industry/Agency	Net Budgetary Position 1981/2	Approach	Recommendations
Industry and Trade	Rolls-Royce (H.C. 389,206)	–£3 m.	* Evidence from chairman and company officers and Minister of State.	* Proposes parliamentary approval be required for major new projects. * Endorses moves towards new engine development (est. £1.5 bill.).
Employment	Manpower Services Commission Corporate Plan (H.C. 195)	* Comm. established 1973 to separate policy making from implementation. * Corporate Plan (1982–6) negotiated through tripartite Board. * MSC estimates 3 m. unemployed 1983 – gov. more optimistic	* Evidence from MSC staff, TUC, CBI and affected groups. * 1 week between evidence and report.	* Keep estimate of 3 m. unemployed under review. * Improve liaison with education authorities. * Insufficient attention to problems of long-term unemployment. * Cttee instrumental in having plan published in 1980/1. Obliged MSC to abandon plans to cut special services to the disabled. * Bipartisan report.

National Coal Board and the power generating industry. The Industry and Trade Committee covers the balance – British Steel, British Rail, British Airways, the Post Office, British Leyland, Rolls-Royce Ltd. In total the nationalized industry sector involved in 1981–2 eighteen organizations with a turnover of £43 billion and a workforce of 1.6 million.[10] Parliamentary oversight of the nationalized industries started in 1958 when, in pursuit of improved accountability without day-to-day ministerial or departmental involvement, the Nationalized Industries Committee was established. The 'scrutiny' inquiries conducted in the 1981–2 session are listed in table 2.4. The Industry and Trade Committee reviewed five industries. The committee conducted lengthy inquiries into BSC and BL in the 1980–1 session.[11] These reports provided the basis for its 1981–2 hearings. These hearings involved evidence sessions to check industry progress against earlier stated intentions. The committee continued this practice in subsequent sessions. Its inquiries into Rolls-Royce, British Shipbuilders and the Post Office were more substantial. These involved assessment of the merit of current levels of public expenditure and of the outlook for the industry. They were not major studies of industry effectiveness or performance. These reviews will be considered in chapter 4. The inquiries considered here involved public evidence by industry leaders in the context of a parliamentary appraisal of current plans.

Only one committee routinely reviewed the budget and proposed programme of a major advisory commission. The Employment Committee examined the proposed Corporate Plan of the Manpower Services Commission before it was endorsed by the government. The publication of a corporate plan by the Manpower Services Commission resulted from pressure from the Employment Committee in the 1980–1 session.[12] The committee gained the agreement of the Secretary of State to the plan being published first in draft. It is not approved by the Secretary of State until the committee has expressed its view. Committee pressure in 1981 had resulted in the Manpower Services Commission reversing a proposal to cut the level of services to the disabled.

Tables 2.1 to 2.4 establish the comprehensiveness of committee coverage of the budget cycle. Our next task is to assess the significance of the subjects the committee tackled.

SIGNIFICANCE OF SUBJECTS

If select committees are to equip members to play a deliberative role, there should be evidence that the topics selected for inquiry are timely and significant. Backbenchers and interest groups need to be informed about issues that are current and that involve important aspects of policy. These inquiries need to be staged in sufficient time to permit judgement of the executive's plans. The committees' capacity should be evident in each component of the budget cycle.

The Treasury Committee alone has responsibility for issues bearing upon the medium-term strategy. The issues that it selected for inquiry were timely and were perceived to underlie important elements of the strategy – for example, are monetary targets desirable indicators of economic health? Should nationalized industries' investments count in the PSBR? The committee pursued at least one major inquiry each parliamentary session. A fifth inquiry in the 1979–83 period concerned civil service effectiveness. It also conducted an important inquiry into budgetary reform. These will be considered in later chapters.

The Treasury Committee's first major inquiry concerned monetary control. It arose from the desire of members to assess the evidence for and against the new approach foreshadowed by the Chancellor after Mrs Thatcher's accession. Early in its term the government issued a green paper signalling its intention to rely on monetary control to achieve its economic objectives. An initial inquiry into civil service pay exposed the committee to the difficulties that would confront the government in adhering to rigid monetary targets.[13] Hence in March 1980 (i.e. about nine months after Mrs Thatcher's accession) it began work.

The committee's second inquiry on nationalized industry financing was a much shorter assay. This inquiry was initiated at a time of controversy about the extent to which nationalized industry investment should be subordinated to the requirements of public sector economic management. In particular, it was disputed whether nationalized industry investment could be considered to 'crowd out' productive private investment.

The committee's third major inquiry on international monetary arrangements, lasted some fourteen months. It originated in the findings of the monetary control report concerning the vulnerability of the domestic sector to pressures transmitted from the international sector. The committee judged attention to exchange rate changes could not be omitted from the medium-term strategy. Indeed, it argued, international developments narrowed the government's capacity to influence domestic outcomes to a degree that called in question the presumptions behind its announced policies. This inquiry was also initiated at a time of widespread concern about the future stability of international monetary arrangements. A number of countries were expected to be in difficulty servicing their debts. A number of major private banks were thought to be overexposed.

The final major policy inquiry of the Treasury Committee in the life of the first Thatcher government concerned the intersection of the tax and welfare systems – an area Mrs Thatcher had publicly claimed to be of paramount importance for future policy.

So far as the annual budget cycle is concerned, the Treasury Committee staged public hearings in parallel with each announcement by the government. In its autumn (November) review, the committee responded to the economic forecast the Treasury is obliged to produce under the Industry Act. As is customary, the Committee took evidence from the Chancellor and from Treasury officials. This evidence is published along with papers from the committee's official advisers. It was available to members of parliament before debate in the House.

The committee also held hearings in conjunction with the budget announcements and release of the Public Expenditure White Paper. The timing of the Public Expenditure White Paper has varied. It was originally intended to be published in draft in November, with a final version in January or February. Earlier publication of public expenditure forecasts is essential if committees are to review proposed departmental spending before final budgetary decisions are taken. The Treasury Committee has repeatedly criticized the government for not tabling this information earlier.[14] The committee also staged hearings in conjunction with presentation of the Summer Supplementary Estimates. These provide the first opportunity for the committee to assess how closely expenditure out-turns are conforming to the government's stated plans.

Inquiries by the committees into departmental estimates were also stimulated by the publication of official papers. The seven committees staging estimates inquiries demonstrate the capacity of committees to critically appraise departmental spending proposals. This capacity would become significant if spending bids were published before the budget was finally determined.

Routine scrutiny reviews of nationalized industries and advisory commission spending and performance were undertaken by the committees on their own initiative. The Industry and Trade Committee acted on its own initiative in staging inquiries on the nationalized industries. The Employment Committee had, as we have seen, gained government endorsement of its scrutiny of Manpower Services Commission proposals before annual budgetary decisions by the government.

CONDUCT OF INQUIRIES

The third area in which we should expect to find evidence of select committee capacity is in the conduct of inquiries. This covers such factors as the adequacy of the evidence collected by committees, the research resources mustered by the committee, the pattern of questioning, and the leadership of inquiries.

All inquiries concerning the medium-term financial strategy were conducted by the Treasury Committee. The collective experience of government gathered on the committee is the first point to note. The Treasury Committee's membership of eleven included four ex-ministers, of whom three had been Treasury ministers. Two members had served on the General Sub-Committee of the Expenditure Committee. The membership was made up of four Labour and six Tory nominees, and one Liberal. Its Chairman, Edward du Cann, had been Chairman of the General Sub-Committee of the Expenditure Committee. He was also Chairman of the influential 1922 Committee (the backbench committee of the Tory Party) and had been a junior Treasury Minister.[15]

The committee's approach to its first major inquiry, Monetary Control, provided a model for all its subsequent inquiries. Seven leading economists were recruited as part-time advisers. These included individuals with access to economic models other than that of the Treasury, and academic economists with outstanding reputations in their particular area of expertise. These advisers were selected by the committee on the advice of the Chairman and Clerk. In identifying potential candidates, Treasury and past Expenditure Committee advisers were consulted. Once selected, the advisers were invited to suggest issues that the committee might investigate and the approach it might take. Their work was co-ordinated by the Clerk.

At the outset, the committee decided to circulate a questionnaire to leading academic economists and central bankers to solicit their views. A detailed questionnaire was formulated jointly by the Clerk and advisers, endorsed by the committee and widely circulated. Detailed replies were received over the ensuing ten months from seventeen economists of international repute, such as Milton Friedman, James Tobin, Sir Alec Cairncross, and Patrick Minford. These replies were published separately while the inquiry was still in progress. Replies were also received from ten central banks, e.g. the US Federal Reserve, the Bank of France, Deutsche Bundesbank.[16] The committee's outreach to other interest groups was less extensive. It sought evidence from the peak employer and employee groups, the CBI and TUC. It did not, however, seek to engage major groups involved with other areas of policy (e.g. peak welfare or education groups) to weigh the implications of the proposed monetary strategy from their perspective. The committee conceived its task primarily in technical terms – an assessment of the theoretical and empirical evidence bearing upon the government's announced approach.

Oral evidence was taken from a number of individual experts, senior Treasury officers, the Bank of England and the Chancellor. All this evidence was published as taken. It amounts to 380 pages. Oral evidence was taken over twelve sessions between 30 June and 1 December 1981, and in all the committee heard thirty-one witnesses. The inquiry occupied the committee over eleven months.

The Treasury Committee's second major inquiry considered whether nationalized industry financing 'crowded out' private sector investment.[17] The inquiry took approximately two months. The nationalized industry viewpoint was advanced through its informal 'Chairmen's Group'. Eight individual industries provided evidence along with the Treasury, the Bank of England and individual experts.

In its inquiry on international monetary arrangements, the committee followed the pattern of the Monetary Control Inquiry. Three expert advisers were recruited. Evidence was sought on a range of issues from international experts and central banks. Economists of international repute such as

Professors Klein, Epstein and Meade responded. In addition, three international banking institutions and two individuals associated with international monetary institutions provided written evidence. This was published in August 1982. The committee took oral evidence on eighteen separate occasions in the eight-month period between June 1982 and February 1983. As well as experts and bankers, witnesses included some major multinationals (Ford and Unilever), the Treasury, Chancellor, and the Bank of England. The committee took evidence in Washington from individuals associated with two American think-tanks – the Brookings Institution and the Georgetown Center for Strategic and International Studies.

The inquiry into the 'poverty trap' was judged by some committee members and advisers to be the least successful of the Treasury Committee's major inquiries.[18] This inquiry was pursued by a sub-committee chaired by the Labour MP, Michael Meacher. The sub-committee submitted a draft report in February 1983. Review of this draft had not been completed when parliament was dissolved in May 1983. Hence the published papers contain the draft report, the minutes covering consideration of this draft, and an alternative report proposed by the neo-liberal Tory, Ralph Howell. The committee's special advisers included an academic, an individual associated with the Centre for Policy Studies and the director of the Institute for Fiscal Studies. The report draws on UK and international theoretical work on the concept of the poverty trap and documents various schemes proposed to eliminate it. These schemes range from a variation of existing arrangements to more radical reconstruction of the taxation/benefit structure. Ralph Howell's minority report draws on the Basic Income Guarantee Scheme sponsored by the neo-liberal 'think-tank', the Centre for Policy Studies.

The committee took evidence from nine representative groups including specialist advocacy and research groups such as the Child Poverty Action Group, and the Low Pay Unit. An ad hoc coalition, Family Forum, also gave evidence.[19] Central peak groups, the TUC and the CBI, the Association of Independent Businesses and the Institute of Directors, provided both written and oral evidence. Evidence was also taken from all relevant departments (Health and Social Security, Treasury, Inland Revenue), and from three academics. This evidence canvassed the experience of other countries – France, West Germany and the US.

The sub-committee report includes evidence on the degree of joint planning between the Department of Health and Social Security, the Treasury and the Inland Revenue. The sub-committee recommends more formal consultation between departments. Its report comments: 'We are left with the impression that there is an absence of any medium and long term objectives for the [taxation and social security] systems and of arrangements for co-ordination between those objectives.'[20]

Ralph Howell's minority report places on public record neo-liberal proposals for restoration of the 'work incentive' through a single benefits structure supported by one income tax/income support scheme. Divisions between members of the sub-committee remained wide. Advisers complained of heavy demands by the committee, incommensurate with the results. The sub-committee chairman was criticized for pursuing personal political interests at the expense of sub-committee consensus. Members of the full committee commented they would be more cautious in future in using sub-committees to pursue important controversial inquiries. They expressed the view that controversial issues need to be handled from the outset by the full committee to avoid rehearsing the arguments twice.

These criticisms granted, it remains that this was the only major public inquiry on an important tax issue during the tenure of a government committed to significant tax reform. In an environment in which recovery is unlikely to free the resources for reduction of the overall income tax burden, change in the pattern and incidence of taxation seem the most likely form of development. The effects of sustained inflation on tax rates and benefits no doubt makes necessary more frequent adaptation of the tax and benefits system. Yet such adaptation inevitably attracts hostility from groups who perceive themselves to be losing. Those who stand to gain are often not mobilized. This report places on the public record the relevant statistical and other information about reform options. It documents international comparisons. It places on the public record the views of some key interest groups. Government needs this information if a coalition of groups is to be mobilized to support change. Groups need such information from government if potential beneficiaries are to be identified and if they are to assess, from their point of view, the equity of alternative proposals. The usefulness of the inquiry in this context will be considered further in chapter 4.[21]

The Treasury Committee's approach to review of the annual budget cycle is also now well established. It has recruited a panel of specialist advisers to help it with this task. As with the major inquiries, the specialist advisers take responsibility for assessing particular aspects of the government's public pronouncements. They suggest questions to the committee and seek additional information on its behalf. The advisers meet with the Clerk and the Chairman immediately after publication of the government's statements, and with the full committee prior to public sessions. They usually attend these sessions to suggest follow-up questions to committee members.

In its 1981–2 analysis, the Treasury Committee undertook an independent assessment of the cash figures for public expenditure to highlight the extent to which public investment was carrying the burden of budgetary contraction. A capacity to probe the implications of government proposals is essential if a plural policy-making structure is to develop. In this situation, the Treasury Committee would counsel individual departmental select committees about aspects of their own estimates that they may wish to re-assess on larger macro-economic grounds.

The expert evidence published with the report includes papers from the committee's specialist advisers who are drawn from the Department of Applied Economics at Cambridge, the Economist Intelligence Unit, and the stockbrokers, Phillips and Drew. Their memoranda offer detailed explanations or critiques of particular aspects of the government's policy and Treasury's supplementary argument. Terry Ward's memorandum draws attention to the difficulties of comprehending the overall effect of budgetary policy when tax and expenditure decisions are made and presented separately. He also analyses the reasons for change in the PSBR and suggests a different set of causal factors to those implied by government. Paul Ormerod explains why the cash planning totals for 1983–4 and beyond 'should be treated with scepticism'. Dr Paul Neild examines the problems for policy caused by the number of variables the government now recognizes to be significant in interpreting economic developments. He argues:

> Since there now appear to be several targeted variables, it is going to be extremely difficult to decide when policy should be changed. If one variable is outside the range and the other within it, will this be a sufficient condition for a change of policy? If one variable is above the range and another below it, will this constitute sufficient conditions for a change of policy?

He also redressed the Chancellor's omission of a forecast of the effects of budget measures on GDP and employment.

In the course of its budget inquiry the committee invited the Treasury to submit a paper explaining the government position on indexation. This approach was followed by the committee on a number of occasions. When the paper is deemed of sufficient interest, it is published as a special committee document. The paper on indexation is a case in point. It explains the government's approach to indexation in the major economic sectors – the tax system, financial markets, and in relation to pay and public expenditure. There are also detailed papers from the major economic interest groups, the TUC and the CBI.

The seven departmental committees approached their estimates reviews in different ways. For example the Defence Committee took extensive evidence from the Secretary of State about the government's re-equipment plans soon after the Falklands' conflict. The Secretary of State's evidence provided the most detailed public account of the government's intentions. He provided tentative indications of the budgetary implications of this programme. The committee formed no judgement about this evidence. However, it subsequently undertook a series of inquiries into the lessons of the Falklands' exercise, including equipment procurement and performance. The Education Committee used the estimates hearing to gain an overview of policy developments. Committee questions related to other inquiries it was pursuing concurrently on specific issues (e.g. school meals). They also covered issues on which it was contemplating inquiries or which were of current public concern (e.g. closure of village schools). Similarly, the full Foreign Affairs Committee took extensive evidence from the Secretary of State but reached no conclusions. Estimates inquiries typically involved two or three evidence sessions.

Reports were compiled within approximately two to three weeks of the hearings.

Only two of these inquiries included evidence from interest groups. The Overseas Development Sub-Committee in its hearings on support for voluntary agencies took evidence from some voluntary groups about the impact of proposed funding cuts. The Social Services Committee provides a pertinent example of the use of interest group evidence to check information supplied by departments. The committee took evidence concerning the use of departmental indicators at the area level. The group concerned represented responsible officers – the Association of Directors of Social Security. They testified, contrary to the department's claim, that the indicators were not being used for local planning.

The Industry and Trade Committee held hearings on five nationalized industries. It adopted a common approach. Evidence was taken from senior executives of the industry, from unions, departments and sometimes the relevant ministers of state. The inquiries were relatively short. In the case of the Post Office, British Shipbuilders, British Steel and Rolls-Royce, formal reports were tabled. In the case of British Leyland, the inquiry took the form of evidence hearings only. The purpose of these hearings was to enable senior management to report progress in meeting particular targets or to explain why performance had failed to meet expectations.

The British Steel Corporation hearings reflect the committee's approach. The committee took evidence in November from a BSC group and in December from the Secretary of State. BSC was represented by its Chairman, Deputy Chairman and three functional managing directors. Questions covered the current state of negotiations with the United States on BSC's alleged dumping, the effect of non-tariff barriers on BSC's export prospects, its severance payments and plant closure programme, its internal arrangements for planning and reasons for its failure to reach forecast production and market share figures. The committee's short report expressed its concern about several of these issues. The primary result of the inquiries was to bring up-to-date information into the public domain. In its inquiry into the Post Office the committee took evidence from the unions, the various users' committees, and private groups pressing for the right to compete for some services on which the Post Office continued to hold a monopoly. The British Shipbuilders inquiry took evidence from management, the Department of Industry, the TUC, the Confederation of Shipbuilding and Engineering Unions, the Engineers and Managers Association, and the Shipbuilding and Allied Industries Management Association. There were three evidence sessions over a six-week period. The report subsequently took four months to finalize.

Finally, in its hearings on the MSC corporate plan the Employment Committee illustrates how systems of functional and parliamentary representation can be bridged. Evidence sessions with the Chairman of the Commission show committee alertness to the danger of a corporatist consensus emerging on the Commission at the expense of the public interest. Committee questioning explored the frequency with which the 'public' representatives acquiesced in an arrangement congenial to union and employer representatives, but not congenial to other groups or to the public. The committee probed how the Commission informed itself about the attitudes of other interests. The committee also sought information on the Commission's relations with the Department of Education and local government. It explored differences between the Commission's and ministers' projections for unemployment. The cross-examination of the Chairman addresses these points in the context of Commission recommendations and proposals. His defence is available for scrutiny on the public record.[22]

FINDINGS

Our next task is to evaluate the clarity of findings and the degree of committee bipartisanship. We begin with the important Treasury Committee reports on the medium-term financial strategy.

The report on Monetary Control was published in May 1981. It offers a comprehensive appraisal of the government's approach and tactics and extends to approximately 116 pages. The committee classifies expert evidence into four schools which it terms 'neoclassical', 'gradualist', 'pragmatist', and 'anti-monetarist'. These schools are separated by their degree of faith in the capacity of monetary control to break inflationary expectations within politically and socially acceptable boundaries. The report discounts the first Thatcher budget as an authentic monetarist experiment. It draws attention to the effects of the exchange rate on domestic activity. The committee's bipartisan report does not disguise its reservations about the government's strategy. It draws attention to the prospects of deep recession inherent in following rigid monetary targets.

> In the medium term financial strategy the government describes a path for the PSBR which it believes to be consistent with progressive reductions in monetary growth. . . . We believe that there are risks attached to such a subordination of fiscal policy to monetary targets. In a recession caused by a fall in private domestic demand, built-in automatic stabilisers tend to raise the PSBR, which, in turn, with unchanged interest rates, may lead to an increase in monetary growth above the target. Meeting MTFS targets may then require either a rise in interest rates or a tighter fiscal stance. Either of these would tend to counterbalance the moderating effect the automatic stabilisers have on the recession. In these conditions, additional sacrifices of output may be made to meet anti-inflationary monetary targets.[23]

The report points to the government's difficulty in influencing the exchange rate. It draws attention to the risk that international pressures beyond the government's control, transmitted through the exchange rate, would work to frustrate its domestic policy objectives. The committee concludes against the possibility of a sharp assault on inflationary expectations through tight monetary controls in a context in which much of the wage and price structure is negotiated and relatively insulated from market forces.

One of the ways in which it was suggested that monetary policy would combat future inflation was by changing inflationary expectations. We conclude that in the light of experience, this view is not valid. It is unrealistic to suppose that negotiated wages and administered prices respond rapidly and automatically to announcements about monetary policy, however credible they may be. The influence of monetary policy on wage and price inflation does not therefore, appear to be primarily through the setting of targets or through expectations but rather in the short term through the lowering of economic activity and the appreciation of the exchange rate.[24]

The committee concludes its bipartisan report with a warning against faith in quick solutions through monetary targets.

The medium term financial strategy was a bold experiment intended to change expectations about the future of the economy . . . we believe that the view that declarations about monetary policy will quickly affect wages and price expectations is unsubstantiated. This clearly will not happen if the monetary targets themselves are not credible. . . . We were warned by other central banks who have pursued monetary targets that the effective use of such devices is by no means a mechanical procedure. It evidently requires a degree of judgement and flexibility in a choice of the monetary aggregate, and in the setting and resetting of the targets to ensure that the pursuit of such an intermediate target is consistent with and not inimical to progress in achieving the ultimate objective of policy on which there is substantial agreement, namely growth, less inflation, and higher levels of employment.[25]

The Treasury Committee report on nationalized industry funding was also bipartisan. The report concludes with reservations about the presumptions behind current policy:

The nationalised and State owned industries now comprise an important sector of the economy. Some of their investments are on the frontiers of new technology. Others, steel and shipbuilding, represent some of Britain's oldest industries. We have already stressed their variety. Not one of them appears to regard the system under which they are controlled as ideal, nor has it seemed to us designed to give the maximum incentive to their efficiency and effectiveness.[26]

An appraisal of this report was subsequently published by M. R. Garner of the London School of Economics. He applauds the extra information which the committee brings into the public domain. He notes that the report makes the issue accessible to non-technical people:

> The rationale of the government's macroeconomic policy . . . has been set out for non-specialists to see and marvel at. The problem of frustrated investment has been brought down from the clouds and given approximate dimensions. Issues associated with the EFLs [External Finance Limits] included the scope of the PSBR and alternatives to the National Loans Fund as means for the industries' financing, have been dealt with sensibly, if sometimes only provisionally. By itself calling for simulations from several economic models, the Committee may have discouraged departments from adopting their economists' theoretical conclusions without first checking their practical consequences and applying a measure of common sense.[27]

Garner criticizes the report on two grounds. First he says it fails to address the problem of the politicization of investment decisions implicit in an arrangement where each industry negotiates its future with its sponsoring department. Second, he criticizes the conclusions for superficiality.

> The Committee failed to set out the basic dilemma the EFL system attempts to resolve. From the industries' point of view it is not acceptable that they should be prevented from proceeding with profitable investment . . . from the government's point of view it is not acceptable that its economic strategy and the finances of the public sector shall be disrupted by unbudgeted financial demands from the industries. It needed to be made plain that the EFL system in its present form is incapable of resolving this dilemma. The Committee's recommendation of more flexibility in the operation of the system is no solution. If it was not prepared to condemn the EFL system, the Committee might at least have explored the possibility of two EFLs for each enterprise – one for capital expenditure and one for the revenue account.

The first report on international lending by commercial banks, was published in March 1983. The report is some fifty pages long. It provides a comprehensive assessment of the default risk. The report concludes that the failure of global recovery represents the principal risk to the international financial system. It endorses steps taken by the private banks to strengthen their capacity to assess individual national borrowers' credit capacity. The committee welcomes the proposed enlargement of IMF reserves. This report was tabled in time for debate of the second Brandt Report in the Commons on 18 April 1983.

The second report of the Treasury Committee on International Monetary Arrangements was published without endorsement by the full committee. The general election of June 1983 prevented finalization of the committee's review of the Chairman's draft. The published documents include an alternative approach to achieving an acceptable international regime prepared by a Labour member of the committee, Dr Jeremy Bray. The draft report was published on 11 May, three weeks before the Williamsburg Summit. The report recommends an approach for the British Government at this meeting. So far as domestic economic management is concerned, the report notes the government's move towards a more pragmatic approach. The committee welcomes this move as consistent with its own earlier findings. The report proposes a strengthened money-supply/exchange-rate policy regime. An appendix offers a comprehensive survey of recent developments in economic theory bearing upon exchange rate fixation.

The Treasury Committee report on the Chancellor's Autumn Statement, like most periodic reports in its first five years, criticized the amount of information the government makes available.[28] The committee has pressed continually for the disclosure of more current and more comprehensive out-turns and forecasts. The committee's goal has been to gain sufficient information to judge economic outcomes and budget options in parallel with the government. In its 1981–2 November report, the committee pointed out that the statement as currently delivered lacked essential information for those seeking to appraise the costs and benefits of emerging budget options. No revenue estimates were provided. There was very little information about expenditure plans. Out-turns related to estimates provided in the previous year's budget, not to the most recently available forecasts. Such information as was disclosed was not on a comparable basis. The figures in the Public Expenditure White Paper could not be reconciled with those in the budget. In its first year of existence the committee was able to undertake its own projections of economic developments by feeding its own data into the Treasury model. Funds for this purpose were provided by the Treasury in the 1980–1 session. Subsequent requests for funds for a similar exercise were rejected. Its discussion of the 1982–5 Public Expenditure White Paper also focused on the question of the adequacy of the information which the government disclosed about levels of service. Whilst endorsing the desirability of cash controls, the committee argued that legitimate concern about levels of service by MPs and members of the public required that volume and cost information should continue to be published. 'Such a presentation would not offer a challenge to the primacy of the cash plans, but is necessary if these plans are to be satisfactorily expressed.'[29]

The committee's report on the budget reflected the conclusions of its Monetary Control Report. The committee noted the modification to the government's economic strategy which had taken place. Its report endorsed this development: 'These changes to the medium term financial strategy represent a further move to greater pragmatism in policy for which we have constantly argued.'[30]

The report reviewed the government's budget judgement. The committee concluded that the government's 'fiscal stance is planned to be no more or less tight in 1982/83 than in 1981/82'.[31] So far as economic prospects were concerned the committee expressed concern at the levels of unemployment which the government's approach accepted. 'That the assumed rate of growth over four years of a cyclical upswing (1981/2 to 1984/5) is insufficient to reduce unemployment significantly is clearly disturbing as it suggests a trend of increasing unemployment over the cycle as a whole.'[32] The Committee applauded the 'overdue' elimination of inflationary gains from capital gains tax.

Three committees indicated a disposition to challenge specific estimates – the Treasury Committee in its review of the Summer Supplementary Estimates, the Energy Committee and the Overseas Development Sub-Committee of the Foreign Affairs Committee. The Energy Committee contested several individual votes. An earlier report on nuclear power spending had criticized the government's failure to support research on energy conservation. In its estimates reviews, the committee criticized the level of government spending on research into enhanced oil recovery, wind power development, and the increase in oil-related payments to the Isle of Man and Northern Ireland. It concluded: 'We believe there are small but revealing indications of a lack of strategy, coherence and logic in the Department's pattern of resource allocation.'[33]

Its major criticism was directed against a vote of £231 million in 1981–2 to the National Coal Board to maintain uneconomic pits. The government had earlier withdrawn its plan to close these pits in the face of threats of industrial action. Its bipartisan report concluded: 'If we had a formal role in the Estimates, we would have been extremely reluctant to endorse the additional expenditure on the coal industry without much firmer assurances from the Department that the underlying strategy is both viable and sustainable.' The committee also criticized the export price for coal levied by the NCB.

In its review of the Summer Supplementary Estimates, the Treasury Committee announced its willingness to challenge particular estimates. Referring to the allocation of £7 million to the European Community's Budget, whose legality the British Government was then contesting in the courts, the committee comments: 'We cannot escape the conclusion that . . . the Government would have been better advised to put the question of the payment of public monies to the judgement of the House before disbursement.'[34]

The Overseas Development Sub-Committee of the Foreign Affairs Committee recommended the restoration of £500,000 to the British Volunteers Programme. It did so after taking evidence from the interest groups concerned. The sub-committee also renewed its criticism of the Department's handling of airport development on the Turks and Caicos Islands. This was the subject of a separate inquiry by the sub-committee. In its estimates report, the committee recommended review of the management of trade–aid programmes. This illustrates one way in which committees can build upon and reinforce earlier findings. It thus allays the concern of some members (mentioned earlier) that estimates inquiries occur too late to be effective. What these inquiries demonstrate, on the contrary, is the opportunity to follow up earlier findings.

The Social Services Committee referred one vote – spending on animal research – for investigation by the Public Accounts Committee. This committee used its estimates reviews to mount a sustained critique of the department's approach to policy planning and to the supply of information. This began in the 1979–80 session. The committee recruited Rudolf Klein from Bath University as an expert adviser. Professor Klein's interest in the National Health Service and in welfare policy generally was long established.[35] He played a leading part in drafting reports which provide a detailed and comprehensive critique of the department's approach to, and priorities for, planning. Reports in the 1979–80 and 1980–1 sessions include a comprehensive review of the availability and presentation of information in the health and social security area.

The 1981–2 report contains detailed information on departmental arrangements to review the National Health Service. It also lists the issues currently under examination by the Policy Strategy Unit. The committee challenges the government's decision not to publish these reports. It criticizes the department for not seeing outreach and public discussion as essential elements of its strategic planning activity.[36]

All these reports reviewing departmental estimates were bipartisan – except for one Labour dissenter on the Energy Committee review of the National Coal Board vote.

Turning to reviews of nationalized industries, the Industry and Trade Committee has evaluated the performance of four nationalized industries on a regular basis. The expansion of the nationalized industry sector had been a marked feature of the past decade. Mrs Thatcher's government pledged to restore the sector's economic health as a prelude to privatizing particular industries. The government began with ambitious targets for the nationalized industries. It sought to convert their total external financing of £2.7 billion in 1979–80 to a £700 million contribution by 1983–4 (in 1980 prices). In the event these targets were not met during Mrs Thatcher's first term. External financing stayed around £2.5 billion in 1980–1, 1981–2 and 1982–3. The major loss-making industries were steel (loss of £500 million in 1982–3); coal (loss of £900 million in 1982–3) and British Rail (loss approximately £900 million in 1982–3).[37] The reports reviewed here are notable for placing the views of management and unions on the public record. They demonstrate the capacity of the committee to mobilize the information necessary to check the government's judgements. In the context of the proposed public investment in aero engine developments and its earlier uncovering of continuing Concorde costs, the Industry and Trade Committee suggests parliamentary committees should endorse long-term capital projects before they are accepted by the government.[38] This proposal was later endorsed in an amplified form by the Committee on Financial Procedure. It attracted some negative press comment.[39] But if committees are to build their role in the budget process, automatic public scrutiny of major proposed capital projects seems the likely initial step.

The committee endorses the government's continued funding of British Leyland. Its hearings and published evidence provide, it says, 'the most comprehensive public explanation of British Leyland's current situation'. The report on the Post Office followed that organization's separation from British Telecom. It is more extensive and places a considerable amount of information on the public record. The inquiry provides political access to various participant groups to place on the public record their appraisal of Post Office service.

The committee's report on British Shipbuilders is sympathetic to the industry's claims. The evidence from the Confederation of Shipbuilding and Engineering Unions is comprehensive and detailed. It includes a candid assessment of industry problems from union witnesses. They blame traditional management practices for current industrial relations. They argue that current manning practices and worker–management distrust are the result of unstable employment conditions. Traditionally, large-scale retrenchment automatically followed the completion of a major project. The report documents changes since the establishment of British Shipbuilders. Since 1977, nine yards, thirty-eight building berths, three engine-building facilities, and three ship-repair centres were closed. Employment was reduced by 20,700.

The committee report criticizes the decrease in Defence orders. It comments:

> British Shipbuilders argued powerfully to us that to sell war ships overseas, the active support and cooperation of HMG, Ministry of Defence and Navy was essential to match the efforts of our foreign competitors. We greatly doubt the adequacy of such support in the past. Recent history of war ship building for the Royal Navy suggests that the U.K. has sought standards of sophistication in war ships that have made the chance of selling them abroad very slight.

As we shall see in the following chapter, several other committees have conducted detailed investigations of particular projects or of ongoing programmes.

IMPACT

The impact of the select committees can be gauged at a number of levels of the policy-making system. The most significant indicator of impact is of course government policy. Treasury Committee members themselves saw monetary control as their single most effective report. They credited it with anticipating economic relationships which the government only subsequently conceded to be significant.[40] The impact on ministers and parliament of the other major policy inquiries of the Treasury Committee and of the estimates hearings is much harder to assess. These reports have been criticized variously as too imprecise or too partisan, or as misconceived.[41] These criticisms in some cases reflect that contention which is the essence of politics. But the merit of these inquiries is also to be found in the extensive additional information they place on the public record, their explication of the political choices inherent in technical disagreements, their explanation of these technical disagreements in language comprehensible to the intelligent layman, their identification of the limited range of choices confronting government, their generally bipartisan character and their relevance to ongoing debates.[42] But no reports were specifically debated in the House. The government's formal replies, which were printed as House of Commons papers, were generally bland. Without the opportunity to advance findings in the political process the committee reviews often faded into obscurity.

A second potential impact is on bureaucratic thinking. Treasury officials credited the monetary control report with introducing them to current theoretical work. The prospect of public cross-examination by well briefed, well informed parliamentarians (however the experience actually turned out) encouraged them to sharpen their arguments. Treasury officials credited this with aiding the substance as well as the presentation of their case. Despite the time involved, those Treasury officers who were interviewed (or who publicly commented) held this to be a positive result.[43] Other committees were evidently also able to 'stimulate' their departments. The Energy Committee's criticism of the Energy Department and the NCB stung the Department of Energy into a speedy reaction. The committee's report elicited a letter from the Secretary of State the day it was published. Ian Lloyd, the Chairman, replied unrepentantly, with bipartisan support from his committee. The correspondence was published. This served as a prelude to a further major inquiry in the 1983–4 session into pit closures.

A third indicator of impact is press attention to committee proceedings and findings. The Treasury Committee has perhaps attracted most attention. Its report on monetary control attracted extensive press coverage.[44] The reports and the hearings of the Defence Committee also attracted considerable publicity. The Secretary of State's evidence, which occurred soon after the Falklands' War attracted national press attention. No less important is the attention paid to the committees by the specialist press, whose coverage of committee activities has been extensive – the *Times Educational Supplement*, for example, carrying full reports of the Education Committee's hearings.[45]

A fourth area of potential impact is ministers' relation with officials. The ability of determined officials to thwart ministers has been well documented.[46] Criticism by the Social Services Committee of the inadequacy of departmental strategic planning was turned to advantage by the then Secretary of State. The committee's criticisms coincided with the desire of a new minister, Patrick

Jenkin, to strengthen strategic planning within his department. He was able to use the select committee's report to encourage a reluctant permanent secretary to establish a policy strategy unit.

Senior administrators can also be influenced by the use of external protagonists or local and regional public servants to check the advice tendered by officers of central departments. The Treasury Committee has deliberately sought to engage experts and (to a lesser extent) peak groups and to tap the views of departments other than Treasury where this is appropriate. The monetary control inquiry shows how this evidence can be marshalled to contribute to strategic policy making. The use of an interest group's evidence to check and discredit departmental evidence (by the Social Services Committee) also illustrates the engagement of interest groups for tactical purposes.

On the other hand, the committees' impact on interest groups has been equivocal. For example, the peak groups the TUC and the CBI were hesitant in their assessment of the monetary control inquiry and the work of the Treasury Committee generally. Their reaction reflected their uncertainty about the role of committees and their place in the policy structure. They could not see any tangible result.[47] Outreach to interest groups was not a major element of other inquiries in this group.

One charge levelled against select committees is that they become 'captives' of the interest groups associated with their inquiries. There are only two inquiries of the twenty reviewed in this chapter that could conceivably fall into this category. One is the Industry and Trade Committee's review of British Shipbuilders. The government rejected the committee's recommendations. It argued that the report amounted to a 'call for more help for the shipbuilding industry through preferential policies and restrictions on U.K. shipping interests'. The second is the Overseas Development Sub-Committee call for additional support (£500,000) for the British Volunteers Programme. In both cases the evidence does not support unequivocal judgements. What is clear is the ability of committees to marshal evidence to dispute ministerial and/or departmental judgements.

The final area of impact occurs within and between committees themselves. Committees have demonstrated the capacity for what might be termed 'committee learning', which occurs at two levels. First, it occurs within committees. We see how one inquiry leads to another or provides additional opportunities to pursue earlier findings. The Treasury Committee inquiries on the medium-term financial strategy and several of the individual estimates inquiries illustrate this (e.g. Social Services Committee). From the point of view of the Treasury Committee itself, for example, the most important immediate consequence of its monetary control inquiry was to provide a framework for assessing the government's annual economic statements. The inquiry informed members about the varying indicators that might be used and the emphasis given to these indicators by the differing economic schools. The principal Opposition spokesman, Peter Shore, stated subsequently that he had found this particular report 'very helpful'.[48]

The second level of committee learning occurs between committees. Here they have developed a formal structure to link their efforts. A Liaison Committee composed of all the chairmen has been established.[49] Through the Liaison Committee an embryo system has been established for transmitting information between chairmen and this system is mirrored at the official level by a committee structure uniting clerks. The most senior parliamentary officer – the Clerk of Committees – acts as secretary of the Liaison Committee, which meets as necessary during the session. For their part, the clerks meet together weekly to review common problems and issues. The promotion structure of the clerks' department gives senior officers the opportunity to provide leadership, or at least guidance. This system has the potential for co-ordinating committee work. For example, reviews of the estimates were suggested to departmental committees by the Treasury Committee. A system exists that allows the Treasury Committee to notify other committees of its specific findings on general budget matters, particularly when these have implications for individual estimates. Naturally, individual chairmen and committees are sensitive about their independent prerogatives but nevertheless a system of communication exists which enjoys the confidence of all chairmen.

THE COMMITTEES AND THE BUDGET CYCLE

What are we to make of the foregoing evidence? That the committees have brought more information about government decisions and government operations into the public domain is generally agreed. There is also general agreement that the committees have had little direct impact on policy. So, the critics ask, what is there to show for a significant commitment of parliamentary, bureaucratic, ministerial and, to a lesser degree, interest group time and effort?

Within the context of the two-party policy-making system it is true that tangible results are hard to find. Committees are typically inquiring, after the event, on issues which parliament generally has little opportunity to influence. But in the context of a policy-making structure in which select committees become catalysts for parliamentary deliberation and provide a political arena for the integration of interest groups, there are some very encouraging, and some cautionary, aspects of the committees' experience.

In their investigations and in their reports there is evidence that committees have crafted a role for themselves in each phase of the budget process. What are the characteristics of this role? First, it offers the potential to bring a much more comprehensive account of the government's perceptions of general interests and priorities into the public domain.[50] All the committees conduct all their significant hearings in public. All evidence both oral and written is printed. Committee votes are recorded with reports, so that the approach of individual members can be identified. The volume of additional information these committees make available is evident not only on the public record but in the publicity that they have received. This information bears upon those determinations of the public interest that are now the private preserve of ministers and departments. This is the kind of information external interest groups require if they are to calculate general interests from their point of view or relate their judgements to those of the government. It is also essential if interest groups are to calculate realistic, not utopian, alternatives.

The second characteristic of the role being crafted by committees is their capacity to mobilize resources to reach a well-founded independent judgement on government proposals. The Treasury Committee in particular has demonstrated an impressive capacity to mobilize the technical expertise to review, explain and, if necessary, challenge the government's budget judgements. It has demonstrated a capacity to work at both 'levels' of the budget process. Its inquiries explore not only the underlying assumptions in the government's medium-term financial strategy but also the government's current tactics and proposals. The Treasury Committee has undertaken both tasks competently. Its inquiries have been timely, its reports succinct and well documented. Its evidence sessions are usually probing and instructive. These features are equally evident in departmental committees such as the Energy Committee and the Social Services Committee.

A third characteristic of the role being crafted by select committees is their potential as independent assessors of policy. The various estimates recommendations and the judgements about the medium-term financial strategy, suggest the committees have drawn clear conclusions about government decisions. Reports place on public record the basis of committee reasoning and the facts judged to be relevant. The government replies to these reports oblige departments to justify their original recommendations and to refute the inferences or judgements the committee may have drawn.

Just as importantly, these reports demonstrate the capacity of select committees to produce bipartisan findings. None of these reports was voted on strictly party lines. Yet it cannot be said that committees have avoided tough issues. The monetary control inquiry, the review of the Manpower Services Commission, the merit of providing additional funds to Leyland and to British Steel, spending on an overseas aid vote – these are the matters on which committees produced precise bipartisan recommendations. If only one or two reports were involved, one could argue that special factors were decisive. But the number of reports with strong, bipartisan recommendations suggests perhaps greater possibilities for bipartisanship than most observers have allowed.

Finally these inquiries illustrate the capacity of committees to become 'brokers' between government, departments, interest groups and individual experts. Government and other interests need to know the detailed rationale behind the position of 'rival' and 'friendly' groups, such as the CBI or the TUC. Through their engagement in Treasury Committee inquiries these peak groups have been obliged to place their detailed case on the public record and, less frequently, to defend their views in public cross-examination. If departments or other protagonists are to calculate negotiating options and weigh trade-offs, this information is essential.

The Treasury Committee's continuing effort to obtain more up-to-date, comprehensive and comparable information indicates the deficient quality of publicly available information. Until clearer, more comprehensive and more timely information is available on a routine basis, committees will be a useful source of information, but not an essential 'conduit' between the government and important interests.

Similarly, the performance of the individual departmental committees was uneven. Seven of the thirteen committees undertook estimates reviews. Three of these produced reports with precise, generally bipartisan recommendations for variations of estimates that could be voted. Six used the occasion to check departmental action on earlier reports or to gather information relevant to possible inquiries. Only one committee has reviewed an advisory commission regularly. The Employment Committee's approach to the Manpower Services Commission is an instructive guide to what committees can achieve. Its sensitivity to the risk of corporatist consensus at the expense of the public interest, reflects the role committees can play in bridging systems of functional and parliamentary representation.

The limited engagement of interest groups in these inquiries is the most significant cautionary factor. One justification for an extended role for select committees lies in their potential to integrate interest groups in policy making in ways that advance the public interest. The Treasury Committee has undertaken extensive outreach to domestic interest groups on only one inquiry – that concerned with taxation and the poverty trap. The Treasury Committee's shorter reviews have not been used to provide access to the views of important sectional interests. The committee has not as a matter of course taken oral evidence from leaders of peak groups such as the General Secretary of the TUC or the Director-General of the CBI or from local government organizations. It has not sought to engage leaders of major welfare, unemployed or rights groups on current budgetary matters. It has sought written evidence only from peak producer groups. Its most impressive and extensive outreach has been to independent experts.

Similarly, individual departmental committees have not, in their estimates reviews, generally engaged more than concerned ministers and officials. In the 1981–2 session, only one committee – the Social Services Committee – checked departmental advice by calling evidence from a practitioner's group (The Association of Directors of Social Security). The reviews of nationalized industries and of the Manpower Services Commission have involved more extensive outreach to interest groups. Clearly, on estimates inquiries time constraints will inhibit the capacity of committees to hear oral evidence. Still, these inquiries do not suggest committees have been eager to engage directly with interests from the relevant policy constituencies in assessing government judgements or proposals.

In sum there are a number of encouraging signs. The shape of an enlarged committee role can be clearly perceived. Committee capacity for bipartisan judgement is well demonstrated. Committee capacity to bring new currents into policy making and to deliver succinct and timely reports is clear. There is evidence of the scope for co-ordination between committees. Committees have demonstrated their sensitivity to overall macro-economic consider-ations. The evidence suggests the crafting of a role for committees has begun, but it remains at a formative stage, with its full potential yet to be tested.

This review of the work of committees in the budget area suggests they could as easily be maintained as impotent ancillaries of the two-party system as become independent agents in a more plural policy-making structure. The movement of structures and attitudes necessary to sustain a plural approach has begun. Its possibilities are evident. Its promise remains unproven in some fundamental respects.

I now turn to assess the extent to which committees have contrived a role in relation to current policy proposals.

Chapter 3

Current issues and the government programme

The second area of policy making to which parliament needs to be introduced if it is to exercise an independent deliberative role involves current or proposed programmes. Here issues arise from two sources: first, from ministers who are responsible for incorporating their government's philosophy and priorities into existing programmes; and second, from the unfolding of existing programmes. Ongoing programmes require adaptation as new needs or unexpected developments emerge. Much of the day-to-day business of government arises from these two sources.

Much of this activity, although financed or directed by central government, is actually executed by others. Local government provides many welfare, education and housing services. Universities provide higher education. The hospitals provide health care. The Manpower Services Commission designs and manages training programmes. Central government provides some or all of the funds for these activities. But often it does not itself directly control their use and application. It sets guidelines, evaluates performance and monitors and co-ordinates overall programme development. But its direct power of control is relatively limited and, when exercised through management systems like cash limits, relatively crude.[1]

The conditions under which policy is developed and implemented derive ultimately from the constitutional conventions associated with the two-party system. The distinctive feature of this system is, as we have seen, the concentration of formal power. Whereas in the budget cycle formal power is concentrated in the hands of the prime minister and chancellor, in the departmental structure formal power of initiative is concentrated in the hands of ministers.[2] Ministers are accountable to parliament for the day-to-day administration of current programmes. They are formally required to take all the important decisions affecting the administration of current programmes or their development. They are also required to authorize and keep themselves briefed about important negotiations between their own department and other departments (such as the Treasury) and relevant independent bodies, (e.g. local government, the University Grants Commission). Ministers are also

deeply involved in preparing Cabinet submissions for ongoing and new programmes.

Because the two-party system works to separate the public political battle
for office (for which parliament is the arena) from policy work (which occurs
between Cabinet, departments and particular interest groups), departmental
activity takes place in private. Ministers will make statements to parliament
about important new developments. But this usually occurs after key decisions
have been taken. Even when they occur before the government finally determines its position, parliamentary debates are rarely based on the merits of the
issue. The merits of particular issues are overshadowed by the battle for
government between the rival parties.

Government backbenchers perhaps have more influence over departmental
policies than over budget decisions. Backbench pressure can be mobilized in a
number of ways. Individual members have access to ministers. Backbench
committees of government members can exert influence on a minister. All-
party groups can be influential in achieving legislative amendment.[3] But
compared to the influence of ministers and departments, backbenchers are
impotent. Even if they possess the will, they lack the information, the machinery and the rationale for a larger role. The two-party system effectively casts
backbenchers as 'lobby fodder'. So far as policy making is concerned, their
primary role is as members of the cast for what is mostly a ritual parliamentary battle.

Interest groups, other levels of government and independent agencies
participate in policy making in varying ways. What now passes for consultation involves an (often elaborate) apparatus for tapping the views of the
relevant groups. Green Papers and White Papers have grown in popularity as
a means of communicating with particular policy constituencies.[4] Advisory
councils are attached to most major programmes. But these relationships
typically take place in private. Submissions are invited on particular proposals. The influences at work which might lead either central government or
the relevant interest group to modify its pre-existing approach are relatively
weak. Departments initiate interaction. They control the agenda. They
control the time scale of negotiations. They control who participates. They
determine next steps and if there is to be any feedback to participating interests.

This is the context in which the new departmental committees have super-
vened. Our task is to establish how effectively they have discharged their role.
The following sections review, in turn, the scope and significance of the
inquiries conducted by the committees, the adequacy of the conduct of
inquiries by the select committees, the precision and bipartisan character of
committee findings and the impact of their reports.

SCOPE AND SIGNIFICANCE

In the 1979 to 1983 period, all except two committees undertook a short
current inquiry of some kind. They are an established element in the pattern of

Table 3.1   Summary of current inquiries

Committee	Legislation/ regulations	Government policy proposals	Implications government decisions	Committee initiated review of programmes	Committee initiated proposals	Information	
Employment	3	2				1	6
Home Affairs	1	1			2	1	5
Foreign Affairs	1		1			3	5
Energy		1	1		1	1	4
Transport		1					1
Welsh Affairs		1				1	2
Social Services		1	1				2
Education				3	6	3	12
Industry and Trade			1			2	3
Defence Committee						1	1
Liaison Committee						1	1
	5	7	4	3	9	14	42

inquiries of the 'average' committee. Such a committee in fact typically undertakes two short inquiries, one long inquiry, plus an estimates hearing in each session. In the 1981–2 session, nine of the fourteen committees undertook thirty-four inquiries concerned with current policy issues. Hence five committees omitted these inquiries. The Treasury Committee cannot be counted because of its preoccupation with the budget cycle. The Agriculture and Environment Committees concentrated on longer-term issues. The Scottish Affairs and Defence Committees undertook inquiries of this kind in other sessions. The Defence Committee undertook one inquiry reviewing departmental action on earlier recommendations of the committee. This inquiry is included in this chapter – although not counted in the above total. Six inquiries from earlier sessions, that are of special interest or that were debated in the House in the 1981–2 session, are also reviewed here.

This area of activity tests partisanship more than any other. Proposals will usually have been endorsed by ministers and by Cabinet before being introduced. Table 3.1 classifies these inquiries according to the aspect of policy making that is involved. Of the thirty-eight inquiries that ended with substantive recommendations, five involved review of proposed legislation or regulations (i.e. committees at work in a pre-legislative mode); seven inquiries involved review of specific government policy proposals before being implemented and four reviewed decisions after their announcement. The committees themselves initiated review of three programmes and nine inquiries that ended in specific proposals on current policy matters. This pattern of inquiries represents full coverage of the range of activities conducted by the executive. It also shows committees responding on their own initiative to current issues.

Table 3.2 analyses the inquiries in terms of the government objectives pursued and suggests the extent to which committees have responded to

Table 3.2   Inquiries responding to government themes

Select Committee	Privatization	Expenditure control	Reduction of union power	Reduced regulation	Total government initiated	Other
Employment			1	3	4	
Transport	1				1	
Home Affairs		1			1	2 (Legal Process)
Foreign Affairs		1			1	1 Canadian Constitution
Energy	1	2			3	
Welsh Affairs						1
Social Services		2			2	
Education		3			3	6
Industry and Trade		1			1	1
Public Accounts		1			1	
	2	11	1	3	17	11

Total inquiries 28 (including 1 PAC Inquiry) (Excluding information only inquiries)

proposals resulting from the translation of government objectives into programmes. The major themes of the Thatcher government are privatization, expenditure control, and a reduction of regulation and of trade union power. Sixteen of the twenty-eight inquiries (approximately 60 per cent) that terminated with specific recommendations originated in these themes. Two inquiries concerned privatization, eleven arose from expenditure control measures, one considered means to reduce union power, and three to reduce regulation.

The pattern of inquiries between committees is also noteworthy. Table 3.1 shows that the Education Committee with twelve inquiries contributed a disproportionate number to the total. Other active committees were Employment (six inquiries), Home Affairs (five), and Foreign Affairs (five).

Tables 3.3 to 3.8 review the pattern of inquiries in detail in each dimension of executive activity. Table 3.3 shows legislation considered by committees in the 1981–2 parliamentary session plus two notable examples of legislative reviews in earlier sessions.[5] The three examples from the 1981–2 session all happen to involve the Employment Committee. Two of its hearings concern proposals for additional regulations. These originated beyond the executive in the Manpower Services Commission and the Commission for Racial Equality. The examples from earlier years involve the Home Affairs and the Foreign Affairs Committees. The inquiries concerned the proposed 'SUS' laws and patriation of the Canadian Constitution.

The second category of inquiries involves government policy proposals (table 3.4). Government policy proposals arise either from the translation of the government's priorities into current programmes or from the adaptation of current programmes to new exigencies. Of the seven inquiries in this category four result from the former cause and three from the latter. These inquiries do not reflect the range and number of government initiatives proposed during the 1981–2 session. Their novelty lies in the fact that they occurred at all. It is not usual practice for the government to give notice of new initiatives on current matters to parliament sufficiently far in advance to permit a select committee inquiry. The government does however often signal its intentions to the various interest groups associated with particular pro- grammes through Green Papers and White Papers. This is the way the select committees learnt of five of these seven policy proposals. The committees conducted their inquiries in parallel with the official consultation process.

These proposals covered a wide range of government activity, for example: a charge on a group who previously received free health care; transfer of vehicle testing to private sector control; sale of the British Gas Corporation stake in an oil-field; a new youth training programme; a proposal to shift the burden of sickness benefits from government to employers in the initial stages of illness. The economic significance of these issues varies considerably. For example: the Wytch Farm Field was valued at up to £450 million; the Youth Training Programme was estimated to cost one billion pounds in a full year; the vehicle testing stations involve annual revenues of around £10 million; the National Health Service charge to overseas visitors was estimated to realise £6 million.

The preceding category of inquiries involved committees reporting on proposals before final decisions were taken by the government. A further group of committee reviews involved inquiries after the announcement of particular decisions. In one case – school meals – this involved review of the impact of a decision implemented in 1980. There were four inquiries into the implications of government proposals in the 1981–2 parliamentary session. They are listed in table 3.5. The subjects covered include the implications of expenditure cuts on higher education and medical services. The Education Committee estimated the likely impact on participation rates and challenged the government's estimates of redundancy costs. In a further inquiry it took evidence from universities sceptical about the fairness of the procedures followed by UGC for allocating cuts. The Social Services Committee calcu- lated the effects of education spending cuts on the availability of medical services.

Four inquiries involved the review of specific programmes. These are listed in table 3.6. With the exception of the Public Accounts Committee inquiry, all followed up the findings of earlier, longer committee inquiries. They thus show committees returning briefly to a subject as a result of new developments or to check that promised action has been carried out. Three of these occurred in the 1981–2 session and one early in the 1982–3 session. This involved an inquiry into pit closures by the Energy Committee. In reviewing specific programmes committees perform a function akin to the Public Accounts Committee. They draw on the presumption that committees exist to extend parliament's scrutiny of departmental expenditure. As we saw in chapter 1, this view has been most potent in the development of a rationale for com- mittees.

Table 3.3 Legislation and regulations (references are to 1981/2 session unless otherwise indicated)

Committee	Inquiry	Approach	Outreach	Findings/Impact on government
Employment (H.C. 153)	Legal Immunities of Trade Unions	* Builds on earlier cttee inquiries: (H.C. 282, 1980/1). * Cttee acts in pre-legislation role.	* Pre-legislation hearing: TUC, CBI, Sec. of State. * Earlier hearings: 3 experts, TUC, CBI, Institute of Directors etc. Written evidence 22 individuals and groups.	* This hearing involves cttee in pre-legislation role. * 1980/81 report split on party lines.
Employment (H.C. 273)	Review of Anti-Discrimination Code (proposed by Commission for Racial Equality)	* Draft code before parliament as required by statute. * Ostensibly negotiated through TUC and CBI via representatives on CRE plus invited comments from other groups. * Cttee concentrates on practicality of requirements.	* Oral evidence from affected interest groups: Assoc. of Independent Businesses, West Indian Standing Conference, Conf. of Afro-Caribbean and Asian Councillors, ACAS, CRE. * ACAS indicates reservations about proposed code.	* Substantial change in code recommended, including: – treatment small firms. – protection of information. * Cttee proposals accepted by gov. * Bipartisan report.
Employment (H.C. 27)	Review of Draft Code on Employment of Disabled (proposed by Manpower Services Commission)	* Draft code from MSC as required.	* Oral evidence MSC and 5 interest groups, written evidence 7 interest groups.	* Endorses MSC approach but suggests further thought re mechanics. Questions continuing need for quotas. * Gov. endorses cttee findings. Refers code back to MSC. * Bipartisan report.

(continued)

Table 3.3—*continued*

Committee	Inquiry	Approach	Outreach	Findings/Impact on government
Home Affairs (sub-committee) (H.C. *559, 744*, 1979/80; H.C. *271*, 1980/1)	'SUS' Laws	* Cttee opposed law. * After Law Commission review, further report (744) foreshadowed private bill to repeal laws.	* Evidence from 'Scrap SUS' campaign; Society for Lab. Lawyers; Met. Police; Soc. for Cons. Lawyers; Runnymede Trust etc. * Campaign for Homeless and Rootless; Met. Police; Assoc. of Chief Police Officers.	* Cttee recommends abolition of 'SUS' laws. * Motion (moved by Opposition spokesman) for approval by House debated on supply day (5.6.80). * Provision repealed in Criminal Attempts Bill (1980/1). * Report approved 4 Cons plus 4 Lab = 8 for; 1 Lab against.
Foreign Affairs (H.C. *427, 295*, 1980/1; H.C. *128*, 1981/2) (Debated Commons 17.2.82; 23.2.82; 3.3.82; 8.3.82)	British North America Acts	* Cttee challenged gov. judgement that 'it may not look behind any Federal request for patriation'. * Canadian Gov. published paper countering cttee conclusions.	* Special adviser Dr John Finnis. * Cttee elicited evidence from 9 UK constitutional experts.	* Cttee questioned gov. view that British parliament bound by Canadian Gov. request. Evoked strong response Canadian Gov. and interest groups UK and Canada. * Major influence on UK parliamentary debate. * Bipartisan report.

71

Table 3.4 Government policy proposals (references are to 1981/2 session unless otherwise indicated)

Committee	Inquiry	Approach	Outreach	Findings/Impact on government
Home Affairs (sub-committee) (H.C. 121)	NHS Charges for Overseas Visitors	* Cttee calls evidence on feasibility from RHAs.	* CRE Council for Overseas Students, NUS, TUC, 7 RHAs.	* Cttee (voting on party lines) finds gov. proposals will not harm race relations. Questions revenue estimate (£6 m.) and suggests modifications and review of procedures.
Employment (H.C. 221)	Youth Unemployment A New Training Initiative	* Gov. abolished compulsory Training Boards 1980. * MSC proposes YWS – modified by gov. to Youth Opportunities Scheme. * Cost estimate £1.1 billion 1984/5.	* Institute of Careers Officers, CBI, TUC, MSC regional staff. * No youth groups.	* Cttee recommended maintenance of supplementary benefit to school leavers to ensure positive start to scheme. * Accepted by gov. (H.C. 425, 1981/2). * Bipartisan report.
Employment (H.C. 348)	Abolition of Industrial Training Boards	* Builds on evidence sessions in 1980/1 (H.C. 51, iii to vi)	* Oral evidence from Sec. of State.	* Cttee publishes evidence to better inform House of reasons for gov. decision.
Energy (H.C. 138)	Disposal of BGC interest in Wytch Farm Field	* BGC opposed to sale. Inquiry allows it to place on record its valuation of £450 m. * Cttee sought written evidence from all the parties after Sec. of State laid Directive before House – June 1981.	* Written evidence BGC and Energy Dept.	* Cttee expresses no judgement on the evidence. Emphasizes need to maximize returns.

(continued)

Table 3.4—*continued*

Committee	Inquiry	Approach	Outreach	Findings/Impact on government
Transport (H.C. 203)	Transfer of HGV and PSV Testing to Private Sector	* Policy proposal issued March 1980. * Ctee investigation H.C. 344 (80/1) negative. Requested more evidence. * Current inquiry while Bill being debated to check gov. argument that industry supports proposal.	* Attitude of affected private sector groups hostile.	* Bipartisan recommendation against transferring testing stations to private sector. * Gov. subsequently abandoned privatization proposal.
Welsh Affairs (H.C. 335)	Establishment of Consumer Advisory Committees – Welsh Water Authority	* Follows lengthy official investigation and reorganization of WWA. * Minister proposed 5 Advisory Committees. * Inquiry duration 9 months.	* Oral evidence 15 groups. * Written evidence 34 groups.	* Establish 7 Advisory Panels. Limit tenure on consumer bodies. Associated proposals re administration. Mostly accepted by gov. * Bipartisan report.
Social Services (H.C. 113, 1980/1)	Income during Initial Sickness	* Gov. proposed shifting responsibility in first 8 weeks of sickness to employers. * Ctee conducted quick inquiry before publication of proposed legislation. * Analysis of published reactions to gov. proposals by special adviser, M. O'Higgins.	* No outreach because of need for rapid determination.	* In current economic climate further burden on employers inappropriate. * Bipartisan report.

Table 3.5 Implications of government decisions (references are to 1981/2 session unless otherwise indicated)

Committee	Inquiry	Approach	Outreach	Findings/Impact on government
Education (H.C. 82)	Expenditure Cuts in Higher Education – Effects on Robbins Principle and on Universities	* Following announcement of higher education cuts cttee issued report on implications. * Builds on 1979/80 inquiry – 'Funding and Organization of Courses in Higher Education'. (H.C. 787, 1979/80)		* Draws attention to costs of redundancy – estimated at £120 m. by 1983/4. Also fall in University Participation Rates – from 75% of qualified applicants to 60% by 1990. * Conservative members divided 2 against, 1 for, report.
Education (H.C. 274; also H.C. 293, 1982/83)	Gov. Reply to Cttee Report on Univ. Funding	* Cttee earlier reported on implications of 13% expenditure cuts, to Univs 1980/1 to 1982/3. Inadequate financing retirements etc. * Builds on report: Funding and Organization of Courses in Higher Education (H.C. 787, 1979/80), which supported establishment of NAB. Followed consultative document 'Higher Education in England outside the Universities' (July 1981).	* Evidence at – Univ. of Sterling – Univ. of Aston at Birmingham. * Evidence from UGC/NAB chairman on method and relations with gov. * All relevant papers from DES on relations between UGC and NAB published in appendix. * Additional written evidence from 7 groups (e.g. Vice-Chancellors' Cttee, AMA, NUS).	* Scepticism amongst affected univs at fairness of process. * £20 m. redundancy allocation versus £100 m. est. by UGC and CVCP. * Probes ambiguous relationship between UGC, NAB and gov. * Evidence only published.

(continued)

74

Table 3.5—*continued*

Committee	Inquiry	Approach	Outreach	Findings/Impact on government
Education (H.C. 505)	School Meals	* Follows gov. decision in 1980 to remove obligation on LEAs to provide free meals except for children of parents receiving supplementary benefit or FIS.	* Cttee visits 1 LEA where free meals abolished. * Sec. of State questioned at second scrutiny session (H.C. 480).	* Proposes DES lead in determining nutritional standards. * Alerts ministers to inadequacy of machinery to inform LEAs who is entitled to free meals. * Bipartisan report.
Social Services (H.C. 191)	UGC Cuts and Medical Services	* Proposed cuts estimated to eliminate up to 300 clinical/academic posts. * Builds on inquiry into Medical Education (H.C. 31, 1980/1).	* UGC, University Hospitals Assoc., individual hospitals, DHSS. * Written evidence from 27 universities and related bodies and 13 medical schools.	* Strong criticism of liaison between UGC and DHS. * Recommends £5 m. additional funding to protect teaching/research. * Identifies specific issues requiring policy: suggests focus for debate within department and throughout profession. * Bipartisan report.

75

Table 3.6 Committee-initiated review of specific programmes (references are to 1981/2 session unless otherwise indicated)

Committee	Inquiry	Background/Approach	Outreach	Findings/Impact on government
Foreign Affairs (H.C. 112) (Debated House of Commons 14.3.83)	Airport Development – Turks and Caicos Islands	* Cttee report (H.C. 26, 1980/1) questioned £5 m. vote for tourist airport development. * Sept. 1982 cttee learned Club Med. failed to meet commitments.	* Evidence ODA, Club Med. etc.	* Questions desirability of tourist development and gov. support for this type of infra-structure. * Condemns Dept for failure to advise cttee of Club Med. failure to meet commitments. * Recommends reduction of estimates – debated 14.3.83 – no vote.
Industry and Trade (H.C. 193)	Concorde	* Cttee report (H.C. 265, 1980/1) first identified ongoing costs of Concorde plus underestimate of total costs. * Further inquiry to review developments: continuing costs £35 m.	* Evidence BA, Brit. Aircraft, Dept.	* Questions reliability of Dept cost estimates. Draws attention to long history of forecasting errors, spread of costs over different votes, etc. Strong criticism of Dept management. * Suggests negotiating points with French. * Bipartisan report.

(continued)

Table 3.6—*continued*

Committee	Inquiry	Background/Approach	Outreach	Findings/Impact on government
Public Accounts (H.C. 269)	Chevaline Improvement to the Polaris	* Arose from discrepancy between 1972 project estimate of £175 m. and 1982 actual cost £1,000 m. * Studies began 1967; detailed planning 1972; significant changes in programme management 1976. * Special request from PAC to C and AG.	* Evidence from MoD	* Defence planners hide inefficiency behind claims of security. Insufficient ministerial control 1970–4. Recommends more parliamentary accountability for major projects of this kind.
Energy (H.C. 135, 1982/3)	Pit Closures	* Short inquiry launched Nov. 82, report 22.12.82. * Followed allegations by NUM, that NCB compiled list of pits for closures. Also cttee criticism in review of Dept Estimates of 50% of Dept spending maintaining uneconomic pits. Criticized monitoring by Dept.	* Evidence NUM, NCB. * Special adviser: Prof. Gerald Manners (Geog. – Univ. College, London). * Written evidence BSC, Blue Circle Inds, German coal industry costs, South Scotland Electricity Board.	* Rejects NUM claim of evidence of 'Hit List' of pits for closure. * NCB not sufficiently forthcoming with information. Current review procedure not adequate. * Bipartisan report, except 1 Labour member opposed. Party division on NUM right of veto over pit closures – SDP member voted with Cons. majority.

77

Unlike the Public Accounts Committee, the departmental select committees can explicitly consider the objectives of programmes. They can also undertake reviews of programmes before completion – as in the case of the Foreign Affairs Committee inquiry on airport development in the Turks and Caicos Islands, and the Industry and Trade Committee inquiry on Concorde. One inquiry actually originated with the Public Accounts Committee. It concerns the Chevaline development of the Polaris submarine. This inquiry is included because of its scope and implications. The Chevaline programme was estimated in 1972 to cost £175 million. Its actual cost by 1982 was £1000 million. The pit closures inquiry also involved continuing and significant sums of money. Although not ostensibly concerned with future spending, the report notes the provision of £250 million in the 1982–3 budget to sustain uneconomic pits.

Another group of inquiries, listed in table 3.7, involves committees taking the initiative in proposing policies to the executive. This is the largest single category of 'current' inquiries and it suggests committees would not be backward in advancing policy proposals if they were to formally share powers of iniative with ministers. This category of inquiries illustrates a novel array of possibilities for committee activity. Ten reports are reviewed. Four of these are from earlier sessions. The Energy Committee report on the Isle of Grain Power Station expresses concern about the extent to which spending on power station construction is beyond CEGB control. One proposes reduced taxes (VAT and the Arts). Two involve proposals for increases in expenditure (Theatre Museum and grant to preserve film stocks). In total these proposals would increase current expenditure by £2.1 million. Two other inquiries involved the committees proposing new procedures to government. These inquiries – by the Home Affairs Committee – were conducted with co-operation from the Minister and his department. One inquiry draws on evidence gathered in an earlier major committee inquiry as a basis for committee opposition to an anticipated policy change (redistribution of maternity benefits). Two inquiries illustrate committee intervention in developments independently of ministerial action (*Times* takeover and a threatened disruption of Promenade Concerts because of industrial action).

Finally, fourteen inquiries, listed in table 3.8, did not end with specific recommendations. The published reports seek to place information before the House. Two involve the committees building their own awareness of current issues and programmes in the process of selecting particular topics for inquiry. Six involve committees bringing information about government into the parliamentary and public arena. Four involve inquiries that were begun but not completed – one was overtaken by events, one was absorbed in other inquiries, and two were not finally resolved. Three inquiries involve committees giving information about their own activities to parliament. This represents one of the few devices available to committees to follow up earlier hearings.

Our next task is to review the conduct of inquiries by committees.

Table 3.7 Committee-initiated proposals (references are to 1981/2 session unless otherwise indicated)

Committee	Inquiry	Background/Approach	Outreach	Findings/Impact on government
Education (H.C. 239)	VAT and the Arts	* During inquiry on arts funding, cttee identified discrepancy between EEC and UK practice on VAT charges. * EEC practice documented; only Denmark and Holland at UK levels.	* Extensive outreach to arts groups in inquiry Public and Private Funding of the Arts. (See table 4.6.)	* Reduce VAT on entertainment. * Bipartisan report. * Gov. rejected this recommendation.
Education (H.C. 240)	Nitrate Problems at NFA	* During inquiries on Arts funding cttee identified risk of deterioration in film stocks. * £695,000 needed for preservation.	* Arose from BFI evidence in Public and Private Funding of the Arts. (See table 4.6.)	* Increase grant above £200,000. * Office of the Arts work with BFI to raise private funds. * Bipartisan report. * Gov. grant increased.
Education (H.C. 472)	Future of Theatre Museum	* Rayner scrutiny recommended cancellation – despite £1.5 m. already spent.	* Evidence from affected parties plus Rayner team consultant.	* Error in facts of Rayner Report plus unqualified policy judgements. Project should continue. * Bipartisan report. * Museum funding continued.

(continued)

Table 3.7—continued

Committee	Inquiry	Background/Approach	Outreach	Findings/Impact on government
Education (H.C. 557)	Further and Higher Education in Northern Ireland	* Builds on inquiry on Further and Higher Education (1980/1) and investigation of effects of cuts in university funding. * Gov. proposed merger of Ulster Polytechnic and new University of Ulster. Steering Group already recommended Vice-Chancellor.	* Evidence from affected interest groups in Belfast and Londonderry. * Witnesses criticized composition of Steering Group, pace of merger and degree of consultation.	* Urges Minister to be flexible in target start-up date of Sept. 1984. * Bipartisan report.
Home Affairs (H.C. 98)	Police Complaints Procedure	* Home Sec. foreshadowed review of existing Board. * Cttee initiated inquiry.	* 3 civil liberties groups; 6 police groups.	* No new independent investigatory body required. Improve and tighten existing procedures. Base process on regions. * Police and Criminal Evidence Bill close to cttee proposals. * Cttee divided on need for independent body. 7 against, 2 for.
Home Affairs (H.C. 421)	Miscarriages of Justice	* Petitions now reviewed by Home Office which advises Home Sec. without public scrutiny. * Justice estimates 200 reviews per year from 2000 petitions.	* Criminal Bar Assoc. Justice.	* Proposes Independent Appeals Review Body. * Proposes less stringent burden of proof. * Criticizes excessive secrecy by HO. * Bipartisan report. * Gov. rejects Independent Appeals Body. Other recs accepted.

(continued)

80

Table 3.7—*continued*

Committee	Inquiry	Background/Approach	Outreach	Findings/Impact on government
Education (H.C. 152, 1980/1)	Future of *Times* Supplements	* No existing machinery for gov. intervention – unless Minister suspects statutory breach.	* Evidence from Rupert Murdoch.	* Murdoch offers public commitments on editorial independence, continuation of papers.
Education (H.C. 722, 1979/80)	Future of Promenade Concerts	* No machinery for ministerial intervention. * Dispute between BBC and Orchestra threatened cancellation of Promenade Concerts.	* Evidence BBC, Musicians Union, Arts Council.	* Cttee re-establishes negotiations between parties. * Dispute subsequently ended.
Social Services (H.C. 85, 1980/1)	Redistribution of Maternity Benefits	* Committee addressed questions of maternity benefits in PNM. Report (H.C. 663, 1979/80). Cttee learned gov. planned legislation.	* No additional evidence. * Specialist adviser, Ken Shuttleworth.	* Maternity Allowance and pay should be fused in single rate. * Increase Maternity Grant. * Bipartisan report – 3 Cons, 3 Lab. * Gov. accepted recs.
Energy (H.C. 770, 1979/80)	Isle of Grain Power Station	Arose from investigation of proposed nuclear power programme.	Outreach reported in table 4.2.	* 'Contractors at the Isle of Grain have enjoyed a blank cheque which the CEGB have been obliged to honour.' * CEGB has failed to assert management. * See table 4.2. * Bipartisan report.

Table 3.8 Publication of evidence (references are to 1981/2 session unless otherwise indicated)

Committee	Inquiry	Approach	Outreach	Findings/Impact on government
Education (H.C. 107)	Information Technology	* Annual library spending cost approx. £560 m. * 1982 designated IT year. Inquiry to establish gov. arrangements for promotion and co-ordination. * Builds on The British Library (H.C. 607, 1979/80) and Info. Storage in British Library Service (H.C. 767, 1979/80).	* Cttee takes evidence from ministers responsible	* Follow-up report planned but not proceeded with.
Employment (H.C. 348)	Work of Dept of Employment Group	* Follows announcement of new scheme for long-term unemployment.	* Secretary of State and Under-Secretary.	* Evidence covers: – Community Enterprise Programme. – Gov. reaction to cttee report on MSC plan. – Abolition of Training Boards. * Cons. members question gov. opposition to CEP.
Education (H.C. 328)	Scrutiny Sessions	* Chairman indicates selection of topics	* 1st session – Sec. of State/Minister/Dept officers. * 2nd session – UGC Chairman, Minister, Dept officers.	* Sec. of State covers: – Curriculum. – Student grants. – Small schools etc.

(continued)

Table 3.8—*continued*

Committee	Inquiry	Approach	Outreach	Findings/Impact on government
Energy (H.C. 224)	Wave Power	* Cttee visited Edinburgh Univ. to take evidence.	* Evidence at Research Unit on support, progress, prospects. (Univ. of Edinburgh).	* Documents: – Evidence on technical and economic feasibility. – Memorandum on Wave Power Research. – Paper by Prof. Salter for Parl. Liaison Group for alternative energy strategies. – Dept. of Energy response.
Home Affairs (sub-committee) (H.C. 106)	Racial Attacks	* Home Office published study 17.11.81.	* Evidence from Assoc. of Chief Police Officers and Met. Police.	* Published for information of MPs.
Foreign Affairs (H.C. 71)	Work of CDC		* Officers of CDC, ODA.	* Published for information of MPs.
Foreign Affairs (H.C. 48)	Evidence Sessions		* Nov. 1981 – Lord Carrington and Sir M. Palliser. * Jan. 1982 – Lord Carrington and Sir M. Palliser. * May 1982 – Francis Pym and Sir Anthony Ackland.	* Evidence covers: (i) Middle East Relations with US NATO Nuclear Role CAP. (ii) Poland. (iii) Falklands.
Foreign Affairs (H.C. 151)	UNDP		* Evidence from: – Administrator. – Deputy.	* Published for information of MPs.

(continued)

83

Table 3.8—*continued*

Committee	Inquiry	Approach	Outreach	Findings/Impact on government
Education (H.C. 58)	Science Policy	* Investigates machinery to co-ord. science policy in gov. Draws on 1972 and 1979 white papers plus Merrison Report on support for academic research 1982.	* Evidence from: – Advisory Council for Applied Research and Development. – Advisory Board for Research Councils. – CPRS.	* Questioning suggests concern at fragmentation within government. * Follow-up report planned but not proceeded with.
Industry and Trade (H.C. 23)	Negotiations for New Multi-Fibre Agreement	* GATT negotiations in progress.	* Minister reports developments in Geneva on return.	* Published for information of MPs.
Welsh Affairs (H.C. 312 etc.)	Welsh Office Functions		* Extensive hearings 1980/1 and 1981/2 into each branch of Welsh Office. What does it do? Who report to? etc.	* Coverage includes: – Transport and Highway Group – Ed. Dept – Land Use Planning Group – Arts Council – Industry Dept – Tourist Authority – Finance Group.

Reports of select committees to parliament

Committee	Inquiry	Approach	Outreach	Findings/Impact on government
Defence (H.C. 55, 1982/3)	Previous Recs of Cttee			* Records all cttee decisions, gov. responses and where appropriate developments since reports – to May, 1983.
Industry and Trade (H.C. 388, 1982/3)	Previous Recs of Cttee			* Records cttee decisions and gov. replies to 1 May 1983.
Liaison Cttee (H.C. 92, 1982/3)	The Select Cttee System			* Documents work on select cttees in 3 sessions 1979/80 to end 1981/2. Also chairman's recommendations for reform of system.

CONDUCT OF INQUIRIES

In their approach to inquiries, committees followed a pattern broadly similar to that we have already discerned in the conduct of budget and estimates inquiries.

Special advisers were appointed by a number of committees – some for the entire session, others for particular inquiries. The former practice was followed by the Social Services and Education Committees. The latter approach was adopted, for example, by the Foreign Affairs and Defence Committees. These advisers were usually academics recruited on a part-time basis to assist full-time committee staff.

Most inquiries involved extensive interest group evidence – usually those groups immediately affected by the proposed policy. The Employment Committee, in its assessment of the Anti-Discrimination Code, took evidence from six interest groups. Evidence from the Association of Independent Businesses concerned the difficulties that would be created for small business. Evidence from the West Indian Standing Conference and the Conference of Afro-Caribbean and Asian Councillors revealed disagreement between members of the ethnic communities about the merit of the proposed Code. The evidence sessions also put on public record the difficulties that might arise in implementing and policing the Code. The inquiry served to bring to public attention the reservations of the official Advisory, Conciliation and Arbitration Service. ACAS had pressed its concerns without effect through private official channels. The select committee hearing placed these reservations on the public record. The review of the Quota Scheme for the Employment of Disabled People was also based on interest group evidence. The committee took oral evidence from five groups and written evidence from seven. Groups giving evidence included the proposing agency, the Manpower Services Commission, and representatives of the disabled, employers and unions. In reviewing the government's proposed Youth Training Initiative, the Employment Committee took evidence from the Secretary of State, the Manpower Services Commission, the CBI, the TUC, the Institute of Careers Officers, two private companies and officers from two MSC programme areas. This inquiry was stimulated by the government's response to an MSC proposed 'Young Workers' Scheme'. The inquiry on proposed NHS charges took evidence from fifteen interest groups including ethnic and student groups who opposed the charges, the Commission for Racial Equality and seven Regional Health Authorities. This latter evidence covered the feasibility of proposed procedures to check patient eligibility and to levy charges.

In reviewing the Trade Union Immunities Bill, the Employment Committee provided access for the trade unions to the policy-making system at a time when the unions were refusing to meet the Secretary of State. The committee took evidence while the government's legislation was before the House. The union movement had refused to negotiate with the government on the grounds that the time allowed was insufficient. The TUC had also expressed the view that discussions would be futile because the government had publicly declared its position to be inflexible. But it lacked a public platform apart from the media, where its point of view could be heard. Labour parliamentarians, of course, represented TUC views in parliament. But the TUC leadership welcomed the opportunity to place its views directly before a committee of parliament. The TUC was represented by a high-level delegation (led by the then General Secretary, Len Murray). Its evidence is available on the printed parliamentary record. Committee questioning by both Tory and Labour members obliged Len Murray to justify his reluctance to enter negotiations with the Employment Secretary.

The government's White Paper on Trade Union Immunities had been the subject of an extensive committee inquiry in the 1980–1 session. Not surprisingly, the committee split precisely on party lines on the question of its desirability. But the inquiry provided a vehicle for placing a considerable volume of evidence from various interests on the public record. The access provided to 'think-tanks' is a notable feature. The appendices include an eighty-page report from the neo-liberal Centre for Policy Studies documenting the case for trade union reform. There is also evidence from eminent jurists contesting the desirability of extending the law into this area. This inquiry exposed the tension in government ranks. Evidence from the Lord Chancellor, Lord Hailsham, supported the principle of the legislation, but questioned its timing.[6]

The duration of these inquiries varied considerably. The larger inquiries lasted up to about three months. Approximately eight inquiries fall into this category. The Employment Committee's investigation of government proposals for a new youth training scheme took some three months between commencement of evidence sessions and tabling of the report. The inquiry on NHS charges also involved some three months from initiation to report. The longest inquiry involved the Welsh Affairs Committee's investigation of Consumer Advisory Committees of the Welsh Water Authority. This lasted nine months.

Some inquiries were as short as two or three days. For example, the inquiry concerned with vehicle testing took evidence one day and reported to the House two days later. The Transport Committee had already conducted an extensive inquiry on this issue during the 1980–1 session. Similarly, the Social Services Committee report on maternity benefits was produced in reaction to a government Green Paper and without evidence sessions. The committee relied on an analysis of public submissions prepared by its special adviser. The report was published before the government's draft regulations appeared.

Committee-initiated proposals were generally the result of short inquiries. The shortest, VAT and the Arts, took only one hearing. Typically these inquiries lasted two or three weeks from initiation of evidence sessions to presentation of reports. Evidence was taken only from groups immediately affected. The reports were specific and succinct.

The origin of the inquiries varied. Some developed from earlier hearings. The Energy Committee decided to investigate pit closures as a result of its earlier inquiry on departmental estimates.[7] The Foreign Affairs Committee inquiry on the Turks and Caicos Islands originated in the same source.[8] The Industry and Trade Committee had conducted an inquiry into continuing Concorde costs in the 1980-1 session. The inquiry reported here involves the committee checking developments since its initial report.

The specific policy proposals initiated by committees all build on earlier work or emerge from a current larger inquiry. They demonstrate the capacity of committees to become familiar with a particular policy area, to track developments and to make timely suggestions. For example, the Education Committee recommendation to end VAT on arts activities emerged from its larger inquiry into funding the arts.[9] In the course of this inquiry (which involved extensive outreach to interest groups), the Education Committee became aware of the discrepancy between British practice and that throughout the remainder of the EEC. Because of its concern to seek government action within the current budget the committee agreed and issued this short report. Similarly, the report on Higher Education in Northern Ireland, which draws the Secretary of State's attention to local concerns, was preceded by a lengthy inquiry into further and higher education throughout the UK.[10] The committee thus judged Northern Ireland issues against the background of this earlier investigation. The Social Services Committee recommendations on maternity benefits had been preceded by a long inquiry in 1980-1 on perinatal and neonatal mortality. This report was one of the few actually debated in the House.[11] It recommended, amongst other steps, a review of maternity benefits. The committee subsequently learnt indirectly that such a review was in progress. It therefore issued a separate report describing the structure of benefits it believed desirable. The government largely accepted these recommendations.

Several of these inquiries responded to representation from interest groups. Select committees provide a public forum in which interest groups claims can be appraised. For example those sponsoring the Theatre Museum claimed the government was improperly repudiating a commitment to fund the Museum. They also claimed the Rayner scrutiny which the government used to justify its decision was inadequately prepared. Similarly the National Film Theatre had pressed its case for a special grant to save its film stocks without success through regular channels. In reviewing miscarriages of justice, the Home Affairs Committee responded to the initiative of a public interest advocacy group – Justice. This organization enjoys a high reputation amongst all parties for its work on law reform. It had ready access to committee members and was supported by the Criminal Bar Association.

Another feature of some inquiries was travel beyond Westminster to gather evidence. The Education Committee in its inquiry on education spending cuts travelled to the University of Aston, Birmingham, and to Loughborough. It took evidence from administrators and staff. These inquiries became the vehicle for exploring the relations between the University Grants Commission, the universities and government, and between the university sector and the National Advisory Board for Local Authority Higher Education. Evidence sessions repeatedly explored the difficulties caused by the bifurcated role of the UGC: first, as agent for the government in determining budgetary cuts for individual universities; and second, as agent for the universities in pressing their case for funding. The change from expansion to contraction of the university sector exposed the difficulties inherent in the private relationships between the UGC, DES and the government. This issue was pursued in the 1982–3 session with a further inquiry into relations between the NAB and the UGC.[12] The Education Committee also travelled to Lincolnshire to see the effects of the 1980 Act on provision of meals by the local education authority. This Act limited the obligation of local authorities to provide free meals to children of parents receiving supplementary benefit or family income supplement.

Written evidence was also deliberately sought by committees to supplement or test departmental views. The Social Services Committee took oral evidence from the Secretary of State, the Minister, the UGC, departmental officers and from representatives of University Hospitals concerning the effects of UGC cuts on medical services. But it also solicited written evidence from twenty-seven universities and thirteen medical schools. The Energy Committee called only for written evidence in its inquiry on the sale of the Wytch Farm field. The Welsh Affairs Committee solicited written evidence from local groups in its inquiry on the Welsh Water Authority.

We have already noted that the Education Committee was the most active of all the select committees in the 1981–2 sessions on current issues. It tabled a total of twelve short reports in this period. This was due partly to the interest and commitment of its Labour chairman, Christopher Price, and partly to the way work was divided between committee members.[13] Price took the lead on education matters. The committee also established an informal sub-committee to lead its inquiries in the arts area. This was chaired by a Tory member, Tim Brinton. The Education Committee used its major inquiries (to be considered in chapter 4) as a vehicle for identifying current issues. The committee was quick to table bipartisan reports on these matters. This suggests possibilities for committee activity that were not explored to the same degree by other select committees. The Education Committee avoided the difficulties encountered by the Treasury Committee in having sub-committee reports adopted without extensive further hearings by the main committee. Members attributed this to the 'committee spirit' which both Christopher Price and Tim Brinton assiduously cultivated.

The Education Committee dominated particular categories of inquiry. For example six of the ten reports in which committees initiated proposals originated in this committee. Similarly, four of the 'information' inquiries involved the Education Committee. This committee entered actively into a range of current controversies, seeking information about developments before deciding whether further inquiry would be fruitful. Its scrutiny sessions with the Secretary of State illustrate this approach. When it decided further work would not be helpful, the committee placed relevant evidence before the House. This was the case, for example, in the evidence sessions on information technology policy.

Committee members attributed the level of activity of individual committees largely to the influence of chairmen. The ability of the chairman to elicit and nourish committee identity was held to be the decisive influence. In every case the chairman formally proposes the inquiry agenda. The party allegiance of the chairman did not appear to influence committee 'activism'. The Education Committee (the most active) was chaired by a Labour member, as was the Employment Committee. The Education Committee staged six inquiries, the other most active committees being Home Affairs and Foreign Affairs, with five inquiries each. Both were chaired by Tories.

There are two examples of committees intervening independently of ministers to protect the public interest. Both involved the Education Committee. Following Rupert Murdoch's bid for Times Newspapers, the committee decided to hold a hearing because of public concern for the future of the supplements. The hearing provided an opportunity for Rupert Murdoch to place guarantees on editorial freedom and on the future of the supplements on the public record. In the second case, the Education Committee helped renew negotiations between the BBC and the London Philharmonic Orchestra. The orchestra had struck over a pay issue. This strike jeopardized the 1981 Promenade Concerts. The committee heard the parties and indicated a disposition towards proposed terms of settlement. The BBC responded positively, negotiations were resumed, and the dispute was subsequently successfully settled.

FINDINGS

How precise were committee findings and what levels of bipartisanship were attained?

The Trade Union Immunities Review reflects the difficulty of reaching agreement within committees on an intensely partisan issue. The committee split in its 1980–1 report exactly on party lines. In responding to earlier elements of the government's reform of trade union law (the draft codes on picketing and the closed shop tabled in the 1979–80 session) the committee produced a bipartisan report. This was on a procedural issue. The committee united in criticizing the amount of time the government allowed for public debate.[14] The committee was fortified in this view by the varying evidence received from the CBI, the TUC and the Association of Chief Police Officers. This judgement is itself an important indicator of committee capacity to find common ground despite disagreement on substantive questions. It could not find similar grounds for bipartisanship in later inquiries on proposed trade union measures. The Home Affairs Committee report on NHS charges also split on party lines. The Energy Committee too failed to achieve bipartisanship in its recommendations on pit closures. The SDP member joined the Conservative majority in opposing an NUM veto of pit closures which was proposed by the Labour member.

All other inquiries that produced precise findings were bipartisan. This covers twenty-one reports on a wide range of issues. Bipartisanship was achieved on the Education and Social Services Committees in their reports recommending action to the government. The inquiries into the proposed Anti-Discrimination Code and the Quota Scheme for the Employment of Disabled People (Employment Committee) also reflect the ability of committees to reach bipartisan conclusions on an issue surrounded by strong interest group feeling.

The potential for bipartisanship is also evident in committee appraisals of government policy proposals. Three of these inquiries reached strong bipartisan conclusions proposing variation of policies. After taking public evidence on the position of school leavers, the Employment Committee recommended that the government continue to pay supplementary benefits to school leavers who failed to join the Youth Opportunities Scheme. The committee recommended this after hearing evidence from the TUC. It concluded that withdrawal of supplementary benefit would mar the launch of the Scheme. This recommendation was accepted by the government. The Social Services Committee used an analysis by its special adviser to point to the impact the government's proposals to vary sickness benefit payments would have on particular employer groups.[15] Its bipartisan report against the government's proposals was adopted. The Transport Committee opposed transfer of vehicle testing to the private sector on the basis proposed by the government. It concluded that there seemed little merit in this proposed privatization exercise. At the least, it recommended that the government should not proceed until industry objections had been resolved. Its evidence sessions in the 1981–2 session allowed it to appraise the extent to which this had occurred. Government legislation was then before the House. Industry reservations have continued to delay implementation of the government's proposals, which were finally abandoned in 1983.

The Welsh Affairs Committee report was bipartisan. But its recommendations relate to administrative arrangements. In his appraisal of the committee, Barry Jones notes it avoided the overtly political issues:

It concerned itself with the more mundane matter of representation of local interests on the proposed consumer committees. Fourteen recommendations were made, but none were of a contentious nature and none raised substantive policy issues. The government was quietly congratulatory of the

committee's efforts and accepted the vast majority of the recommendations.[16]

Committees generally reached precise conclusions although not all inquiries
proposed specific remedies. In some cases committees were content to draw
the attention of the House to some particular developments. The Education
Committee documented the impact of cuts on university participation rates
and staffing. It drew attention to extra funds it judged could be required to
meet redundancy schemes. But it did not propose any variation to the then
current expenditure programme. The Social Services Committee strongly
criticized the lack of liaison between the Department of Health and Social
Security and the University Grants Commission. But the criticism was general
– the committee did not propose a specific variation to current policy. By
contrast, the school meals inquiry identified deficiencies in departmental
administrative arrangements and proposed more precise guidelines be issued
by the DES. In three cases – VAT and the Arts, Higher Education in Northern
Ireland, and Redistribution of Maternity Benefits – the committee reports
proposed change in some specific current policy or procedure based on their
independent assessment of the issue.

The Concorde and Chevaline reports included strong criticisms of departmental accounting procedures. These allow programme costs to be spread
around a number of estimates and votes thus preventing them from coming to
the direct attention of parliament. Both these cases have provided evidence
which has been used subsequently by parliamentarians arguing for additional
financial information for the House.[17] These two cases also caused their
committees to argue for explicit powers of scrutiny over long-term capital
projects. The Public Accounts Committee concluded that the mismanagement of the Chevaline Project points to the desirability of giving parliament
the opportunity to scrutinize projects as they unfold. It judged that the project
passed beyond ministerial control between 1970 and 1974.[18] Similarly the
manner in which continuing Concorde costs were distributed amongst differing estimates led the Industry and Trade Committee to recommend select
committee responsibility for appraisal of major programmes before initiation
and throughout their life.[19]

The Foreign Affairs Committee hearing on expenditure on airport development in the Turks and Caicos Islands also included strong criticism of the
sponsoring department – in this case the Overseas Development Administration. The committee questioned the impact on the island's society of tourist
development on the scale predicted. It questioned the use of government aid
funds to provide commercial infra-structure. This report was one of the first
debated in the House under the new estimates day procedures. This debate, in
March 1983, long after the expenditure complained of had actually taken
place, occurred on a 'take note' motion.[20]

In seven of the ten inquiries in which committees initiated policy proposals, they identified a gap or problem in present policy making and recommended remedial action. The government either had not acknowledged that a problem existed (VAT and the Arts, nitrate problem at the NFT, higher education in Northern Ireland, miscarriages of justice), or lacked the power to act (*Times* Supplements, Promenade Concerts). In the case of the Isle of Grain power station the Energy Committee sought to place on public record proposals for bringing power station construction costs under control. In the course of its inquiry on nuclear power, the committee discovered that due to mismanagement and industrial problems the Isle of Grain station was four years behind schedule. The committee calculated construction delays had added 20 per cent to project costs.

IMPACT

The impact of reports can be assessed at a number of levels. First there is evidence of the role committees might play in bridging systems of functional and parliamentary representation.[21] This was apparent in the way Tory and Labour members of the Employment Committee approached their inquiry on the Anti-Discrimination Code. The Anti-Discrimination Code had been unanimously endorsed by the Commission for Racial Equality. This Commission includes both trade union, CBI and ethnic representatives. Committee questioning led by both Conservative and Labour backbenchers identified features of the Code which the Committee subsequently held to be contrary to the public interest. Both Tory and Labour members expressed strong concern about the dangers involved in disclosure and reporting of ethnic identity.[22] Labour members expressed doubts about the likelihood of trade union observance in practice. Tory members expressed concern about the impact of the Code on small business. The government accepted the committee's bipartisan report. It invited the CRE to redraft the Code to take account of committee reservations. Similarly, in the case of the Quota Scheme for the Employment of Disabled People, committee members questioned the continuing need for specific quotas. The government endorsed the committee's suggestions and referred the Code back to the Manpower Services Commission.

There are two notable examples of committees successfully undertaking a pre-legislative role. Both involve inquiries from earlier sessions. One concerned the Home Affairs Committee and its inquiry on the 'SUS' laws. The other concerned the Foreign Affairs Committee with its inquiry on the British North America Acts. Both these inquiries involved the select committees reaching bipartisan conclusions contrary to those of the government on important current issues. Both committees were chaired by Tories with a majority of Tory members. In the case of the 'SUS' laws the committee took extensive evidence from the coalition of interest groups − the 'Scrap SUS Campaign' − opposed to the then existing legislation. It also took evidence from individual ethnic, police and civil liberties groups. This evidence persuaded the committee that present provisions should be repealed. This was first brought before the House with the agreement of the Opposition in a supply debate in 1980. Anne Davies notes:

> Although moved by Opposition spokesman Merlyn Rees the motion debated was 'that this House notes with approval the Second Report from the Home Affairs Committee Session 1979–80' (HC 559). The performance of all the committee members speaking in the debate was impressive, in particular that of the Conservative chairman, Sir Graham Page. For the Government, William Whitelaw moved an amendment drastically weakening and qualifying the motion and for this he was challenged by the chairman: 'I wish that my right Hon. friend the Home Secretary had noted with approval the report of the Select Committee. . . . He is asking a lot when he asks me to accept it as nothing more than showing a need for a change in the law without a commitment to what that change may be, and when he asks me to pledge myself to do no more than look forward to the Law Commission report, and to public response' (col. 1777, *Hansard*, 5 June 1980). When the vote on the Government's amendment was taken all the Committee members present voted with the Opposition.[23]

The government was subjected to further private pressure from its backbench. The committee returned to the subject in its fourth report.

> No Committee of this House can escape its continuing responsibility for the recommendations it has made. It therefore follows that, if there is no measure to repeal 'sus' foreshadowed in the next Queen's Speech, members of the Committee will themselves place such a Bill before the House.[24]

The government finally agreed to abandon the objectionable provisions in its reform of the Criminal Attempts Bill in the 1980–1 session. Partisans of both sides claim to be happy with the outcome. Opponents of the 'SUS' provisions see it as a victory for their campaign. Protagonists for the regulations argue that the new provisions provide police with sufficient powers for their purposes.[25]

The Foreign Affairs Committee inquiry into the British North America Acts involved a challenge to the government's interpretation of the role of the British parliament in the patriation of the Canadian Constitution. The Canadian Federal Government proposed new arrangements for amending the Canadian Constitution which were contested by some Canadian provinces. The British Government held it had no power to do other than accede to the request of the Canadian Federal Government. The Foreign Affairs Committee took evidence from nine leading UK constitutional jurists. This evidence led the committee to conclude that the British Government should interest itself in the merits of the issue. This elicited a strong reaction from the Canadian Government. In the event, the committee's view prevailed in the

House. The matter was debated on four separate occasions. Sir Anthony Kershaw, in his report to the Liaison Committee summarized the committee's role in the following terms:

> The first of the Reports on the British North America Acts . . . not only made an important contribution to the 'patriation' debate in Canada, and, I believe, contributed significantly to changing the Canadian Government's approach to the subject, but also influenced HMG's thinking. Moreover, this series fulfilled the primary purpose of such Reports in that when the Canada Bill came before the House, the First and Third Reports were relied upon heavily in debate by both Government and backbench Members.[26]

In a subsequent appraisal, Bruce George and Michael Woodward conclude:

> One cannot with any precision say what would have happened to patriation had not the First FAC Report come out as it did. It legitimised opposition and magnified it, provoking greater interest among MPs and more pressure on Ministers. It assisted the opposition in Canada and supported the FCO and Canadian High Commission who must have been warning the Canadian Government of the unease in the British Parliament; had there not been the 'November accords', the Bill would undoubtedly have had a rough passage, and may have faced defeat. The care and thoroughness with which the Report was prepared, and the bipartisan support for its conclusions within the Committee, allied to the timing of its deliberations, meant that Parliament had to consider the issue, however much the Governments of both Britain and Canada denounced the relevance of its findings. The Committee's proven record in performing its core functions with a certain degree of consensus and relatively little partisanship created an influence and standing vis-à-vis the Commons that facilitate this outcome.[27]

Other inquiries illustrate the capacity of committees to produce bipartisan policy proposals that could be voted, despite their relative impotence in the present policy-making structure. For example the Education Committee urged that VAT in Britain for entertainment and arts activities be brought into line with other EEC countries. The report documented EEC practices. Only Denmark and Holland were found to follow the UK approach. The same committee recommended extra funds for the National Film Theatre to preserve its archive from deterioration. The NFT estimated this work would cost £695,000. The government, which also received direct representations from individual members and from other sources, subsequently provided additional funds.

An inquiry can provide the basis for committee members to exert later private pressure on ministers as an issue unfolds. This is illustrated in the report of the Energy Committee on the value of the Wytch Farm Field. This was one episode in a protracted tussle between the government and the BGC over sale of the latter's share of this asset. The government originally announced its plan to require sale of BGC's interest in June 1981 and introduced the necessary orders. In July the Energy Select Committee sought written evidence from British Gas and the Department of Energy. The committee did not report on this evidence until February 1982. By this time the report was relevant to negotiations between BGC and the Department of Energy about the value of the field. The report takes no firm position except to stress the committee's view that a sale should only take place which realizes the full value of the field. This issue was resolved early in 1984. In reporting agreement to sell the BGC stake for £215 million *The Times* article notes: 'The new settlement clearly reflects taxation changes made in the budget and follows pressure from the Commons Select Committee on Energy to ensure the price was raised accordingly.'[28]

Other reports were influential because they brought information or judgements to the attention of the executive which had not been available through regular departmental channels. This was the case in both the Employment Committee report on the Youth Training Scheme and the Social Services Committee report on income during initial sickness. By contrast the Transport Committee in its report on privatization anticipated difficulties which the government was loath to recognize. These committees acquired information through their outreach to interest groups (Transport and Employment Committees) or through fresh analysis of data (Social Services Committee). These outcomes suggest the potential contribution of a select committee inquiry when staged prior to a final decision being taken by the government.

Beyond government, the publicity which inquiries and reports attract can help to build understanding of policy issues within particular policy communities. The publicity which the Treasury Committee has attracted in the national press was noted in the last chapter. Here we see illustrated the capacity of committees to attract extensive coverage in the specialist press. With interest group politics an important dimension of successful policy making, the specialist press becomes a potentially significant bridge between government and the various policy communities. This is illustrated in the attention accorded the Education Committee.[29] In the case of the Transport Committee, the Road Haulage Association journal included detailed reports of its activities.[30] Neither of these committees was extensively reported in the national press. Understanding of issues by interest groups can also arise from appearances before the committees. We will consider this potential impact of committees in more detail in chapter 5. To be noted here is the comment of the chairman of the Welsh Affairs Committee in his report to the Liaison Committee:

> the evidence sessions have forced organisations to clarify their standpoints and submit them to critical scrutiny and the reports have brought home to the House and to government in a formal way the particular needs and requirements of Wales. In addition, these form fairly comprehensive reference works for opinion formers in the Principality.[31]

The three reports of committees about their own work represent one avenue for committees to track progress in the implementation of their recommendations. Such reports, particularly in association with further evidence sessions from ministers or departmental officers, allow committees to bring pressure to bear on government or the relevant department. In the current situation, where the floor of the House is barely accessible to committees, published reports of this kind represent one of the few devices available to committees to apply further pressure. The reports from the Defence Committee and the Industry and Trade Committee list committee inquiries and reports and subsequent action by government. The report of the Liaison Committee represents an account of the select committee system generally in its first three years. The report lists all the inquiries held, and includes detailed comments from individual chairmen appraising the work of their committees. This report also suggests additional reforms to strengthen committee powers.[32] The appointment of additional sub-committees is proposed. The report laments the lack of committee access to floor debate. It is the only published document of the Liaison Committee – the committee (discussed in the last chapter) through which individual chairmen co-ordinate their activity and raise common problems or issues.[33]

Finally, the 'information' inquiries which concluded with no report, represent much deeper and more intensive scrutiny of ministers than is available in question time. They allow issues which are of concern to particular members or particular policy communities to be explored in public. These concerns are not necessarily addressed in the debates between the parties in the House. The Foreign Affairs, Employment, Welsh Affairs and Education Committees all conducted 'scrutiny' sessions involving the appropriate Secretary of State and senior departmental officers. In the case of the Education Committee for example, two hearings were held in the course of the year. These hearings ranged over current developments in relation to the curriculum, student grants and closure of small schools. The Foreign Affairs Committee staged three hearings. It met Lord Carrington twice and, after his resignation, Francis Pym. Topics reviewed covered current developments – at the first session, the Middle East, relations with the US, NATO's nuclear role and EEC agricultural policies; at the second session, Poland; and at the third session, immediately after Lord Carrington's resignation and whilst the Falklands war was still in progress, Francis Pym reviewed the government's objectives and tactics in this conflict.

COMMITTEES AND CURRENT POLICY MAKING

The foregoing inquiries show the committees moving rather less coherently towards a role in current departmental policy making than in their approach to the budget cycle. No single departmental committee has the focus of the

Treasury Committee. Few have as experienced a membership as that committee. No other committee numbers as many determined or astute parliamentary reformers amongst its membership.

Partisanship has influenced effective committee work in this area. Yet there are a surprising number of reports – twenty-one to be precise – which represent committees tackling current issues and reaching bipartisan conclusions. Committees reached precise bipartisan conclusions on proposals from independent advisory commissions, on the details of proposed initiatives (e.g. should supplementary benefits be continued for school leavers who do not join the Youth Opportunity Programme), and on mismanaged or wasteful programmes (e.g. Turks and Caicos Airport Development, Concorde). The Industry and Trade, Energy and Foreign Affairs committees have been most active on expenditure matters. These inquiries realize the aspirations of the Tory reformers. They show the select committees exposing mismanagement and waste in government. They reinforce the case of those parliamentarians who wish to build the role of committees in authorizing major projects. The extent of bipartisanship is a positive pointer to the potential of committees as vehicles for building backbench support for policy initiatives.

In six cases committees played an important role in the subsequent development of policy – 'SUS' abolition, Anti-Discrimination Code, British North America Acts, the retraining initiative, and perhaps police complaints and judicial review procedures. Three of these were not in the 1981–2 session. The inquiries from the 1980–1 session on the 'SUS' bill and on the British North America Acts, indicate possibilities for select committees operating in a pre-legislative mode. They reflect the possibility for blending interest group evidence, expert appraisal and committee deliberations and judgement to build parliamentary and, through the media, public understanding of an issue. But there is hardly sufficient evidence of other committees working in a similar vein, or indeed of the same committees undertaking similar inquiries on other issues, to conclude that there is widespread support for extension of pre-legislative work by committees. Similarly, in the array of committee-initiated proposals, the work of the Education, Home Affairs and Social Services committees, points towards possibilities for committee activity that were not followed up by other committees. Two relevant inquiries were conducted by the Education Committee concerning the Promenade Concerts and the takeover of the *Times* Supplements. These possibilities for novel committeee roles were not imitated or extended by other committees or followed up by the Education Committee itself on other occasions. These inquiries together reflect the potential of committee inquiries to bring within the parliamentary domain the various facets of policy work that are now usually conducted in private between ministers, departments and interest groups. They reflect the potential of committees to contribute in a positive way to this process.

Finally, there is no strong evidence that committees have been 'captured' by their interest group 'clients'. As in the inquiries reviewed in chapter 1, the evidence is at best ambiguous. Is one to say of the Home Affairs Committee, for example, that it was 'captured' by the 'Scrap SUS' coalition? Or of the Education Committee that its proposals on VAT for the Arts, or the Theatre Museum or the Film Archive are a sell-out to special interests? What is clear is that there is no general disposition amongst committees to propose increased spending. In several cases the political wisdom of government decisions is questioned. These sometimes involved expenditure reduction (e.g. privatizing vehicle testing, income during initial sickness). But committees assemble their evidence carefully and their judgements are prudently argued. Similarly there are sufficient examples of committees questioning expenditure (e.g. power station construction costs, Turks and Caicos airport development, Concorde, pit closures, Wytch Farm Field price) to negate any suggestion of committee irresponsibility or capture by interest groups.

In sum, a number of aspects of the inquiries reviewed here point towards a developing role for committees in policy making. First, committees have been involved in all phases of policy development. They have undertaken pre-legislative and pre-policy scrutiny as well as reviews after the announcement of new policy or to check the effectiveness of a change some time after implementation (e.g. school meals). Second, the committees have sought evidence directly from the relevant interest groups. This evidence has decisively influenced their judgement in nine inquiries. The interest groups provided new information to the committees. Six of these reports were subsequently substantially accepted by the government.

This needs to be weighed against the generally cautious approach of the committees to partisan issues, and the dominance of the Education Committee in this band of inquiries. Taken together the evidence leads to less sanguine conclusions concerning the development of a committee role in current policy making than in the budget area.

At least one of the causes of the variation between the role of committees in the area of current policy and in the budget area is the absence of a well developed rationale for committee work. The Treasury Committee draws on a body of published work arguing the case for a role for committees in expenditure. This grounds select committee work securely in the historic powers of parliament.[34] This literature was reviewed in the first chapter. The case for a committee role in policy areas beyond the scrutiny of public expenditure has not been comprehensively articulated in the Study of Parliament Group or amongst parliamentarians. Development of a role for committees would bring them into conflict with the fundamental canons of the party system.

There is much less community of view about the legitimacy of a committee role on matters beyond public expenditure. Without a conceptual base further development is hardly likely to be evident in practice. Development of the notion that backbenchers have independent deliberative responsibilities would seem to be a prerequisite for a widened select committee role on current policy issues.

Chapter 4

Strategic policy making

The third dimension of policy making to which parliament requires access if it is to have an independent deliberative role involves strategic assessments. This covers reappraisal of ongoing or proposed programmes and forward planning. Both activities turn ultimately on an appraisal of the community's general interests. They both involve assessment of the public interest in particular cases. Alteration or adaptation of established programmes now occurs only rarely. The past history and continuing significance of the issues that are the subject of the inquiries reviewed later in this chapter confirm this. Most of the issues continue to be unresolved. The alteration of programmes frequently invites Opposition attack. It requires acceptance of the need for change by one or another powerful established interest group. As Samuel Brittan observes:

> Interest groups have acquired a stranglehold over the political process – whether these are the unions, the professions, the farm lobby, the pensions industry, the home owners' lobby, the heavy exporters' lobby (usually known as overseas aid), council employees and all the rest. The fact that most of us belong to one or more of these lobbies does not reduce their perverse effect. But the commitment to defend, keep and protect goes into areas which make no economic sense, from any point of view.[1]

Forward planning, on the other hand, involves matters that are not yet the subject of partisan dispute. These are issues that can reasonably be expected to grow in economic, social and therefore political significance. Significant political actors – departments, political parties, interest groups and the media – need to be introduced to these issues in sufficient time to allow a coherent and politically acceptable response to be formulated. Sir John Hoskyns is the most recent, but far from the only, critic of the failure of present policy-making arrangements to handle strategic questions:

> Where are the thinking and the planning going on? Nowhere. Whitehall is not organised to do it. Ministers cannot, in the odd day at Checkers unsupported by training, method or organization. The only department which

might attempt such work is the Cabinet Office. But it co-ordinates. It lacks
the competence for strategic leadership, which would in any case compromise its political neutrality. The 'think-tank' no longer exists. In organ-
isational terms government is a creature without a brain. . . . Strategy in
Whitehall can be defined as 'the thinking we should have done three years
ago but do not have time to do today'.[2]

It is not as though attempts have been lacking over the past decade to try to
improve the capacity of the policy-making system to handle such issues. The
Central Policy Review Staff was one administrative innovation conceived to
strengthen the ability of the Cabinet and the Prime Minister to focus on such
questions.[3] The introduction of senior outsiders as ministerial advisers, the use
of 'think tanks' to define strategic objectives, the introduction of Policy
Strategy Units to departments, the development and growing use of the white
paper and green paper consultative system, and the strengthening of staff support for the Prime Minister, all reflect the effort to improve the capacity of
central government to handle strategic policy making.[4] Yet, as Sir John
Hoskyns's and Samuel Brittan's observations suggest, none of these
approaches has proved successful. These attempts all take the current political
framework for granted.

This framework derives from the current theory of policy making. According to this theory the political parties are the exclusive agents for the community's general interests. They do this by framing a programme which
embodies their version of the public interest. This programme is presumed to
be adequate to guide policy making and to mobilize interests. The definition
championed by each party should be capable of gathering a majority coalition. Writing in 1965, Samuel Beer distinguished the creative, opinion-
forming, role of British political parties in the following terms:

> It has been said that a principal function of a major party is to aggregate the
> demands of a large number of groups in the electorate. Where party govern-
> ment is as highly developed as in Great Britain, I wish to emphasise the role
> of the party is much greater. Party does not merely aggregate the opinion of
> such groups. *It goes a long way towards creating these opinions by fixing
> the framework of public thinking about policy and voters' sense of the
> alternatives and the possibilities.* . . . The parties themselves, backed by
> research staffs, equipped with nationwide organisations, and enjoying the
> continuous attention of the mass media, have themselves in great part
> framed and elicited the various demands to which they then respond.[5]
> (emphasis added)

To justify their predominant role in defining general interests, the parties
must be able to mobilize consent. Their role here is most visible at elections.
But the support then mobilized needs to be sufficient to sustain the government throughout its life. The presumption that parties can mobilize sufficient

support to sustain the government, allows ministers in government to act as the exclusive political agents for the community's general interests. This underwrites the concentration of the power of initiative in policy making in their hands. Ministers translate their party's priorities into existing and new programmes. Ministers are thus the political champions for their party in three equally important dimensions of public policy: first, in translating their party programmes into policy; second, in reviewing existing programmes to ensure they continue to be effective and relevant; third, in providing essential political leadership to forward planning. Their role as exclusive agents for the community's general interests requires them to discharge these three tasks.

As the last chapter demonstrated, the party government model continues to dominate current policy-making practice. Parties continue as leading proponents of general interests. The rival parties champion their alternative conceptions before the electorate. Having obtained an endorsement, one party proceeds to implement its conception in government. Its rival maintains public visibility for its alternative view through its role as the official opposition. Parliament provides a public forum for the expression of opposition. The forms and procedures of the two-party system reconcile the principle that the government should be accountable, with the no less valued principle that considerable concentration of political power is necessary to allow the executive to do its job.[6]

In the two-party system, parliament is conceived as the setting for a 'continuing election campaign'.[7] The public face of politics is based on contest for office between the parties. This struggle for office often distorts debate about the merit of issues. The 'benefit' of focusing public attention on debate between adversarial parties is to leave policy making as a 'private' activity between ministers and departments. The 'private' character of policy making and the concentration of the power of initiative in the hands of ministers presumes elections settle the 'political' dimension of policy making. 'Private' policy making presumes the parties are the exclusive agents for general interests and that they are capable of mobilizing sustained majority support.

Various reasons have been advanced for the failure to handle fundamental programme review and strategic issues. Some critics, such as Sir John Hoskyns, blame an indolent civil service culture. They arraign the power of the service to thwart government. Departments themselves have become defenders of established programmes. Their responsibility for particular programmes means they are gathering information about their impact and evaluating demographic and other factors bearing upon public need. Departments are in a favoured position to advise ministers about the desirability of modifying or expanding current programmes in the light of changing circumstances. Further, the extension of professionalism in government has resulted in a greater recruitment of individuals qualified in particular disciplines such as economics, social administration, health administration, and urban planning. These disciplines have (often tacit) normative as well as positive dimensions. Expertise creates policies. Departments now act as agents for general interests alongside ministers. Their privileged access to ministers reinforces their effectiveness in this role.[8] Under the influence of their advisers, ministers frequently abandon or obfuscate programmes their parties have championed to the electorate.[9] They do so because government provides them with information they were denied in opposition or because they are 'captured' by their advisers, or both. This suggests, incidentally, the extent to which information essential to formulate a judgement about the public interest remains confidential within government.

Another explanation for the failure to handle strategic issues adequately is ministerial overload.[10] Ministers are the central agents of political initiative. According to the party model, ministers are charged with the task of translating their party's conception of the public interest into policy. This gives them the responsibility of reviewing ongoing programmes, handling current issues and managing strategic issues. These responsibilities sit alongside a range of other tasks. Ministers are accountable to parliament for their day-to-day administration of departmental programmes. This requires them to sign an endless stream of correspondence covering representations from fellow parliamentarians, members of the public, and from the organizations dependent in one way or another on the programme for which the minister is responsible.

There are, in addition, the internal decisions relating to the administration of current programmes or their development. Further, a minister needs to authorize, and keep himself informed about, important negotiations between his department and other departments (for example, the Expenditure Division of Treasury on expenditure bids). He needs, as well, to participate in the formulation of Cabinet submissions for new programmes. Finally, he is a member of Cabinet or some Cabinet Committees.[11] He must prepare himself to participate in these administrative activities. He needs to leave time for political and parliamentary tasks. Political tasks might involve meeting interest groups, making speeches, attending functions. Parliamentary tasks involve participation in debates, question time and meetings with backbench committees.

These are the routine duties that confront any minister. The workload associated with all these tasks flows automatically. The day a minister assumes office, he becomes immediately subject to this flow of paper, this array of responsibilities and all the associated duties.[12] No department will be able to pursue fundamental programme review or the analysis of strategic issues without ministerial leadership. Without political input, public servants will lack critical information about public preferences or critical guidance about acceptable choices or remedies. Ministerial overload or ministerial turnover makes it most unlikely most ministers will be able to discharge all their political responsibilities.[13]

But even if a minister finds the time to sponsor debate on strategic issues, the logic of the party system often frustrates him. He is beset by political danger. This was illustrated during Mrs Thatcher's first term by the leak of the CPRS paper exploring the cost implications of maintaining unaltered the full apparatus of welfare state programmes.[14] Despite her own publicly expressed concern about these matters, Mrs Thatcher judged the political implications to be sufficiently threatening to require affirmation of her commitment to the current array of programmes. The government repudiated the paper publicly. The Chancellor subsequently tabled a Treasury paper assessing future expenditure implications. Compared to the general concerns voiced by the Prime Minister, this was a tame document. It did not suggest that government expected future resource requirements of current welfare state programmes to be an unacceptable burden. It did not suggest that government anticipated the need to change programme structures. It confirmed the existing array of programmes and expressed the government's view that resources would be adequate to maintain them.[15] Mrs Thatcher returned to this issue in her second term. Her Secretary of State established four task forces to review aspects of the social security system. The task forces met in private. Private evidence was taken from sixty-two interest groups. The Government published two Green Papers in May 1985. These Green Papers omit information essential to determine the ultimate impact of the changes the Government proposed. The fate of these proposals remains to be determined in the political market-place, despite Mrs Thatcher's eight years of office.[16]

There is some truth in the argument that the civil service enjoys excessive power and that ministers are overloaded. But recent analyses suggest these explanations of policy failure do not go to the heart of the matter. The third, and ultimately the decisive, reason for the failure to handle fundamental programme review and strategic issues arises from the new role of interest groups.[17] In the theory of the current system, interest groups are subordinate to the parties. Interest groups may be consulted on options. They may be consulted on implementation. In return for consultation and influence they may be expected to organize their members to support the Government.[18] But in participating in consultations, interest groups do not enjoy a role as of right in the policy process. The experience does not expose them to the 'social learning' that is focused on parliamentarians. It does not provide them with the institutionalized assurance that they will have a second chance to advance their claim. Lack of access to policy making often forces interest groups into conflict. As the next chapter will show, their attachment to their sectional objectives is often reinforced by the present consultation process. In pursuing their objectives (either by direct advocacy to ministers or departments or by exploiting their ability to mobilize support in the electoral system), interest groups frequently impose their sectional demands. They are able to do this because of the government's anxiety to achieve results, or because of the government's fear of opposition attack and electoral backlash, or both.[19]

This suggests that the failure to deal with strategic issues will not be corrected by further administrative reform. Rather, it suggests deficiencies in attention to the 'politics' of policy making. Looked at another way, it suggests the parties have lost their role as exclusive agents for the community's general interests. It suggests the failure to handle strategic issues in fact reflects the power of interest groups to assert their claim to participate in this activity. This perspective suggests that policy making requires attention to 'interest group politics' as well as party politics. So the questions to be considered here are: do these inquiries show the potential of select committees to handle interest group politics in its most important dimensions – fundamental programme review and forward planning? Second, is there evidence of select committee capacity to renew parliament's deliberative role?

Before turning to individual groups of inquiries, I want to review the overall pattern. Table 4.1 shows that in the 1981–2 session some thirty-two inquiries were staged (plus some instructive inquiries from earlier sessions debated in the 1981–2 parliamentary year or initiated in that year). Of these, fifteen involved fundamental reappraisal of existing programmes, and seventeen involved forward planning in one of its dimensions. Only one committee (Welsh Affairs) failed to conduct an inquiry of this kind in the 1981–2 session. The committees conducted on average at least one inquiry in this category each parliamentary year. The Energy Committee is listed as undertaking five inquiries. This represents inquiries initiated in earlier years and debated in the 1981–2 session (one inquiry), or inquiries initiated in the 1981–2 session but completed in later sessions (three inquiries). The following sections deal in turn with each broad category of inquiry. These are distinguished because each concerns fundamental aspects of policy making.

REVIEW OF MAJOR PROGRAMMES

Major programmes share a number of characteristics. They involve very significant public expenditure. They can take ten or fifteen years from conception to completion. The burden they impose on public expenditure can vary significantly between initiation and implementation. The assumptions on which they are based are critical and can vary as the project unfolds. In their appraisal of the management of public expenditure, Heclo and Wildavsky criticize the apparent incapacity of government to review major programmes once they are endorsed by Cabinet.[20] They conclude that such programmes acquire a life of their own. Constituencies are created with privileged access to ministers and with a vested interest in the programme's preservation. Ministers are reluctant to repudiate established commitments because of the charge of incompetence which they can attract from the opposition, because of the political benefits to be gained from being associated with major visible phases of the project (e.g. a first flight, opening a hospital, a power station, or a university), because of the fear of interest group reaction or some combination of these reasons.

Heclo and Wildavsky conclude policy making is biased towards large programmes which, once announced, seem to be impossible to modify or

Table 4.1 Select committee inquiries on strategic issues, 1981/2

Committee	Fundamental programme review			Forward planning		
	Major proposed programmes	Adequacy programmes/ policy	Adequacy administration/ management	System-wide reviews	Role of central government	Emerging issues
Transport (3)	2			1		
Energy (5)	1				2	2
Defence (3)	1	1	1		1	
Education (3)		1		1	1	
Social Services (2)				1	1	1
Scottish Affairs (3)				1	1	1
Employment (2)					1	
Environment (3)			1		1	2
Agriculture (2)		1				
Ind. and Trade (2)		2				
Home Affairs (2)		1	1			
Foreign Affairs (1)		1				
Treasury (1)			1			
Total (32)	4	7	4	4	7	6
	Total fundamental programme reviews (15)			Total forward planning reviews (17)		

This covers inquiries completed in 1981/2 or inquiries for which a significant number of evidence sessions were held in 1981/2.

cancel. They suggest a preferable approach would be to submit large programmes to regular review. These reviews could be at various stages in the
passage of the programme from conception to implementation. Such a system
would require a political mechanism for reviewing programmes without the
competence of the current government being impugned. Unlike an internal
review, a political review would open the possibility for reconsideration of the
fundamental principles underlying the project. Are these possibilities realized
in the select committee inquiries?

To answer this question the following sections review in turn the scope and
significance of the inquiries conducted by the select committees, their conduct
of these inquiries, the adequacy of the committees' findings and their impact
on government.

Scope and significance

For the purpose of analysis, select committee reviews of major programmes
can be classified into three groups: first, review of proposed programmes;
second, review of ongoing programmes or policies; third, evaluation of particular public sector agencies.

The committees' review of four proposed programmes are listed in table
4.2. These programmes all involve large expenditures over a protracted
period. Two of these enquiries were begun in earlier sessions. The Transport
Committee conducted its major review of the proposed Channel link in the
1980–1 session. This project, it was estimated, would cost between £1.3
billion and £4.5 billion at 1981 prices. The project has a long history in Anglo-
French relations. At the time, the most recent official appraisal had occurred
in 1975. Thereafter, various committees examined alternative schemes. A unit
to monitor developments was established in the Department of Transport in
1979. The project received a political boost in 1981 after a meeting of UK and
French ministers. This meeting endorsed intensive review of seven options.
The Transport Committee's 1980–1 report concluded that the most promising
proposal appeared to be a single-track rail link. The committee's report in
1981–2 placed the most recent analysis on the public record. This comprehensive study, by Sir Alec Cairncross, questioned the viability of a fixed link.

The Defence Committee's full review of Strategic Nuclear Weapons Policy
also occurred in 1980–1. The Trident project was estimated to involve expenditure of £7.5 billion over ten years at 1981 prices and exchange rates. This
was a major inquiry with extensive outreach, independent expert evidence,
and witnesses from the defence planning and the intelligence communities.
R. L. Borthwick, in his appraisal of the committee's work comments:

> The topic is one that the Government would probably have preferred the
> Committee not to have dealt with. . . . Attempts were made at the outset to
> limit the Committee's terms of reference by excluding consideration of
> alternative forms of replacement and the costs involved. . . . A further

attempt to limit the enquiry was made towards the end of the Committee's investigation, when Parliament had approved the choice of Trident to replace Polaris, by trying to have the Committee's final report confined to implementation of that decision.[21]

The third inquiry also involved the Transport Committee. The committee conducted an extensive inquiry into mainline railway electrification. This built on an electrification review conducted by the Nationalized Industries Committee in 1976–7. Several members of the committee had been involved in the earlier inquiry. The fourth inquiry, on the Nuclear Power Programme, began in the 1979–80 session and ended in the 1980–1 session. The Secretary of State anticipated a ten-year programme of power-station construction at a cost of £15 billion.

Seven inquiries reviewed the adequacy of existing programmes and policies. These are listed in table 4.3. All these inquiries involve the review of some significant aspects of government activity. Unlike the reviews of specific programmes examined in the previous chapter, these inquiries involve broad ranging evaluations of the adequacy of ongoing programmes. These reviews provide the opportunity for a bipartisan committee to reappraise the grounding principles on which programmes or policies are based. The ability of politicians to challenge the political foundations of programmes if they so choose, distinguishes these inquiries from those conducted by the Public Accounts Committee. In fact two of these seven inquiries are critical of the basic framework within which current programmes are conceived – immigration from the Indian subcontinent and protection of the research base in bio-technology. The other five inquiries criticize the details of present arrangements but not the basic foundations of policy.

These reviews concern programmes that share a number of characteristics. First, they have survived both Tory and Labour governments, thus implying bipartisan support for their broad thrust. The current array of measures to assist exporters had evolved since the early 1960s. Similarly aid measures for Northern Ireland were established during both Tory and Labour governments. The British Army of the Rhine fulfils a NATO commitment.

Second, they involve a complex array of direct grants, other incentives and consultative machinery. The effort to encourage bio-technology involved both an elaborate consultative apparatus and a number of specific aid programmes administered by the various Research Councils. Responsibility was shared between the Department of Industry and the Department of Education. Five separate committees advised these two departments and the UGC.[22] Although industry aid to Northern Ireland was administered by the Northern Ireland Office, some forty individual programmes were involved. The Department of Industry maintained an interest in this programme. ASEAN trade involved trade officials on site, the Export Credits Guarantee Department, the Foreign Office and the British Overseas Trading Board.

Table 4.2 Proposed major programmes (references are to 1981/2 session unless otherwise indicated)

Committee	Inquiry	Background/Approach	Outreach	Findings/Impact on government
Transport (H.C. 207)	The Channel Link	* 1975 Expert Cttee reported on scheme. * Thereafter various cttees and inquiries reviewed scheme. * SNCF and BR proposed single-track rail tunnel. In 1979 Channel Tunnel Unit with 12 staff set up by DoT. * Joint working party set up after Anglo-French summit 1981. * 7 schemes under consideration costing between £1.3 bill. and £4.5 bill. at 1981 prices. Sir Alec Cairncross invited to assess commercial viability.	* Major report of Transport Cttee with extensive outreach. H.C. 155, 1980/1. * Recommended more investigation single-track rail link. * H.C. 155 lasted 10 months. Oral evidence from 21 groups in UK and 8 groups in France (3 volumes).	* Puts on public record analysis by Sir A. Cairncross concluding against fixed link. * H.C. 155 bipartisan report.
Transport (H.C. 317)	Mainline Railway Electrification	* Proposal for electrification review by Nationalized Inds Cttee 1976/7. * BR/DoT assumptions reviewed and confirmed by Cttee. * Cttee denied access to critical CPRS Report.	* Inquiry whilst ASLEF strike – evidence from leaders. * Evidence suggests disbandment of key construction team without further project. * Special adviser Dr S. Glaister, LSE.	* Endorses association of new investment with productivity gain. * Recommends London to Leeds electrification proceed now. * Report bipartisan except para. 18 re responsibility of unions, Cttee divided 3 Lab. against, versus 1 Lab., 1 SDP, and 2 Cons for.

(continued)

Table 4.2—*continued*

Committee	Inquiry	Background/Approach	Outreach	Findings/Impact on government

Energy (H.C. 114, 1980/1)	Nuclear Power Programme	* Follows Parliamentary Statement 18.12.79.
		* Cost £15 bill. over 10 years.
		* Separate report on lack of control of construction costs during main inquiry. (See table 3.7.)
		* Main report 99 pages; evidence and appendices 2,600 pages (4 volumes).
			* Evidence from 19 industry and nuclear groups, incl. Friends of the Earth, Ecology Research Group, Scram, Pandora etc. Also 5 individual experts.
			* 6 Specialist advisers
			  – 3 from Science Policy Research Unit, Sussex,
			  – 2 Imperial College,
			  – 1 Assoc. Nuclear Services.
				* Report questions planning assumptions. Criticizes lack of public debate and CEGB control of construction costs.
				* Inadequate cost calculations on conservation.
				* Report bipartisan.
				* Debated Commons 1.2.82.
				* Gov. weakened commitment to major construction programme.

Defence (H.C. 266, 1981/2)	Strategic Nuclear Weapons Policy	* Builds on H.C. 36, 130, 1980/1. This involved review of Trident proposal in context of options for nuclear weapons strategy. Majority endorsed programme. Cost £7.5 bill. i.e. approx. 5% Defence vote, 1985 to early 1990.
		* Since June 1981, several developments:
		  – March 1982 Paper on UK Trident programme.
		  – Paper from specialist adviser on developments and options.
			* Report to cttee by Dept on follow-up action since 1980/1 inquiry.
			* Background paper by adviser, Prof. L. Freedman on issues and options also published.
				* Ministers' evidence discloses preferred option 640 class sub + D5 type missile.
				* Notes gov. decision to use US facilities to prepare and refurbish missiles.
				* Notes action to acquaint UK Defence contractors of offset bid opportunities.
				* Major report (H.C. 36, 130, 1980/1) divided on party lines.

109

Table 4.3 Adequacy of programmes/policies (references are to 1981/2 session unless otherwise indicated)

Committee	Inquiry	Approach	Outreach	Findings/Impact on government
Industry and Trade (H.C. 195, 1982/3) (most evidence 1981/2)	UK trade with ASEAN	* ASEAN growth 78/81 = 7% p.a. UK market share 3.5%. * Support from BOTB and ECGD. * Builds on inquiry Imports and Exports (H.C. 109, 1980/1). * Malaysian gov. recently adopted deliberately anti-British purchasing approach.	* Visited 5 ASEAN nations. Evidence from 30 officials, businessmen etc. * Special adviser Garel Rhys, Univ. College, Cardiff.	* Identifies best export prospects (high tech., capital goods, services etc.). * Some evidence of tardiness by ECGD. * Extend tenure in posts to 5–6 years. Extend opening hours etc. * Bipartisan report.
Home Affairs (sub-committee) (H.C. 90)	Immigration from Indian Subcontinent	* Administrative orders used to mask political decisions. * Builds on inquiry British Overseas Citizens (H.C. 158, 1980/1).	* Hearings in Bangladesh and India from affected individuals and groups.	* Increase entry vouchers by 1200 in 1983 and 1984 to clear queue. * No division on strict party lines. On key points, report bipartisan.
Industry and Trade (H.C. 398)	Gov Support for Trade and Industry in Nth. Ireland	* Industry support est. £205 m. 1982/3. * Housing support £400 m. * Currently 40 different schemes. Principally standard capital grants scheme; selective financial assistance scheme.	* Evidence from affected depts and interests.	* Maintain special treatment. * Need more housing. * Emphasize services. Cttee criticizes monitoring of De Lorean investment. * Media report suggests cttee sees industry incentives as failure. * Gov. reply H.C. 85, 1982/3.
Defence (H.C. 93)	Allied Forces in Germany	* Follows BAOR reorganization plus cut in RAF manpower of 2500.	* Cttee visits troops on site in West Germany. * Meets with counterpart cttee in Bonn.	* Criticizes lack German-speaking officers. * Notes high morale, strength of units etc. * Bipartisan report.

(continued)

110

Table 4.3—*continued*

Committee	Inquiry	Approach	Outreach	Findings/Impact on government
Foreign Affairs (H.C. 47)	Caribbean and Central America	* Arose from ongoing review of major regions where British political commitments still substantial.	* Expert evidence 5 academics, 3 private groups, Oxfam, Latin American Bureau etc. (Total 12 individuals and groups).	* More consultation with allies on Central America; Support multilateral, bilateral aid for Costa Rica. * Use Brit. influence against Nicaraguan expansion. * Specific proposals to exploit trade opportunities. * Bipartisan report.
Agriculture (H.C. 41)	Financial Policy of EEC and Member States to Less Favoured Areas.	* Tests feeling of some British farmers that they are unfairly disadvantaged by some national schemes (e.g. Dutch cross subsidy). * Reviews effectiveness of MAFF in seeking EEC grants.	* Oral evidence 22 groups: – Ag. depts – NFU, Landowners Assoc. – Nature Conservation Council etc. * Cttee visited 14 farms UK also France, West Germany.	* Create Min. of State for Rural Affairs to deal with LFAs. * 42 specific recs concerning new policies or changed existing policies. * Bipartisan report (1 Cons. dissenting). No division on party lines.
Education (H.C. 289)	Protection of Research Base in Bio-Technology	* Responsibility shared between SERC, Med. RC and Ag. RC. * Spinks report 1980, Merrison 1982. * Science and ind. disappointed at blandness gov. response. * Current spending est. £10 m. * 4 specialist advisers. * Duration 5 mths. * Builds on inquiry of former Science and Tech. Cttee. * Ind. needs raised urgency of issue.	* 30 written submissions from associations, depts, advisory bodies. 15 answers to tech. questionnaire. * Oral evidence Royal Society, ICI etc. (6 groups).	* More research spending through UGC and NAB (to match level of research councils). * Links between DoI and UGC required. * 21 individual recs mainly concerning how leadership and co-ordination should be strengthened within gov. * Bipartisan report.

Third, these programmes involve a significant government interest, substantial current expenditure, or affect a considerable number of people. For example, the Industry and Trade Committee noted the value and growth of ASEAN trade to Britain. British exports were estimated to be worth £1 billion in 1982. The UK share equalled approximately 3.5 per cent of total ASEAN imports. The British share had fallen from 10 per cent in 1970 and 6 per cent in 1979. Over this same period ASEAN GNP growth equalled some 9.5 per cent annually. Government support for Northern Ireland development amounted to some £205 million annually. The British Army of the Rhine cost some £1.3 billion annually, equal to 9 per cent of the total defence budget. Direct support for bio-technology amounted to some £11 million. Additional funds were involved through the Medical Research Council's £17 million allocation to basic research and through the direct funding of university research activity. In reviewing immigration from the Indian subcontinent, the committee considered whether the government was using administrative orders to escape its responsibility to British passport holders. The number of UK passport holder heads of household in the Indian immigration 'queue' was estimated at in excess of 5000.

The last group of four inquiries assessed the adequacy of established administrative arrangements or approaches. These are listed in table 4.4. This is a form of scrutiny which has only recently been attempted by departments themselves.[23] Ministers, who ultimately carry responsibility for such matters, are usually too preoccupied by current issues or policy development or Cabinet or other commitments to undertake this kind of work. In his evidence to the Treasury Committee, Michael Heseltine commented:

Politicians who recognise the scale of the present bureaucracy *need a degree of political involvement in the management of the bureaucracy. . . .* There was a point that the bureaucracy grew from the fact that politicians took the decisions and the Civil Servants administered them. If you had a very small department, that was perfectly acceptable. Everyone knew about things. Through your physical presence in the department you would know what was going on and it was easy to get the feel for it. The fact of the matter is that today I have personal responsibilities for 45 thousand people working for me all over the world in a massive range of offices doing a massive range of things. I am responsible for every last one and everything that everyone says. I am responsible for any mistakes they might make.[24] (emphasis added)

Michael Heseltine's remedy was the MINIS system − as the acronym implies, a computer-based management information system for ministers.[25] This provided him with information about staff deployment and the progress of staff reduction plans. He subsequently introduced a variant of this scheme to the Defence Department. The government used its response to the Treasury

Table 4.4 Adequacy of administration (references are to 1981/2 session unless otherwise indicated)

Committee	Inquiry	Approach	Outreach	Findings/Impact on government
Defence (H.C. 22)	MoD Organization and Procurement	* MoD ministerial structure revised June 1981. * Defence equipment budget 1981/2 £5.4 bill. PAC Chevaline inquiry revealed difficulties in holding cash limits. Total defence vote 12.3 bill.	* Evidence from Treasury, DoI, 9 industry groups, 2 academics, industry personnel. (Written and oral evidence from 50 individuals and groups.)	* As procurement more complex, central control reduces. Yet delegation thwarts accountability. Customer/contractor rels need to be reformulated. * Numerous individual recs. * Bipartisan report.
Treasury (H.C. 236)	Efficiency and Effectiveness in the Civil Service	* Civil Service mgt focuses on admin costs – 12% total costs. * MINIS system explained. * Should C & AG have enlarged responsibility for effectiveness audits? * Builds on Civil Service Inquiry H.C. 54, 1980/1; H.C. 535, 1976/7.	* Evidence from 6 depts.	* Ministers should choose permanent secs. * Make C & AG accountable to parliament. * Empower select cttees to seek C & AG inquiries. * Endorses PAC proposal to establish National Audit Office. * Bipartisan report.

(continued)

Table 4.4—*continued*

Committee	Inquiry	Approach	Outreach	Findings/Impact on government
Home Affairs (sub-committee) (H.C. 46)	Commission for Racial Equality	* Racial Disadvantage Inquiry (H.C. 424, 1980/1) disclosed unsatisfactory CRE mgt control. Confusion between promotion and adjudication. * Budget £8 m.	Oral evidence Dept plus 3 outside groups. * Written evidence 45 groups including rights and advocacy groups.	* CRE management needs reconstructing. * Organization unhappy and lacking leadership. * Bipartisan report (only division concerned scope of para. 19.).
Employment (H.C. 400)	Health and Safety Executive	* Established after 1972 report on Health and Safety at Work (Robens Report) by Health and Safety at Work Act, 1974. * Safety Cttee established 1978 and regulations issued. * EEC flow on legislation added to regs.	* Evidence from CBI, TUC etc. Former concerned by costs arising from EEC flow-on regulations. Also Chemical Inds. Assoc., Royal Society for Prevention of Accidents, Cttee on Safety of Nuclear Installations, Soc. for Prevention Asbestosis etc.	* Criticism from Sir Bernard Braine noted. Detailed consideration deferred to subsequent inquiry. * All decisions, orders, regulations issued by Commission listed. * Report suggests strengthened outreach and publicity. * Report reviews *modus operandi* of Commission. Notes its consultative arrangements with unions, employer research groups, etc. * Bipartisan report.

114

and Civil Service Committee report on the civil service, to announce what it described as the Financial Management Initiative.[26] This involves an attempt to upgrade the capacity of individual departments to manage their resources more efficiently. It seeks to introduce a standard reporting framework to allow ministers and accounting officers to identify resources used against targets. It also seeks to strengthen Treasury capacity to monitor departmental efficiency. Techniques to help departments manage their resources better are not inconsistent with an extended role for parliamentary select committees. But select committees have a capacity for unfettered judgement that distinguishes their work from that of departments or ministers. Departments will naturally be hesitant about reviews that undercut major areas of their responsibility or that threaten the prerogatives of senior officers. Ministers will be wary of reviews that could produce uncomfortable political outcomes. Select committees are less constrained by these factors.

This is illustrated in the four inquiries reviewed here. The inquiry on the Commission for Racial Equality involved the appraisal of an organization with high political visibility. The committee was very critical of current management and policies. A bipartisan committee can express criticism that would be difficult for an individual minister. Similarly, in reviewing Ministry of Defence organization and procurement, the Defence Committee had the opportunity to investigate organizational structures and practices up the highest level of the department. Departmental officials would presumably have been inhibited in a parallel investigation. These inquiries involve review of activities that absorb a significant volume of public expenditure or that are politically sensitive. Defence procurement annually costs around £5 billion of a total defence vote in 1981–2 of £12 billion.

Taken together these fifteen inquiries, all involving review of major existing or proposed public expenditures, reflect comprehensive committee coverage of all aspects of programme approval and review. Our next task is to appraise the conduct of inquiries.

Conduct of inquiries

The conduct of these inquiries provides evidence of select committee capacity to identify significant topics, engage interest groups, gather expert evidence and reach conclusions within a reasonable time.

First, their origin demonstrates the capacity of committees to respond, on their own initiative, to change in external circumstances. The inquiry on ASEAN trade arose from the Malaysian government's curtailment of British imports. The review of immigration rules originated in a broad-ranging inquiry into British overseas citizens conducted by the Home Affairs Committee in the 1980–1 parliamentary sessions. This inquiry identified disquiet amongst overseas citizens. It questioned the fairness of the approach then being followed by the government. The review of bio-technology policy responded to the scientific community's disappointment at the blandness of the government's reaction to the Merrison Report. The Defence Committee inquiry on organization and procurement followed revision of the ministerial structure in June 1981. The MoD had been criticized for procurement management in the Public Accounts Committee report on the Chevaline project (reviewed in chapter 3). In addition, the Defence Department had failed to adhere to its cash limits for the previous three years. The inquiry on civil service effectiveness followed an earlier major inquiry of similar scope conducted by the Expenditure Committee in 1976–7.[27] Finally, the Home Affairs Committee inquiry into the Commission for Racial Equality also arose from earlier work by its Immigration Sub-Committee. This inquiry concerned racial disadvantage and was conducted in the 1980–1 session. The sub-committee encountered dissatisfaction with the management of CRE programmes. There was disagreement within the Commission about how vigorous and 'political' its advocacy should be. Concern was expressed that advocacy cut across the Commission's responsibility for investigating alleged discrimination. The Commission had a budget of approximately £8 million. Its governing body consisted of fifteen individuals nominated by the government.

All these inquiries involved extensive outreach to interest groups, in many cases on the committee's own initiative. For example, the Education Committee solicited thirty written submissions from scientific and professional associations, official advisory councils, research groups and individual companies involved in the bio-technology area. The Agriculture Committee took evidence from twenty-two groups for its inquiry on policies towards less favoured areas. These groups included the Agricultural Departments, representatives of farmers and conservation groups. The Foreign Affairs Committee took evidence from twelve individuals and groups in the course of its inquiry on trade/aid policies in the Caribbean. These included five individual experts, three aid and research groups, a bank and a trading company. These inquiries provided a vehicle for academic and other expert opinion to be weighed side by side with current departmental thinking.

The Defence Committee held fifteen evidence sessions. It heard the Chief of the Defence Staff, the Secretary of State, the Permanent Under-Secretary and the various Defence Boards. Oral evidence was also taken from the Treasury, from the Department of Industry and nine industry groups (ranging from the Society of British Aerospace Manufacturers to individual defence suppliers such as Plessey and Rolls-Royce). Written evidence was taken from fifty individual companies and groups. The report fills three volumes. The appendices include six detailed procurement case studies covering the following weapons: Clansman, Seawolf, Tow, Tornado and Hawk, and types 21 and 22 Frigates. The Treasury Committee also took extensive evidence from departments,

including the DHSS, MoD, Internal Revenue and Customs. It obtained information about current US practices and the role of the General Accounting
Office. It took evidence about developments in Australia and Canada.

The Energy Committee took evidence from nineteen industry groups,
including reactor suppliers, construction firms, the Central Electricity Generating Board, and the Department of Energy. It took evidence from environmental groups such as Friends of the Earth, Ecology Research Group, Scram
and Pandora. The Amalgamated Society of Locomotive Enginemen and Fire-
men gave evidence to the Transport Committee inquiry on Mainline Railway
Electrification whilst in the middle of a major manning dispute. Union
members were on strike at the time of the hearing. Committee questioning
probed union attitudes to efficiency and to redundancy.

A number of these inquiries involved select committees travelling to interview affected interests or groups on site. The Defence Committee visited
several army bases in Germany. It also held discussions with its counterpart
committee in Bonn. The Home Affairs Committee held hearings in Bangladesh and India. It took evidence from groups representing affected British
overseas citizens. The Industry and Trade Committee took evidence from
British trade officials and businessmen in every ASEAN capital. This same
committee held evidence sessions in Belfast in connection with its inquiry on
regional aid to Northern Ireland. The Agriculture Committee visited fourteen
farms in the UK and inspected less favoured agricultural areas in France and
West Germany. A sub-committee of the Home Affairs Committee visited the
US to review the approach of the Race Relations Office in the Justice Department. The committee took evidence from commissioners and staff.

In duration, these inquiries ranged from three to eleven months. The
Education Committee inquiry on bio-technology lasted five months. The
Agriculture Committee inquiry lasted eight months. The Home Affairs
inquiry, including the visit to Bangladesh and India, lasted six months. The
inquiry on MoD organization took eleven months and that on civil service
efficiency and effectiveness nine months.

In framing options and analysing government proposals the committees
mobilized impressive expert resources either by engaging individuals as special
advisers or by inviting specialists to give evidence. The Defence Committee's
published evidence includes searching analysis of UK policy options by nine
independent experts, including Professor Ian Bellamy, Mary Kaldor, and the
International Institute for Strategic Studies. In the 1981–2 session the Defence
Committee took evidence from the Secretary of State on developments. His
evidence concerned the government's preference for a 640 class submarine
and D5 missile. These changes were estimated to increase the cost of the programme from £5 billion at July 1980 prices to just under £7.5 billion at September 1981 prices. The committee report, which endorses the government's
approach, includes a lengthy paper from a committee adviser, Professor
Lawrence Freedman, analysing government options. The bio-technology

inquiry circulated a detailed questionnaire to fifteen experts. This question-naire sought their assessment of the current state of research in the UK and the principal gaps and deficiencies. This evidence is all published. The Energy Committee took evidence from academic experts on the safety and efficacy of nuclear power. It took conflicting evidence from individual experts on the merit of PWR and AGR reactors. The report places this evidence on the public record. It exposes, if it does not resolve, the dilemma faced by political decision-makers when technical experts are at odds.[28] The Transport Committee was denied access to a CPRS report on mainline railway electrification. The committee accepted the government's decision under protest.

Findings and impact

Some findings were accepted by the government. This was the case in the important inquiry into the Commission for Racial Equality. The Home Affairs Committee's bipartisan report was strongly critical of the manage-ment and programmes of the Commission. It suggested that Commission management should be reconstructed. The committee commented:

> The Commission's gravest defect is incoherence. The Commission operates without any obvious sense of priorities or any clearly defined objectives. There are few subjects on which they prove unwilling to pronounce and few projects on which they are unwilling to embark. Where specific policy objectives have been established, they are rarely translated into concrete activity. Commission staff respond to this policy vacuum by setting their own objectives and taking independent initiatives, which not surprisingly peter out or go off at half-cock. A distressing amount of energy which should be channelled into a coherent and integrated programme leading to clearly-defined objectives is thus frittered away.

Some committees proposed action more radical than that subsequently adopted by government. This was the case in the Treasury Committee's report on civil service effectiveness. The committee analyses the approach of the departments to the management of resources. The report criticizes depart-ments for concentrating cost-reduction effort on administrative costs — covering only 12 per cent of total programme costs. The report includes extensive evidence on the workings of the MINIS system in the Department of the Environment and its applicability throughout government. The committee reviews staff development practices and compares the UK situation with that of other countries. The report and associated evidence fill 1400 pages in three volumes. There is extensive information about current management practices and approaches within the civil service. The committee recommends that ministers be given the right to choose their own permanent secretaries. It recommends that the Auditor General be accountable to parliament and it invites parliament to empower select committees to commission inquiries by the Auditor General. It endorses the Public Accounts Committee proposal to establish a National Audit Office on the model of the US General Accounting Office. There are a number of individual recommendations concerning staff development and the extension of MINIS throughout government.

As mentioned earlier, the government chose to launch its Financial Management Initiative in replying formally to this report. Members of the Treasury Committee subsequently played a key role in negotiation with the government on control of the Auditor General. This was reviewed in chapter 1. The Treasury Committee inquiry served the purpose of building bipartisan support for this development amongst a key group of backbenchers – for example Tories such as Terence Higgins, Edward du Cann and Labour members such as John Garrett and Dr Jeremy Bray. As was noted, back-benchers were successful on this occasion in obliging the executive to modify its position. However the government would not concede the Auditor General the right to scrutinize local government and nationalized industries.

Some reports, although not formally accepted by government, proposed action which paralleled that subsequently adopted by government. The Energy Committee's final report on Nuclear Power questions CEGB planning assumptions. Evidence challenged the accuracy of CEGB estimates of forward demand. The committee judged these estimates to be over-optimistic. It also criticized the Energy Department's lack of attention to conservation. The report emphasizes the contentious character of nuclear power and the need for public discussion and consultation. The government subsequently established a public inquiry into the proposed Sizewell Station. The proposed programme has since been scaled back significantly.[29] In the course of the inquiry, the Energy Committee determined that power station construction costs had passed beyond CEGB control. It tabled an interim report on this issue (which was reviewed in the last chapter). Both the interim and final reports were bipartisan.

Most of the reports were simply ignored. This was the fate of six reports that terminated with specific recommendations. The Employment Committee's assessment of the Health and Safety Executive was critical of the tripartite character of the Commission. It suggested strengthened outreach and publicity. The report attracted criticism from the TUC. It failed to elicit more than a perfunctory response from government. The government rejected key committee suggestions on mainline railway electrification, immigration from the Indian subcontinent, policy towards less favoured areas, on bio-technology research and on civil service reform. Did these recommendations involve a 'sell-out' to interest groups? The evidence is mixed. The Agriculture Committee is very sympathetic to rural interests, but its key recommendations involve the organization of Agriculture Departments and the British approach to the EEC. There are some proposals that would entail extra spending but these are not the core of the report. The report on mainline railway electrification envisaged more spending. But it could fairly be represented that the committee's judgement of the evidence varied from that of ministers. In releasing the report the (Labour) chairman commented:

> Although the case for electrification does not depend on productivity improvements, there is in my mind no doubt that the railway industry cannot expect further major capital expenditure – which means the spending of the taxpayer's money – unless it demonstrates that it can and will set its own house in order and ensure that full advantage is taken of investment already made to improve the railway infrastructure.

The committee further reviewed developments in the 1983–4 session. The Education Committee recommendations on bio-technology research might similarly be interpreted as a different judgement of the evidence presented, rather than an unquestioning acceptance of interest group views.

The level of bipartisanship is instructive. There were divisions on some recommendations on the Home Affairs Committee report on immigration from the Indian subcontinent. But none of these divisions were on key points. This report offered trenchant criticism of the current approach. Another critical report, that on bio-technology, was wholly bipartisan. There was some Conservative dissension in the report on less favoured areas by the Agriculture Committee. But this involved a disagreement amongst Conservative members, not a partisan split of the committee. Similarly the Transport Committee tabled a bipartisan report recommending immediate electrification of the London to Leeds line and steps to hold key construction and design teams together.

The Defence Committee was not able to reach bipartisan agreement on strategic nuclear weapons policy. Its Tory majority generally endorsed the approach proposed by the government. They criticized the government for not providing sufficient information to allow the impact of this project on the rest of the defence programme to be assessed. Labour members tabled a minority report. The Defence Committee did not specifically return to this subject during the first Thatcher government. It has however continued to monitor developments in its general evidence sessions with the Secretary of State and in its review of departmental action on earlier reports.[30] The committee has not yet judged that developments require reopening of the issue.

The Defence Committee's report on organization and procurement was mostly bipartisan. The report draws attention to the difficulties of reconciling central control and accountability with complex, protracted programmes. The committee suggests no innovative solution. It offers thirty-three specific recommendations. Some members of the committee considered this to be amongst the least successful of their inquiries. They expressed the view that the time and effort absorbed by this inquiry far exceeded the possible impact or merit of the conclusions.[31]

Only one report, that on Nuclear Power, was debated in the Commons. This debate occurred on an adjournment motion and resulted from private negotiations between the minister, the Energy Committee Chairman and government business managers. Speaking for the government, the Minister of State complimented the committee on the quality of its research and findings. He referred specifically to the informed level of debate, crediting this to the committee report. The contributions from both government and opposition speakers dealt with the merits of the issue and eschewed political point scoring.[32]

The impact of these reports can be variously assessed. At one level their impact can be positively interpreted as a considerable extension of the accountability of departments to parliament. The inquiries reviewed here show bipartisan committees assessing complex public investments and major areas of administrative activity. These committees make a bipartisan judgement about the merits of the proposed projects. Through the committees the views of departments, technical experts and interest groups are placed on the public record. Furthermore, the inquiries concerned with proposed programmes oblige members and interest groups to address the fundamental political issue – should the programmes go forward. This issue is to be distinguished from subsequent argument concerning particular phases of a project. The committees provide a forum within government, but independent of departments, where a department's interpretation of the public interest can be presented to parliamentarians and interest groups, and where interest groups' interpretations of the public interest have the chance of modifying executive or departmental approaches.

The fact that a parliamentary committee can mount such an inquiry may be expected to provide a stimulus to the civil service. At another level, the inquiry provides opportunities for external groups to gain access for the investigation of their grievances by a body potentially of equivalent status to departments – a body that draws on the prestige of parliament. This is illustrated, for example, in the Home Affairs Committee inquiry on immigration from the Indian subcontinent. Here groups representing British overseas passport holders were interviewed on their home ground in Bangladesh and India and their associated groups were heard in the Palace of Westminster in London. Similarly, in the case of the bio-technology inquiry, dissatisfied professional groups were given the opportunity to place their views on the public record, to hear the government's position expounded and to see the government's representative cross-examined.

But even the immediate impact of such reports will remain unclear until all committees adopt the practice (now followed by the Defence, Transport and Industry Committees) of periodically checking action on their findings by conducting further scrutiny hearings with departments. Ultimately their impact will be ambiguous until committees enjoy more direct power to pursue their findings on the floor of the House.

FORWARD PLANNING

A second, and distinct, category of strategic appraisal involves forward planning. The central need in the review of major programmes is a political mechanism capable of mobilizing sufficient consent and of proposing action without necessarily impugning the competence of the executive. Forward planning requires the capacity to oblige all relevant interests to come to terms with emerging issues and, as necessary, to alter their current behaviour and relationships.

When the polity was relatively homogeneous and when parties were the primary vehicle for citizen representation, mechanisms to identify widely shared values were not required. This task was carried out within political parties supplemented, if necessary, by private negotiations between ministers and by interest groups. The various protagonists accepted the fairness of elections as the procedure for determining which party élite would occupy the government benches. Electoral victory gave that élite authority to make its will prevail. Once, however, groups other than political parties conceive themselves to have an interest in determinations of the public interest (and acquire the organizational skills and political reach to prosecute their interest) a mechanism is required to introduce issues to the various groups and to elicit their views before final decisions are taken by the executive. This mechanism needs to oblige the varied interests to weigh issues realistically, rather than wishfully, and thus begin the process of 'social learning' which is an essential (although, as we shall see in chapter 6, far from the only) element in mobilizing consent.[33]

In the present policy-making system there is little capacity to give leadership on such matters. Parties generally lack the research resources. Even if they possessed the resources, they lack the capacity to engage departments. Further ideological estrangement prevents them engaging some interest groups. For their part, ministers, including the Prime Minister, are often too busy with day-to-day matters to devote time to strategic questions beyond their current programme. Even if they could, the political hazards associated with speculation about policy change may make action by them imprudent. Finally, departments do not have the authority or the skills to mount ongoing inquiries which are politically credible. Hence, in dealing with emerging issues, select committees are potentially creating a new capacity in the policy-making system. Without dialogue about such issues between key participants it will not be clear whether particular issues deserve a place on the public agenda. Nor can progress be made in handling the issue as it unfolds until all the interests concerned accept their new responsibilities. In assessing the performance of the select committees, inquiries will be considered from the familiar perspectives: their scope and significance; the adequacy of their conduct; the adequacy of findings and of their impact.

Scope and significance

Inquiries that concern forward planning in one or another of its aspects can also be classified into three groups. The first category involves system-wide reviews. These arise where responsibility for an outcome is shared between groups and levels of government. The second category covers inquiries concerning the role of central government, where this is in dispute. A third category concerns inquiries which assess emerging issues in their 'purest' form. These arise when protagonists urge the inclusion of a new issue on the political agenda and when no agreed definition of the issue exists.

The inquiries that involve system-wide reviews are listed in table 4.5. The organizations concerned could be different agencies in central government or different levels of government (e.g. Transport in London) or between central government, local government and independent private interests (e.g. Medical Education, Secondary Schools Curriculum). Under present arrangements central government would formulate its own views about how the matter should be handled. It would do so through information assembled by departments and perhaps after private consultation with interest groups. Counsel between departments is private. Official inquiries might have to be held to gather facts and judgements. But the key political decisions are typically taken in private by ministers on the advice of senior departmental officers, endorsed by Cabinet and then announced. The select committee inquiries reviewed here supplement these internal private inquiries held within government.

All these inquiries have in fact been preceded by lengthy departmental and official investigation. What is not agreed is how responsibility for action will be shared amongst participants. The issues span the life of both Tory and Labour governments. They have proved intractable to both. For example, the medical education inquiry was preceded by two major government sponsored reviews. The previously most recent large-scale review had been conducted by the Merrison Royal Commission in 1979. The CPRS had reviewed medical manpower issues in a report in 1980. The secondary school curriculum review was initiated by former Prime Minister Callaghan with a speech on educational standards in 1976. Thereafter several working parties were established. This culminated in March 1981 in a DES publication, 'The School Curriculum', which stimulated the inquiry we are considering here.

The second category of inquiry explores the role of central government. System-wide reviews involve areas where the responsibility of central government to define tasks and set priorities is acknowledged. A system-wide review is necessary when the way responsibilities are to be shared between levels of government, or between government and other responsible institutions or interest groups needs to be clarified. Another band of issues concerns questions at one remove. Should government have a role? What should it be? In the seven inquiries in this category (listed in table 4.6), four review the first

Table 4.5 System-wide reviews (references are to 1981/2 session unless otherwise indicated)

Committee	Inquiry	Approach	Outreach	Findings/Impact on government
Transport (H.C. 127)	Transport in London	* Covers activities of London Transport Exec., BR, London County Bus Services, GLC and Trunk Road Development. * Annual exp. est. £900 m. Revenue from passengers £546 m. * Builds on 'The Roads Programme' (H.C. 27, 1980/1) 'scandalous state of London system'.	* Oral evidence from 33 orgs and interest groups. * Written evidence 70 interest groups and orgs. * Cttee travelled to USA, Canada, Germany, France, Denmark. * Specialist advisers: Former Vice-Chairman London Transport Board; Dir. of Institute of Transport Studies (Leeds University).	* 37 separate recs. A comprehensive package: – New co-ordinating authority indep. of GLC. – Annual London Road Priority Action Prog. – Annual Public Transport Action Prog. * Gov. announced intention to reform London Transport – March 1983. * 3 divisions on report on fundamental matters. Basically bipartisan.
Education (H.C. 116)	Secondary School Curriculum and Exams	* Debate on curriculum initiated by PM in 1976. March 1981, DES published proposals 'The School Curriculum'. * Inquiry based on: – declining school population; – new 16-plus exam; – critical period 14–16 years.	* Oral evidence from 38 groups including: – 10 prof. groups; – 10 gov./regional groups; – 4 rights groups. * Written evidence 68 groups. * Evidence in Denmark, Sweden and Finland.	* 64 recommendations covering: – curriculum; – school governance; – DES planning; – religious education, etc. * 43 divisions on report. None on strict party lines. * Divisions concerned philosophy of central management of curriculum development, religious education, status of working-class and popular culture etc.

(continued)

Table 4.5—*continued*

Committee	Inquiry	Approach	Outreach	Findings/Impact on government
Social Services (H.C. 31, 1980/1)	Medical Education	* Long history of inquiries from Todd Royal Comm. 1968, Merrison Royal Commission 1979. * CPRS on medical manpower 1980. * PNM inquiry (H.C. 663, 1979/80) introduced Soc. Serv. Cttee to issue. * 138-page report; 3 vols; evidence and appendices 1200 pages. *Inquiry 8 months duration.	* Outreach to teaching hospitals, colleges, UGC, DHSS etc. * 4 specialist advisers: Prof. J. H. Clark; Dr Engelman (Health Economics); N. Hendry; Prof. J. Parkhouse.	* Sees leading role for Education Cttee of GMC in producing system-wide change. Proposes consultant contracts should be held at district not regional level. * Debated Commons 18.6.82. * Bipartisan report. No divisions.
Scottish Affairs (H.C. 178, 510)	Rural Road Passenger Transport and Ferries	* Scope deliberately confined to 'provision and financing of Rural Road Passenger Transport and Ferries'. * Inquiry 5 months duration.	* Oral evidence from 8 groups; written evidence from 19 groups. * Specialist adviser: G. Mackay (Consultant), Prof. T. Cabery.	* 25 recs. including: – experimental fund to encourage cost-cutting innovations; – more exchange of info. re unconventional remedies amongst local authorities; – maintain local control. * Report substantially bipartisan (2 divisions on party lines). * Debated Scottish Grand Cttee. Report 20.7.82. * Gov. rejected proposal for full road equivalent tariff on ferry services. Exposed retreat from electoral commitment.

Table 4.6 Role of central government (references are to 1981/2 session unless otherwise indicated)

Committee	Inquiry	Approach	Outreach	Findings/Impact on government
Employment (H.C. 39)	Homeworking	* Most homeworking not covered by Employment Protection Act (1978). * 200,000–400,000 estimated covered by HSC Draft Code. * Homeworking increasing in typing, market research, card punching etc. * Labour appointed Advisory Cttee – not met since 1979.	* Evidence from CBI, TUC, individuals, local gov. in 1980/1 session. * Written evidence DHSS, Inland Revenue, Assoc. of County Councils, Low Pay Unit, Leicester Outwork Campaign, 3 homeworking contractors.	* Recs MSC establish register. Review mission of Homeworking Advisory Committee. * Gov. rejects report. * Bipartisan report.
Energy (H.C. 337)	North Sea Oil Depletion Policy	* Academic evidence airs differences between market and non-market approach. * Inquiry over 12 months. * Special advisers: A. Kemp; Prof. G. Manners; J. Surrey. * Follows achievement of oil self-sufficiency in 1980.	* BNOC, Minister, Dept, academics pro and con deindustrialization (14 witnesses).	* Need more information. * Suggests evidence for deindustrialization inconclusive; criticizes tax regime; suggests limit gov. role to monitoring developments. * Gov. accepted desirability of minimum intervention. * Bipartisan report.

(continued)

126

Table 4.6—*continued*

Committee	Inquiry	Approach	Outreach	Findings/Impact on government
Environment (H.C. 40)	Private Rented Housing Sector	* 1980 Housing Act sought to encourage private rented sector. * Previous cttee inquiries: Council House Sales (H.C. 366, 1980/1). * Report documents differences between British, US and EEC tax and subsidy schemes. * Low returns – decreasing no. of rental units. * Survey results of 1978/9 not available till 1981/2.	* Written evidence from approx. 145 groups: – 28 local authorities; – 3 building societies; – 33 individual associations (NUS, Society for Co-op. Housing); – 39 academics and experts; – 16 rights groups.	* Returns so low sector will continue to decline. * Rental Act needs to be recast; also rent subsidies. * Gov. reply and cttee responds – point of disagreement: are enough people affected to create issue for gov.? * 11 divisions in cttee in finalizing report. Concerns emphasis between tenant rights and landlord returns.
Agriculture (H.C. 406, 1980/1)	Animal Welfare in Poultry, Pig and Veal Calf Production	* Cttee responds to public concern e.g. Dean of Westminster Working Party, 1980; Expansion of Animal Rights Movement. * Specialist adviser: Prof. D. Coleman, Manchester Univ. and 3 other Professors, 1 consultant. * Cttee visited Germany, Denmark and EEC in Brussels. Also 9 individual farms.	* Oral evidence 23 groups. * Written evidence 61 individuals and groups. * Detailed memo from MAFF concerning action and non-action on Brambell Report (1964).	* Recommends EEC regulation curbing unfavourable practices in each area. Suggests phase-in periods up to 5 years to eliminate existing practices. * UK should take lead in EEC context. Specific recs covering pigs, vealers and poultry. * Report approved after 9 divisions – pro: 3 Lab., 1 Cons.; anti – 3 Cons. * Commons adjournment debate 19.11.82.

(continued)

Table 4.6—*continued*

Committee	Inquiry	Approach	Outreach	Findings/Impact on government
Scottish Affairs (H.C. 96, 184) (Debated Scottish Grand Committee 15.2.82)	Youth Unemployment and Training	* Apprenticeships fallen $\frac{1}{3}$ 1972 to 1980. * Youth unemployment 28% of total (versus 16% 1970/4). * Inquiry lasted 9 months. * Scope deliberately confined to adequacy MSC special programmes and skill training in craft apprenticeships.	* Cttee visits West Germany. * Evidence from 22 groups (employers, unions, youth groups, etc.). * Special advisers: Alan McGregor, Prof. L. Hunter, M. Maclennan, (Univ. of Glasgow).	* Cttee suggestions closely matched gov. proposals – announced 2 days after publication of report. * Proposes major upgrading in vocational training of young people through extension of role of gov. * Report substantially bipartisan.
Education (H.C. 49)	Public and Private Funding of the Arts	* Office of the Arts transferred from Duchy of Lancaster to DES, Jan. 1982. * Gov. proposed arts less dependent on public subsidy. * Current spending £200 m. * Policy now co-ord by office of Arts in DES. * Specialist adviser: John Myerscough. * Duration 21 months (Jan. 1981 to Oct. 1982).	* Visits to Italy, Germany, Denmark, US. * Oral evidence 45 groups. * Written evidence around 85 individuals and 65 groups.	* 77 individual recs proposing significant extension of central administrative and financial role. * 'Umbrella' inquiry spawned 5 single-subject reports. * Bipartisan report.

(continued)

Table 4.6—*continued*

Committee	Inquiry	Approach	Outreach	Findings/Impact on government
Energy (H.C. 401)	Energy Conservation in Buildings	* Arose from Nuclear Power inquiry which concluded Dept. no clear idea of cost-effectiveness of spending on nuclear plant versus conservation. (H.C. 114, 1980/1 – also Industrial Energy Pricing Policy H.C. 422, 1980/1).	* 11 submissions from economic and other interests (e.g. loft insulation contractors). * 13 submissions central, regional, local government. * (Total of 46 submissions: 17 oral and 29 written).	* Create Energy Conservation Agency or Commission. * No. of consequent recs. * Energy Efficiency Office subsequently established in DoE. * Bipartisan report.

question – homeworking, private rented housing sector, animal welfare in poultry, pig and veal calf production, and energy conservation in buildings, and three consider the second question – public and private funding of the arts, youth unemployment and training, and North Sea oil depletion policy.

The third category of inquiry involves review of issues being proposed for the political agenda. Six inquiries of this kind were conducted in the 1981–2 session. These inquiries are listed in table 4.7. In all cases, these issues involve matters of great potential significance for policy makers. An issue such as the age of retirement or the method of funding local government affects all levels of government and a wide range of interests. An inquiry such as that into the future of Prestwick Airport affects a number of authorities and interests in a particular region. The combined heat and power inquiry explores the political, economic and managerial issues associated with this method of energy conservation. The Treasury Committee inquiry on the relation between the poverty trap, tax levels and income support arrangements is also within this category. This inquiry was mentioned in chapter 2.

Three of these inquiries were not completed in the 1981/2 session. Two involve the Energy Committee and one the Environment Committee. These three inquiries were completed before the election in June 1983, although in two cases the published reports were still partially in draft. The analysis that follows concentrates on two inquiries completed in the 1981/2 session (Age of Retirement, Method of Funding Local Government), the Prestwick Airport Inquiry (the report was tabled early in the 1982/3 session) and the Treasury Committee review of the structure of personal income tax and income support.

Conduct of inquiries

In assessing the conduct of inquiries, I will review in turn their origin, the adequacy of committee research, the duration of inquiries, and the engagement of interest groups.

Some inquiries were triggered by interest group pressures, some by member interest and some by ministerial or departmental concerns. Sometimes all sources played a part. The Social Services Committee had been subject to TUC pressure on the age of retirement. The reduction of the age of retirement in France was also cited by the committee as one of the factors that renewed pressure in the UK. The Treasury Committee inquiry on income support reflected the concern of individual committee members. Individual Tory and Labour members shared an interest in this issue, but for different reasons. There had also been pressure from interest groups, particularly the Child Poverty Action Group. The neo-liberal think-tank, the Centre for Policy Studies, had also been promoting the issue. Committee members were responsive to the argument that the government could not rely on economic recovery to provide opportunities for tax reform. The Prestwick Airport inquiry

Table 4.7 Emerging issues (references are to 1981/2 session unless otherwise indicated)

Committee	Inquiry	Approach	Outreach	Findings/Impact on government
Social Services (H.C. 26)	Age of Retirement	* Inquiry reflects gathering pressure for lowering retirement age to ease unemployment plus lowering of retirement age in France. Inquiry duration 15 months. * Specialist advisers: M. Fogarty (PSI) and H. Billings (formerly DHSS). * Cttee visited Belgium and France.	* Evidence from 29 groups: – 6 gov. depts/indep. authorities; – 3 umbrella pensioner and advocacy groups (National Pensioners', Age Concern, Help the Aged).	* Move towards notional common pension age of 63. * Cttee divided 3 Lab. – 3 Cons on merit of flexible age of retirement. Lab. Chairman voted with Cons. * Gov. subsequently appointed inquiry to review age of retirement – DHSS based. * Sir David Price adopted report as basis for private member's bill; debated Commons 25.11.83.
Environment (H.C. 217)	Method of Funding Local Government	* Inquiry based on Green Paper 1981. * Long history of reports/inquiries (1971, 1976, 1977). * Domestic rates generate 16% local authority revenue. Est. £5 bill. rev. * Impact study on local income tax by CI. * Dept analysed 1150 replies to Green Paper.	* Outreach to 15 groups including 4 depts, 4 umbrella groups. * Duration 5 months.	* Retain domestic rates. * Supplement through LIT. No local sales tax. Local LIT would reduce central grant and individual tax. Gov. begin review of LIT concept. * Report comments 'almost without exception the witnesses were more concerned with the autonomy of local Gov. and the accountability of local councillors to the electorate than with the domestic rating system. The Green Paper was seen as an inadequate starting point for a discussion of local Gov. finance.' * Cttee divided 7 times. Cons. divided on LIT versus earmarking income tax for local gov. Other divisions on strengthening local fiscal responsibility.

(continued)

131

Table **4.7**—*continued*

Committee	Inquiry	Approach	Outreach	Findings/Impact on government
Scottish Affairs (H.C. 423, H.C. 62, 1982/3)	Future of Prestwick Airport	* Duration 6 months. * Specialist adviser: G. A. McKay. * Traffic decline at Prestwick raised questions about its future. Cttee responded to local concern. Kyle council established Prestwick Working Party early 1982. Working Party encouraged by DoT-sponsored report by Adam Smith Institute on free ports.	* Extensive outreach to local authorities, BAA operators, users (12 groups). * Cttee visited free ports at Miami, Shannon, Hamburg, Baltimore and also EEC Brussels.	* Report 1982/3 (H.C. 62). * Gov. response H.C. 225, 1982/3, proposes establishment of free port. Gov. established working party. 3 or 4 experimental free ports foreshadowed 1982/3 budget. * Bipartisan report – no division on critical issues.
Energy (H.C. 603, evidence only)	Combined Heat and Power	* Marshall Cttee established 1974. Reported 1978. Recommends further work on CHP. Feasibility study £700,000 versus nuclear R & D £150 m., solar £6 m. * Cttee inquires to establish reasons for delay in gov. action. * Cttee visits US, Scandinavia, West Germany.	* Oral evidence 20 individuals and groups. * In evidence Sec. of State announces issue of consultation paper concerning removal of statutory barriers to private elec. generation. Expected to boost industrial CHP. Also selection of consultants to investigate nine promising lead city areas.	* Evidence question 887 on Sec. of State announcements. Rost: 'I am sure [this] has nothing to do with the fact the Cttee is investigating the subject.' * Completed 1982/3.

(continued)

Table 4.7—*continued*

Committee	Inquiry	Approach	Outreach	Findings/Impact on government
Environment (H.C. 234, 1983/4)	Problems of Management of Urban Renewal	* First phase of inquiry focused on initiatives in Merseyside. * Second phase concerned inner city policies; third phase role of private sector.	* Extensive outreach to councils.	* Report on Merseyside initiatives 1982/3 (H.C. 18).
Energy (H.C. 108) (continued 1982/3)	Energy R & D		* 14 evidence sessions.	* Inquiry incomplete when parliament dissolved.

133

responded to local government, unions and citizens' groups. The inquiry on combined heat and power responded to pressure from a small group of professionals. They argued that this initiative was being thwarted by institutional inertia. The local government inquiry was stimulated by a departmental Green Paper and pressure from the ACA and AMA.

The system-wide reviews in particular had generally been preceded by extensive official inquiries which documented the need for action but which had not resulted in that action. The inquiry conducted by the Education Committee into the secondary school curriculum focused on the experience of students in the fourteen to sixteen age range. The committee selected this topic because 'the 14 to 16 age group has been a major, perhaps the major focus of the very considerable public discussion of the curriculum that has taken place in recent years.' The inquiry was triggered by the government's announcement of a new exam system at the 16-plus level. This had been preceded by five years of public and official discussion. Following Prime Minister Callaghan's 1976 speech, teacher representation on several key committees of the Schools Council was reduced. Discussions were initiated which led to the production of a discussion paper 'The School Curriculum' by Mrs Thatcher's government in March 1981.

Similarly the medical education inquiry arose from the Social Services Committee's 1980–1 review of perinatal and neonatal mortality. In the course of this inquiry the committee became aware of the ratio between junior doctors, registrars and consultants in hospitals and the difficulty of many patients in seeing consultants. On the other hand, the committee noted the long hours and patient-management responsibilities of junior doctors and registrars. This issue had been the subject of a number of earlier inquiries. The Todd Royal Commission in 1968 commented. 'Because many registrar posts meet service rather than training needs, the availability of a post in which suitable training will be received has become haphazard. . . . There are many more doctors in junior hospital posts than ever hope to become consultants.'[34]

The select committee specifically addressed the question of why earlier inquiries had failed to produce action:

Despite the apparent agreement between the Health Department and the profession on the need to increase the number of career posts at a greater rate than the number of junior posts; and despite restrictions on the number of new registrar and senior registrar posts which health authorities can create, the very opposite has happened. Why? . . . The BMA blames a series of financial constraints on health services (although the NHS found money to engage an additional 8 thousand hospital doctors between 1971 and 1979 of whom just over 2 thousand were consultants); the Hospital Junior Staff Committee and the regional medical officers saw the problem as one of intransigence on the part of consultants who expect to be supported by a team of junior doctors; the former Chief Medical Officer, agreed that resistance amongst consultants . . . to the resulting change in consultant work load was a principal factor.[35]

The transport in London review originated from the Transport Committee's earlier inquiry on departmental public expenditure. In its 1980–1 appraisal of the department's vote, the committee referred to the 'scandalous state of the London system'.[36] It calculated annual expenditure by the various authorities at some £900 million – with annual revenues of £546 million. It noted the spread of responsibility for London transport between the London Transport Executive, British Rail, London County Bus Services, the Greater London Council and the Department of Transport.

Inquiries concerning the role of central government had not typically been preceded by an extensive range of official inquiries. This is consistent with the character of the issue. Government could not be expected to stage an array of inquiries where its own role is in dispute. The committee inquiries were usually triggered by some influential external interest or interest group concerned about how the role of government should be defined. In the case of the home-working inquiry, the concerned interest was the trade union movement. In the case of the North Sea oil depletion policy inquiry it was the neo-liberal concern to limit government's role, reduce regulation and expand the role of market forces. The Scottish Affairs Committee inquiry into youth unemployment and training and the Education Committee inquiry on private and public funding of the arts responded to interest group concerns. The Agriculture Committee inquiry into animal welfare responded to agitation from animal rights groups.

The committees gathered and assessed factual information by a variety of approaches. All the committees recruited one or more part-time specialist advisers to aid their work. The Scottish Affairs Committee was aided by a professor and lecturer from the Department of Social and Economic Research at Glasgow University and a lecturer from the Department of Political Economy of the same University. The Agriculture Committee was assisted by a Professor of Agriculture, Horticulture and Animal Husbandry from Bristol and a Professor of Agricultural Economics from London University. It was also advised by the Director of the Bureau Européen des Recherches. The Arts Committee was advised by an associate of the Policy Studies Institute and three individuals associated with a theatre group, an arts association, and the organization concerned to increase business funding of the arts. The Energy Committee drew its specialist advisers from the Institute for Science and Technology at the University of Wales and the Science Policy Research Unit at Sussex. The Environment Committee was aided by a member of the Joint Unit for Research on the Urban Environment, University of Aston in Birmingham, a member of the Sociology Department from Essex and a member of the Department of Land Economy at Cambridge.

'Think-tanks' and research institutes played a larger role as 'brokers' for policy options in the inquiries concerned with emerging issues than in any other band we have considered. In the inquiry on income support both the Institute for Fiscal Studies and the Centre for Policy Studies provided special advisers and detailed, costed alternative proposals to the committee. The Centre for Policy Studies provided evidence of the work disincentives in present arrangements. This was advanced as the basis for a radical reconstruction of income support structures. On the Prestwick Airport inquiry, the Adam Smith Institute gave evidence about the findings of its study, sponsored by the Department of Trade, into the feasibility and requirements for free-trade zones. The Research Unit of the Institute of Directors also provided written evidence on this subject. The local government finance inquiry heard evidence on alternative cost calculations from the Institute for Local Government Studies. The Policy Studies Institute provided a special adviser and alternative cost calculations to the age of retirement inquiry. In this use of research institutes, the select committees illustrate their potential role as 'clients' for such bodies. The institutes need access to the policy-making system if they are to achieve impact. But their independence is jeopardized if they become private advisers to departments.

Departmental studies were also an important source of factual evidence. The evidence and memoranda published with the age of retirement inquiry include papers from the DHSS on the cost of the two major options being considered – reduction of the female age of retirement to sixty and gradual reduction of the male age to an optional sixty-three. Ultimately, this evidence was decisive. In the inquiry on local government finance, the Department of the Environment placed on the public record its most recent assessments of the revenue potential of alternative revenue sources for local government – local sales tax, poll tax, more extensive use of direct charges, or a local income tax. The review of Prestwick Airport considered complex evidence on BAA pricing policy. It used this evidence to respond to local criticism that Prestwick landing charges were set uncompetitively. Finally, the inquiry on the poverty trap and income support heard evidence from the DHSS and Inland Revenue on the options for varying present arrangements and the associated costs.

All these inquiries look towards practices in other countries as an important source of evidence. The Education Committee inquiring into the funding of the arts visited Italy, Germany, Denmark and the USA. The Transport Committee travelled to the US, Canada, Germany, France and Denmark to study the co-ordination of transport planning in other large urban centres. The inquiry on private rented housing drew on the committee's analysis of how other countries handled this sector. The Scottish Affairs Committee visited West Germany to gather information on apprenticeships and training.

We spoke to officials of the Federal Ministry responsible for the various aspects of vocational training, and their counterparts in the Land ministries of North Rhine Westphalia. We also met representatives of both sides of industry and visited a vocational school and training centres of different kinds. The experience was not only valuable as an opportunity of seeing another system at work; it also gave us the chance to put the UK and more particularly the Scottish response in a wider perspective.

The Agriculture Committee records a similar view about the merit of its visits – to a research institute at Celle and to see federal officers in Bonn in Germany; to the responsible minister; to the official councils for the poultry and pig industries; the animal protection association; five individual farms in Denmark; and to EEC officials in Brussels. The Energy Committee visited the US in the course of its inquiry and held discussions with the Department of Energy in Washington, the American Institute of Architects, the Pacific Gas and Electric Company and the California Public Utility Company. The Energy Committee also visited Oslo to review the tax regime applied by 'a country at roughly the same stage of the development of its oil reserves'. The committee met the Minister for Energy, the Director-General of the Norwegian Petroleum Directorate and the President of Statoil. The Social Services Committee travelled widely throughout Britain to teaching hospitals and universities to take evidence on site. It received oral evidence from most of the Royal Colleges, these being the bodies responsible for post-graduate training.

Each category of inquiry included extensive outreach to departments, ministers and interest groups. Apart from ministers and the departments immediately concerned, this covers other official bodies, functional groups and political advocacy groups. Functional groups cover employer, employee and professional organizations – all those organizations which derive power and influence from their role in the system of government-sponsored services. Advocacy groups cover moral rights, environmental and service advocacy groups. The outreach of the seven inquiries concerned with the role of central government is reviewed in table 4.8. The homeworking and North Sea oil inquiries both sought out the least number of interest groups – 20 and 18 respectively. The private rented sector and the arts funding inquiries attracted most, with 155 and 110 respectively. The arts inquiry heard oral evidence from 45 groups. The animal welfare inquiry took oral evidence from 23 groups. In total these inquiries attracted oral evidence from 144 groups and written evidence from 331 groups, a total of 475 witnesses. The range of groups is illustrated in table 4.9 which lists some of the groups giving evidence to the Agriculture Committee's animal welfare inquiry. Despite the extent of this outreach programme, some inquiries neglect important elements of potential constituencies. For example, the Education inquiry touched all the arts interest groups but it failed to engage groups that might have been sceptical about a deeper government role. There are a number of academics, research institutes (e.g. Institute for Economic Affairs, Centre for Policy Studies) and perhaps private sector groups whose point of view might have been tapped.

Table 4.8 Interest group engagement – role of central government

Inquiry	Committee	Ministers	Depts	Other levels of gov.	Advisory bodies	Economic prod. groups	Services groups	Rights advocacy	Environment advocacy	Service advocacy	Think tanks/ experts	Other	Total
		Central government		Functional groups				'Issue' groups					
Homeworking	Employment	1 / 2*		2 / 1*	2	7 / 3*		1*			1		13 / 7*
North Sea Oil Depletion Policy	Energy	1 / 1*	2			6 / 3*					5		14 / 4*
Private Rented Housing Sector	Environment	1 / 2*		3 / 45*		3 / 24*	8*	2 / 25*		12*	1 / 24*	5*	10 / 145*
Animal Welfare in Poultry, Pig and Veal Calf Production	Agriculture	1			5	7		6			4		23 / 61*
Youth Unemployment and Training	Scottish Affairs	2		3 / 9*	6	6 / 3*	4 / 3*	4*			1	1*	22 / 20*
Public and Private Funding of the Arts	Education	1	3 / 8*	6 / 11*	3	14 / 15*	12 / 28*			5	1 / 3*		45 / 65*
Energy Conservation in Buildings	Energy		2 / 5*	2 / 4*	3	7 / 11*		3	2*		7*		17 / 29*
													144 / 331*
													Total 475

* Written evidence.

138

Table 4.9 Illustrative outreach to interest groups – role of central government

Inquiry	Committee	Departments	Advisory groups	Economic groups	Rights groups	Experts	Other
Animal Welfare Inquiry	Agriculture	Agriculture depts	* Farm Animal Welfare Council. * National Consumer Council. * Agriculture Research Councils. * Agriculture Training Board. * Meat and Livestock Commission.	* National Farmers Union. * NUF of Scotland. * Ulster Farmers Union. * Nat. Assoc. of Veal Producers. * British Poultry Federation. * Nat. Pig Breeders Assoc. * Volac Ltd. * Farming Union of Wales.† * Brit. Soc. of Aviary Production.† * Nat. Fed. of Meat Traders.†	* Uni. Fed. for Animal Welfare. * RSPCA. * Central Council for Scotland SPCA. * Farm Animal Welfare co-ordinating executive. * Nat. Fed. of Consumer Groups. * Nat. Fed. of Womens Inst. * Compassion in World Farming.† * Animal Health Trust.	* Royal Group of Vet. Surgeons. * British Vet. Associations. * Prof. P. Wilson. * Prof. D. Coleman.	* Farm and Food Soc.† * Nat. Council of Women. * The Vegetarian Soc.†

† Written evidence: not a complete list.

Similarly, the energy conservation inquiry did not take evidence from important environment groups, although the findings were sympathetic to environment interests.

The outreach associated with inquiries concerned with system-wide reviews is displayed in table 4.10. The Scottish Affairs Committee inquiry on rural road passenger transport involved the least number of groups – 27. Transport in London engaged a total of 103 groups, the secondary schools' inquiry 106 groups, and the medical education inquiry 106 groups. As an example of the groups covered by a single inquiry, table 4.11 lists all the organizations giving oral evidence to the transport in London inquiry. The four inquiries in this category together took oral evidence from 121 groups and written evidence from some 221 groups.

The Education Committee contrasts its approach of outreach and consultation with that adopted by the Department of Education.

The publication by the department of state responsible for education of a national statement of what should be offered and experienced in our schools is, by any account, a major event. One might expect to find much in such a statement to ponder as a means of discovering more about us and our time, about our particular strengths, weaknesses and predilections and about how we see ourselves adapting to the major changes which are occurring in all advanced industrial countries. The first noteworthy feature of The School Curriculum is perhaps the way it was produced. It has not been written by a group of experienced professionals as was the case in Scotland where a committee of educationists were set the task under the chairmanship of the rector of a high school. This document has instead been drafted by departmental civil servants and merely modified in discussion with other interested official parties.[37]

Contrasting the approach of the Munn Group, commissioned by the Scottish Education Department, and the DES, the committee comments: 'The Munn report considers that the wealth of public discussion and the various pressures on the schools are the starting point of a proper analysis and are not to be deflected into occasional qualifying paragraphs.'

In pursuit of its inquiry, the Education Committee heard evidence from 38 groups including professional groups, LEAS and individual schools. It received written evidence, much of it unsolicited, from 68 groups. The report documents international practice with detailed tables contrasting the approach to leaving age, exams, curriculum, dispersal of responsibilities and streaming practices, in France, West Germany, Denmark, Finland, Norway, Sweden, Japan, and, in the US, California, Minnesota and New York.

The outreach associated with emerging issues inquiries is reviewed in table 4.12. In undertaking review of programmes, or in system-wide reviews, com-

Table 4.10 Interest group engagement – system-wide reviews

Inquiry	Committee	Central government		Functional groups				'Issue' groups			Think-tanks/experts	Other	Total
		Ministers	Depts	Other levels of gov.	Advisory bodies	Economic prod. groups	Services groups	Rights advocacy	Environment advocacy	Service advocacy			
Transport in London	Transport	1	2	6	2	14		2	4		2		33
				35*		7*		2*	4*	15*	7*		70*
Secondary School Curriculum and Exams	Education	1	4	2	9	2	9	4		2	2	3	38
				2*	12*	6*	23*	11*		1*	13*		68*
Medical Education	Social Services	1	3		2		32	4					42
			5*			23*		3*		33*			64*
Rural Road Passenger Transport and Ferries	Scottish Affairs		2	5	1								8
				9*	3*	5*				2*			19*
													121
													221*
												Total	342

* Written evidence.

Table 4.11 Illustrative outreach to interest groups – system-wide reviews

Inquiry	Committee	Ministers	Departments	Local Regional Government	Advisory groups	National Industries	Economic groups	Environment advocacy groups	Individuals/ experts
Transport in London (Oral Evidence)	Transport	Sec. of State.	* Dept of Transport. * Home Office.	* Greater London Council. * London Boroughs Association. * Metropolitan Police. * Westminster City Council. * Borough of Southwark. * Borough of Enfield.	* London Transport Passenger Cttee. * Transport Users Cons. Cttee for London.	* Brit. Railways Board. * Nat. Bus Company. * London and County Bus Services. * London Transport Executive.	* London Chamber of Commerce. * CBI (London Region). * ASLEF. * NUR. * Transport Salaried Staffs Association. * Brit. Road Fed. * Confed. of British Road Passenger Transport. * Freight Transport Association. * Road Haulage Association. * TGWU.	* Transport 2000. * London Amenity and Transport Association. * RAC. * AA.	* Ralph Bennet. * David Scott-Hellewell.

Table 4.12 Interest group engagement – emerging issues

Inquiry	Committee	Central government		Functional groups				'Issue' groups			Think tanks/ experts	Other	Total
		Ministers	Depts	Other levels of gov.	Advisory bodies	Economic prod. groups	Services groups	Rights advocacy	Environment advocacy	Service advocacy			
Age of Retirement	Social Services	1 / 5*	5		2	10 / 4*	2 / 3*			3 / 2*	6 / 8*	11*	29 / 33*
Method of Funding Local Government	Environment	1	4	4		3*	1 / 2*	1 / 3*		2*	4	4*	15 / 14*
Future of Prestwick Airport	Scottish Affairs		6	1 / 6*	3	2 / 9*							12 / 15*
Combined Heat and Power (incomplete)	Energy	1	1	4	2	8				1	3		20
Structure of Personal Income Tax and Income Support	Treasury		3 / 2*		2*	5 / 1*	3*			3*	3 / 8*		11 / 19*
													87 / 81*
												Total	168

* Written evidence.

Table 4.13 Illustrative outreach to interest groups – emerging issues

Inquiry	Committee	Departments	Advisory groups	Economic groups	Clients/service groups	Experts/think-tanks	Services advocacy	Other
Age of Retirement	Social Services	* DHSS. * Dept of Employment. * Management and Personnel Office. * Treasury. * Gov. Actuary. * Environment.† * Home Office.† * MoD.†	* Occupational Pensions Board. * Equal Opportunities Com. * Nat. Ind. Chairmen's Group.† * MSC.†	* Nat. Association of Pension Funds. * TUC. * Life Offices Association. * Soc. of Pension Consultants. * CBI. * Nat. Fed. of Self-employed and Small Businesses Ltd. * Inst. of Personnel Management. * Association of Consulting Actuaries. * GMWU. * Iron and Steel Trades Confed. * Building Soc. Association.† * Electrical, Telecom and Plumbing Union.† * Fed. of Business and Prof. Women.† * Union of Indep. Companies.†	* Nat. Pensioners' Convention. * Nat. Fed. of Old-Age Pensioners Association. * Royal Association for Disability. * BMA.† * Association of Dtrs of Social Serv.† * Public Service Pensioners Council.†	* Prof. C. Cooper. * G. Walker. * M. Johnson. * Inst. of Actuaries/Faculty of Actuaries. * Centre for Policy on Aging.† * D. Groves (Lancaster Univ.). * H. Parker† (CPS) (EEC). * Dr W. Keating. * BIM.† * Policy Studies Institute.† * Dr J. Ashton.† * Inst. of Fiscal Studies.† * T. A. Salter.†	* Age Concern. * Help the Aged. * Pre-Retirement Association.† * Nat. Association of Widows.†	* WRVS.† * Oxford Cons. Association. * Womens Nat. Com.† * Cons. Women's Nat. Ctee.† * Fawcett Soc.† * Nat. Lab. Women's Group. * East Kent Retirement Association.† * Soropodist Intern. * London Association for Pre-Retirement.† * Nat. Fed. of Women's Institutes.† * Nat. Council of Women of GB.†

† Written evidence.

144

mittees are usually probing established interest-group/departmental networks. When they deal with emerging issues, committees are providing a context in which such networks can be created. They do this through their invitation to provide evidence. Interest groups can approach the committees as a result of the publicity the inquiry attracts. Alternatively, the committees can seek evidence from particular groups. On the basis of the evidence received, the committees judge whether the issue deserves to be on the public agenda or whether further evidence or investigation is required. They thus prepare the ground for the later initiatives of ministers, opposition spokesmen, or interest groups. The age of retirement inquiry engaged the largest number of interest groups (table 4.13). The committee heard oral evidence from twenty-nine groups and took written evidence from a further thirty-three individuals and groups. It also heard evidence from interest group coalitions. For example, the National Pensioners' Convention is an umbrella organization founded by the TUC, the National Federation of Pensioners, and Age Concern. Similarly the Scottish Affairs Committee heard evidence from an *ad hoc* umbrella group, the Prestwick Action Committee.

A final characteristic of all these inquiries is their lengthy duration. The transport in London inquiry was of some eighteen months' duration; the medical education inquiry lasted eight months; the rural road transport inquiry, five; the secondary schools inquiry, seventeen; the homeworking inquiry lasted some three months; the arts inquiry, twenty-one; the energy inquiry, twelve; and the youth unemployment inquiry, five months.

Findings and impact

These reports blend complex questions of fact with normative issues. Normative considerations lead differing protagonists to give differing emphases to particular facts. This complicates the analytic task. At the same time it provides the committees with bases for their political judgements which leave open the possibility of later action by the proponents of the position which is not accepted. This is illustrated in the age of retirement inquiry. This inquiry heard evidence that earlier retirement would be justified on the grounds of social justice. With high and continuing unemployment, several interest groups advanced this as a remedy. The bipartisan report rejects the argument that earlier retirement would significantly affect unemployment and publishes the technical basis for this judgement. It is open to protagonists to reject this argument if they can marshal better evidence. Social justice was also an element in the case of a variety of protagonists in the structure of income tax inquiry. Both the neo-liberal Centre for Policy Studies and welfare advocacy groups such as the Child Poverty Action Group grounded their submissions on this value. Because of the election, committee deliberations were not concluded. Majority and minority reports from each perspective were published. At the least, this served to clarify the issues dividing the two approaches.

The homeworking inquiry was unable to establish precise numbers of people actually engaged in this activity. This was the ground subsequently used by the government to reject the report. But this leaves the way open for those concerned to raise the issue again if they can gather further information or produce another indicator of the significance of the activity. The private rented sector inquiry identifies shortage of information as a central obstacle to policy assessments or political judgement. Similarly the energy conservation inquiry attempts to value potential savings from the more widespread adoption of economy measures. By contrast, consideration of alternative policy towards oil depletion in the North Sea turned on normative questions about the role of government. The facts of the situation were clear. The significance of these facts depends on the theoretical framework within which they are interpreted. The inquiry itself approached this issue from a practical perspective. Its deliberation took place in the context of practical alternatives. Thus it was able to reach a bipartisan conclusion.

The degree of bipartisanship amongst committees was striking. This was evident in each category of inquiry. All the inquiries involving system-wide reviews tabled essentially bipartisan reports with clear policy recommendations that could be voted. The transport in London report was essentially bipartisan. It proposed a new co-ordinating authority independent of the GLC, and substantial representation from local government. The secondary school curriculum report ends with sixty-four individual recommendations covering curricula, role of central government, consultation and so forth. There were a number of divisions in the committee in approving the report, but none on strictly party lines. The approach subsequently announced by the government followed some committee proposals, particularly concerning the curriculum and exams. But the government programme so far announced is less comprehensive. It contemplates more central direction than the committee envisaged.[38]

Five of the seven reports on the role of central government were substantially bipartisan. This includes the report on energy conservation which was critical of the current regulatory, tax and assistance regime, and that on oil depletion policy which recommended a reduced role for government. There were a number of divisions in the Environment Committee in settling its report on private rented housing. These divisions concern the balance between tenant rights and landlord rights. The report was otherwise substantially bipartisan. The committee subsequently responded on a wholly bipartisan basis to the government's rejection of its central recommendations. Similarly, the Agriculture Committee report involved divisions between Conservative members on some recommendations, but none on strictly party lines.

The reports on emerging issues were bipartisan except for the income support sub-committee report. The chairman's draft recommended abolition of the married man's tax allowance and reassignment of these funds to other purposes. This step was seen as a key element in any programme of structural tax reform.

The impact of these reports varied, at least in the sense that subsequent policy development vindicated or rejected their approaches. Four were largely rejected by the government – arts funding, homeworking, private rented housing sector,[39] and transport in London. The government's own plans for London Transport envisaged more centralized arrangements with local government a minor participant. The government also rejected a single authority with responsibility for all transport modes. Implementation of the government scheme has (at time of writing) yet to commence. It has attracted fierce opposition from local authority groups.[40] The private rented housing sector report stimulated three industry groups to form a Joint Land Requirements Committee to establish likely future needs. The committee was formed by the Homebuilders Federation, the Royal Town Planning Institute and the Housing Research Federation. In announcing its foundation, the sponsoring bodies said they were responding to criticism of the Environment Department in the select committee report: 'It is hard to believe that any major department can put forward in Cabinet or interdepartmental negotiations the arguments for its programme without an estimate for its requirements and the consequences which would follow from different expenditure options.'[41]

Four reports were consistent with subsequent developments. The youth unemployment report was followed by the announcement of the government's new scheme which the Department and the MSC had been developing while the committee inquiry was in progress. The government accepted the Energy Committee's recommendations on its role in relation to North Sea oil depletion. The Energy Department, while rejecting the proposals for establishing a separate Energy Conservation Commission, subsequently established an Energy Efficiency Office. Conservation interest groups see the inquiry as the critical influence in producing this result.[42]

The immediate impact of these inquiries reflects the relative impotence of committees. The Social Services Committee saw its recommendations included in a private member's bill which was debated in the Commons in November 1983. Its report stimulated the relevant TUC policy committee to review and reaffirm its position. It did not succeed in stimulating wider debate throughout the trade union movement. In pursuit of its own programme, the government subsequently embarked on a major revision of social security arrangements.[43] The government announced in 1984 that it would establish a free port at Prestwick.[44] But the Scottish Affairs Committee's recommendations were only one element in the policy process.

The inquiry on medical education was one of the few reports actually debated in the Commons. As noted earlier, this was on a motion which imposed no course of action on government. The committee's report called for an increase in the number of consultants and reduced responsibilities and workload for registrars. With the concurrence of the new chairman of the Education Committee of the General Medical Council, it envisaged leadership in change and adaptation being provided by him. The committee's report was endorsed enthusiastically by the Hospital Junior Staff Committee of the BMA and the Medical Women's Federation. It was received more cautiously, but endorsed, by the BMA as a whole. Consultant organizations did not comment separately. The chairwoman subsequently spoke at several medical conferences. It is not yet clear what role, if any, the inquiry may have played in easing immobilism in the medical system. The committee is contemplating a follow-up inquiry to identify developments, if any.

The select committees and strategic policy making

A number of features of these inquiries point to the potential of select committees to renew parliament's deliberative role and in the process integrate interest groups in strategic policy making. In a multi-party parliament, the review of established programmes requires that majority parliamentary support and at least some influential interest groups be reconciled to government proposals. Forward planning requires that interest groups have independent opportunities to champion their agendas through the political process, thus introducing parliamentarians to their concerns. Interest groups need to be engaged by people whom they perceive to be politically influential and legitimate but independent of current programmes.[45] Ministers and departments need information about hostile, friendly and undecided interest groups. On the basis of this information ministers or departments may vary their approach. Different approaches by ministers will vary the deployment of interest groups. Ministers and departments can also solicit tangible support from the positively affected groups. The select committees might offer a context in which parliamentary opinion can be explored and in which the process of mobilizing interest group consent can commence. In these various ways policy-making immobilism might be overcome.

There is evidence from the inquiries we have reviewed of the potential of select committees to provide the necessary context. First, nearly all the select committees have tackled these inquiries. They have tackled the right band of issues. They have tackled a variety of inquiries that involve reappraisal of existing programmes. They have tackled an impressive array of inquiries concerned with emerging issues. Their inquiries cover all aspects of this array of issues.

Second, in selecting these issues, they have demonstrated their openness to influence from departments and interest groups. They have shown a capacity to widen the access of both to the political process, and a capacity to register and act on concerns from either source. To pick just two examples, the inquiry on energy conservation was stimulated by the persistence of conservation groups against the opposition of the department; and the inquiry on local government finance was stimulated by a government White Paper on 'Alternatives to the Domestic Rate'. The committees have also demonstrated the capacity to take the initiative themselves when they judge this is required by the public interest (e.g. nuclear power station construction, assessment of the Commission for Racial Equality).

Third, the inquiries show committees engaging influential groups be they business interests, trade unions, departments or advocacy groups. They introduce these groups to new information and new perspectives. They do so in a context that focuses participants on the public interest. Select committees, as agents of parliament, offer a unique forum. Particular parties lack the capacity to engage all the relevant interests. Departmental and public inquiries do not provide access in a public and political setting. They do not test the scope for bipartisanship. The select committee inquiries reviewed here possess these capacities – for example, age of retirement, the secondary schools curriculum, medical education, private rented housing sector.

Fourth, on a number of these issues, the committees have demonstrated their capacity for independent bipartisan judgement. If the political system is to make public choices that can be implemented (particularly involving change to established programmes), it must demonstrate the capacity to process contentious issues in a bipartisan fashion. The present political structure encourages partisan dispute. This is stimulated by the needs of the ritual conflict between government and opposition. In a more plural system this conflict would continue – but in a modified form with scope for more bipartisanship on individual issues. This the select committees can be seen to produce in, for example, the transport in London inquiry or the Prestwick Airport inquiry. Equally inquiries like that into the Commission for Racial Equality or the proposed nuclear power programme are pertinent examples of committees reviewing current or proposed programmes and reaching a bipartisan conclusion. The danger in a more plural structure is that excessive partisanship would be replaced by a committee 'sell-out' to interest groups. Several reports have attracted this charge (e.g. arts funding, support for less favoured areas, railway electrification).[46] A number of other reports have reached conclusions unfavourable to important interests (e.g. Health and Safety Commission, nuclear power, Commission for Racial Equality, age of retirement). The available evidence in relation to 'strategic' inquiries is insufficient to draw any general conclusion about the pattern of committee behaviour. It is, however, sufficient to demonstrate that there has been no general 'sell-out' to interest groups.

Fifth, committees have demonstrated the ability to come to grips with complex and contentious issues in a systematic fashion. An impressive volume of evidence has been accumulated and placed on the public record (e.g. strategic nuclear weapons policy, combined heat and power, private rented housing sector). International comparisons have been thoroughly documented (e.g. efficiency of civil service, secondary schools curriculum, age of retirement). Expert opinion has been brought to bear in a way precluded by the present system (e.g. defence inquiries, poverty trap and income support inquiry, agriculture inquiries).

What is lacking is evidence of the ability of the select committees to follow up their findings. Ministers have the authority to pursue issues. They can produce consultative papers, make public speeches, produce Cabinet submissions, make parliamentary statements, or meet with particular interest groups. These options give them the capacity, if they were to recognize the need to devote much more attention to interest group politics, to achieve considerable impact on interest groups and on public opinion more generally. Their control of the initiative in policy making gives them the authority to shape the policy agenda. There is limited evidence in the inquiries we have reviewed of select committees undertaking, or even wanting to undertake, follow-up action. This is evident in the approach of the Energy Committee and the Social Services Committee. For example, on both medical education and the age of retirement, the Chairwoman of the Social Services Committee, Renee Short, sought to advance the committee's findings through the political process. In the former case, this involved seeking parliamentary debating time and speaking at a number of medical conferences. In the latter case, this involved seizing the opportunity to introduce a private member's bill and seeking to promote debate, particularly within the TUC. Both efforts came to nothing. Committees have little capacity to obtain floor debates and no opportunity to propose bills on their own initiative. Habits and attitudes nourished by the two-party system work against further committee-initiated activities. The main avenue currently available to committees is further hearings to review government responses to their reports. So far, this has proved a relatively ineffectual means of advancing an issue.

For committees to have more access to parliamentary debate, additional days would need to be allocated to this purpose. Further, at least some debates would need to terminate with motions that impose a course of action on the government. This would require a redefinition of the role of backbenchers and of the confidence convention. These are essential steps if committees are to be effective in creating parliamentary opinion and as intermediaries between interest groups and the political process. At least some of the powers of initiative now concentrated in the hands of ministers need to be shared with committees. Such developments all lie ahead. The inquiries reviewed here suggest possibilities. Their lack of impact illustrates the distance that needs to be covered to convert these possibilities to actuality.

Chapter 5

Select committees and interest groups

The past three chapters have assessed the roles select committees have been crafting in the budget cycle and in relation to current issues, to fundamental programme review and to emerging issues. We have weighed their performance in the context of the capacity of select committees to restore parliament's deliberative role. The extent to which interest groups have been engaged by these inquiries has been noted. I want now to look more closely at the role of interest groups in the current two-party system and at the impact of the select committees on them.

The current collectivist or two-party policy-making structure presumes the existence of strong political parties. As we saw in the last chapter, political parties are the vehicles for advancing competing conceptions of the public interest to the electorate. In the formal presumptions of the collectivist system, political parties integrate interest groups behind their overarching interpretation of the public interest. Of course interest groups speak out authoritatively on political issues. But in collectivist lore interest groups are held to have a role in policy making on the initiative of the executive. The parties act as intermediaries between political aspirations and political legitimacy. Those who hold political authority may acknowledge their need for advice or guidance from one or another of the ubiquitous interest groups in specific cases. But in this relationship independent interests enjoy a legitimate role, by invitation so to speak.

Interest groups lack an independent claim to participate in the specifically political aspects of decision making. Even when consulted, they generally do not participate deeply in the discussion of the issues associated with determination of the public interest. Such discussions typically occur between departments and within cabinet committees. These relationships prevail as a result of the premise that political authority can be conferred only through political parties.

The role of interest groups in policy making has been the subject of increasing attention in recent years. Perhaps the most influential current analyses, at least amongst the partisans, are those of neo-liberals. In 1975, Samuel Brittan published his essay 'The economic contradictions of democracy'.[1] Brittan argued that the pursuit of self-interest by sectional groups and the growing expectations of government that they nourish, posed the central threat to liberal democracy. Following the work of American public choice theorists, principally Mancur Olson,[2] Brittan's analysis absolved the political structure of any positive role in this process. 'The disruptive effects of group self interest arise from elementary economic logic and are not directly affected with the political structure.' He defined the 'liberalism' of contemporary liberal democracy in terms of basic freedoms – expression, association and assembly. He did not draw any link between particular policy-making structures and the differing capacity to manage interest group politics displayed by particular polities. Indeed he followed Schumpeter[3] in conceiving policy making as a process that confines participation – to bureaucrats, politicians and parties. He rightly inferred that 'policy formulation is on this model a task for politicians and officials. If the electorate does not like the result, it does not buy it again.' The notion that interest groups might be independent actors in policy making is explicitly rejected in Schumpeter's analysis. Brittan considered interest group accommodation only in the context of the log-rolling model. He dismissed this approach because of its capacity to produce an accommodation between interests contrary to the public interest.

In 1976, James Douglas coined the phrase 'the overloaded crown' to characterize contemporary government.[4] He reviewed sympathetically those analyses which conceived extension of the role of government as the principal cause of the contemporary erosion of its authority. Like Brittan, Douglas was sensitive to the political difficulties associated with contraction of the role of the state. But both articles implied this as the desirable remedy. Both authors were particularly concerned at the excessive power of trade unions.

These – and other less cautious analyses – fortified Mrs Thatcher's bid for office. In the event she has sponsored legislation to lessen the legal privileges of trade unions. She has however not been able to do more than modify marginally the role of government. Most of her government's political energies have been concentrated on holding down the rate of increase of spending on major programmes. She has indicated that the broad structure of the welfare state and managed economy will remain unchanged. Hence, the strategy of restoring central authority by contracting government – and thus reducing the sphere of interest group politics – has been unsuccessful.

Neo-liberals are not the only group to have paid attention to the rise of interest groups. There is a considerable body of Marxist and orthodox analysis.[5] This work assesses the role of interest groups in current policy making and the significance of trends towards corporatism. The neo-Marxists concentrate on the delegitimation of government. They trace this to the development of new forms of economic and political conflict. These conflicts are not between classes but between groups, ostensibly from the same class. In Anthony Birch's words: 'The significance of this development is that the out-

cation. First, a number of groups now employ officers full-time to monitor activities at the House of Commons. For example, the Council for the Protection of Rural England, the British Medical Association, and Age Concern all employ individuals in this capacity. In some cases these individuals are 'donated' by their sponsoring organization to serve as secretary of the relevant all-party group. For example, Age Concern's representative also serves as secretary of the Commons All-Party Pensioners' Group. The National Children's Bureau employs an officer as secretary of the all-party parliamentary group for children. Similarly, MIND serves the Mental Health Group, RADAR the group concerned with the disabled, and the Law Society, the legal affairs group. Through their contact with MPs, interest groups are better placed to organize delegations to members, propose amendments to legislation in standing committees and float parliamentary questions. The interest groups become much better informed about developments and much better equipped to intervene effectively at tactical moments in the legislative process.

Second, a number of interest groups have developed research capacities and specialized information sources which allow them to extend their advocacy efforts. This reinforces their capacity to campaign on particular issues. It also provides them with the capacity to assess proposed government initiatives. For example, SHAC (the London Housing Bureau) processes some 6000 inquiries from tenants each year. Its access to information about tenant conditions surpasses that of the DHSS. When the government proposed to cut housing benefits in 1983, SHAC was able to show that the impact would be significantly different from that envisaged by the Department.[11] The government was forced to modify its proposals. The savings subsequently achieved were very modest. Similarly the Low Pay Unit regularly publishes on tax expenditure and the tax significance of fringe benefits.[12] The London Transport and Amenity Association recently published a report entitled 'National Cost of Company Cars'. This report advocates a change in tax deductibility provisions.

In this context the growing number of 'think-tanks' is to be noted. Such bodies originated in the United States to serve the needs of that country's fragmented and porous political structure. There has been a remarkable germination of think-tanks in recent years in the UK. New bodies in the past five years include: The Institute for Fiscal Studies; the Centre for Policy Studies, the Adam Smith Institute, the Social Affairs Unit and the Employment Institute. The Institute of Directors has established a research unit with three full-time members. Both the Social Democratic Party and the neo-liberal movement have been sustained intellectually by such organizations. I shall return to the significance of this development in the following chapter.

A third development in recent years is the practice of interest groups joining together in *ad hoc* coalitions to promote issues of common concern. Age Concern for example has joined with thirty-two other organizations including the Child Poverty Action Group, Jewish Welfare Board, Liberal Party,

London Boroughs Association, Association of County Councils, Association of District Councils, Help the Aged and the Royal College of Nurses to form the Dignity in Death Alliance. This coalition seeks an increase in funeral benefits. A petition with a million signatures was presented to the Prime Minister in January 1981. The coalition has stimulated four Early Day motions in the Commons. Age Concern is currently a member of five other *ad hoc* coalitions: on VAT, fuel poverty, aid to families, invalid care and benefits cuts.

Some of the coalitions reported in the press in one month early in 1984 are as follows. The National Health Service Consultation Association joined NUPE, Age Concern and MIND, to press for extra spending on the National Health Service and to resist cuts foreshadowed in the Sainsbury Report.[13] Greenpeace and the National Union of Seamen formed a coalition to oppose radioactive waste dumping at sea.[14] Hopgrowers and TGWU joined forces to oppose an increase in excise charges on beer.[15] The TUC has also been active in both promoting and joining other interest groups in single-issue coalitions. The 1982 TUC Congress Report lists three major *ad hoc* interest group coalitions formed by the TUC: Jobs for Youth, Education Alliance, Pensions Alliance.[16] A paradigm interest coalition is the Maternity Alliance. It is an umbrella organization uniting fifty interest groups including the trade unions, advocacy groups such as the Child Poverty Action Group, Abortion Law Reform Association, Asian Community Action Group, Patients Association, and shared concern groups such as the Association of Breastfeeding Mothers, and the Birth Control Campaign. The Alliance had an income in 1982–3 of just under £50,000, including a £20,000 grant from the DHSS. Its activities include supporting campaigns on issues such as fuel deductions, the level of maternity allowance, child support and child benefit. The Alliance also provides information to employers, trade unions and the general public concerning various aspects of pregnancy, motherhood and child care.

Particular interest groups have also extended their lobbying activities to political parties. A number of groups now stage 'fringe meetings' at party conferences. For example, at the Tory Party Conference in Blackpool in October 1983, such activities were conducted by Age Concern and the Council for the Protection of Rural England. Senior officers of Age Concern regularly meet the Secretary of State for Health and Social Security at a conference breakfast. This leads to an exchange of correspondence recording progress on the current range of issues on that organization's agenda.

I want now to examine one specific aspect of the way interest groups are integrated in the current system. How do current consultation processes affect the 'social learning' of interest groups?

INTEREST GROUPS AND THE TWO-PARTY SYSTEM

Consultation with interest groups has been a rapidly growing element of policy making over the last decade. Various new devices for outreach have been adopted. The question that concerns us here is the impact of the consultative process on what might be termed the 'social learning' of interest groups. For example: are interest groups treated as protagonists with a legitimate concern for the public interest? Does the consultation process deliberately seek to have an impact on an interest group's perception of an issue? Does the process identify or seek to mobilize potential interest group coalitions who might help to defend the public interest? For interest groups to be admitted to the political phases of decision making, their contribution would need to be an element of an ongoing process. They would need to have a role in defining the issue, in defining the acceptable range of alternative solutions, in picking a specific solution, and in evaluating implementation.

As a tacit acknowledgement of the new representational role of interest groups and the growth of interest group power, governments have adopted more extensive consultative arrangements.[17] This process may be more or less public, and more or less extensive, depending on the issue and on the time frame in which government seeks action. As part of this process, government might establish an independent commission or inquiry to investigate a specific issue. Mrs Thatcher has not chosen to establish any Royal Commissions. A number of fundamental reviews have however been launched through semi-public inquiries. For example, a major review of the National Health Service has been conducted. The Minister for Social Security has undertaken four inquiries covering all aspects of the social security benefits structure.[18] These inquiries all report privately to ministers in the first instance. Government may also issue Green Papers or consultative documents. The Green Papers and White Papers issued during Mrs Thatcher's first term of office by the major 'programme' departments are listed in appendices 1.1–1.3.

Consultation on some current or emerging issue often involves informal discussions with interest groups already known to a department. These discussions are private. They may or may not be preceded by the publication of a discussion paper outlining the government's intentions. For example, in the four years from 1979 to 1983, the Treasury issued twenty discussion papers, four draft regulations, three drafts of proposed legislation, and two Green Papers on various matters related to taxation.[19] These public documents range from relatively specialized issues (e.g. 'foreign-to-foreign leasing') to issues of general concern (e.g. Green Papers on taxation of husband and wife and on corporation tax). In the case of Green Papers, these documents usually set forth the issues and range of options as perceived by the government. In other cases, they set forth government proposals (e.g. draft regulations on car benefits, draft legislation on capital allowances for small workshops).

Replies to the Green Paper on Taxation of Husband and Wife were reviewed by John Kay and C. Sandler of the Institute for Fiscal Studies. They identify a substantial gap between the views of interest groups and of the sponsoring department. I quote them extensively not only to establish the distance that divides the department from its interest group respondents but also to emphasize its basis: a political judgement about the politics of tax reform.

On examining the submissions to the Green Paper, the first and most striking feature is the sharp divergence between the balance of argument in the Green Paper, and that of the overwhelming majority of those who responded. While the former devotes much of its space to modifications and amendments to the present system, the latter almost unanimously declare themselves in favour of a radical change. . . . Hardly any submissions support more modest proposals – such as optional independent taxation – of the kind discussed at length in the Green Paper. The Green Paper goes as far as accepting the anachronistic nature of the present arrangement for the taxation of husband and wife, but then goes on to reflect that . . . 'the surprise, to most who study the matter, lies in discovering how difficult it is to find a better system than that we have today'. This statement sets the tone of the rest of the document and five chapters elapse before the question of changing to an independent tax system is even considered.

The Revenue's 'surprise' is not widely shared. 33 out of 37 organisations who expressed views are in favour of Mandatory Independent Taxation, which implies the abolition of the Married Man's Allowance. The key debate revolves around the question of how to use £3,000 m that the abolition of this allowance would save, and the identification of those households which should, and should not, be protected from the resulting losses. There are two main schools of thought here. There are those who favour retaining some element of the family-based tax unit, in the form of a fully or partially transferable tax allowance, and those who favour an entirely individual system of taxing earnings, accompanied by increased cash benefits for those with children and other dependents. Within each of these camps there is a variety of bodies, with differing objectives, concerns and priorities, but this central issue is clear.

Turning back to the Green Paper itself, however, this clarity is not reflected. Rather than attempting to provide a streamlined and simplified overview, the document has a tendency to complicate and obscure, thus preparing the way for a cautious and conservative approach to the question of change. Discussion is limited in any case by the Green Paper's narrow terms of reference, and its inability to consider its topic either in relation to the social security system, or within the wider context of public policy and society as a whole.[20]

The Treasury provides further evidence of the character of its day-to-day interactions with interest groups in commenting on consultations associated with the 1982 Finance Act:

In the 1982 Finance Act there were a total of 129 sections and 14 schedules dealing with matters for which the Inland Revenue are responsible, of which:
- 12 sections and 1 schedule reflected the straightforward budget decisions on the rates of tax and personal allowances, etc.

- 94 sections and 11 schedules were the subject of either formal consultations or more or less informal consultation with those principally concerned prior to the publication of the provision in the Finance Bill (73%)
- 23 sections and 2 schedules (18%) were not subject to consultation

The figures above are concerned with consultation on particular topics prior to the publication of the Finance Bill. A further important stage of the consultation takes place after the publication of the Bill when there are discussions with the representative bodies and individual tax payers who have a special interest in particular clauses. In addition there are normally discussions with the bodies such as the CBI, CCAB, ABCC and the Law Society across the whole range of the Finance Bill.[21]

In all cases, interest groups are invited to react to the issue from their point of view and to communicate their reactions privately. These are the decisive features of the consultation – interest groups are invited to react to the issue from the perspective of the gains and losses their members will sustain. Their response is private. There is no public forum where faulty argument, or transparently sectional argument, could be exposed or where the argument of one interest group could be used to test, check or refine that of another.

Sir William Pyle, the former Head of the Department of Education and Science, describes a similar private and 'technical' process in relation to the rate support grant negotiations between his Department and representatives of local government: 'The starting point currently is the government's decision about the level of expenditure which it would like to see the local authorities observe . . . in the finance year that is immediately ahead.'[22]

Sir William identifies what he sees as the central obstacle to deeper engagement by local authorities in the financial process:

Local authorities in particular and others also can talk in general about aspirations, aims and objectives, but to do serious analytical work does require staff and facilities, which they are not organised to have. Therefore I have not seen evidence of their ability to respond to these things in the way that I wish they could respond . . . the complexities of the problems are such that the interest groups are not really organised – they have not got the staff – to do this sort of consultative policy planning.[23]

Sir William draws upon the two-party system's preference for concentrated power in looking to peak groups to speak for, and to shape the opinion of, their members:

I suppose that local authorities would say that their associations speak on their behalf and voice their views. After all, this is the way a vast amount of our public business is conducted. The government deals with the CBI, and not with all its constituent members; the government deals with the TUC and not with all its constituent unions. This is a basic structuring of our institutional life, is it not, that you have representative spokesmen for various interest groups?[24]

An elaborate Green Paper consultation affecting local government resulted from a 1981 Department of the Environment paper 'Alternatives to the Domestic Rates'. The history of government action on this issue stretches back to the Allen Committee Report of 1963. The Allen Committee commented on the regressive nature of rates. Its report led to the introduction of rate rebates in 1966 and a review of the structure of local government. This inquiry was headed by Sir John Maud. The Maud Report was the basis of the reorganization of local government carried out by the Conservative Government in 1972–4. The 1976 Wilson Government initiated a further review of the financing of local government with the appointment of a committee chaired by Sir Frank Layfield. Layfield, like Maud, favoured a strengthening of local government autonomy, a prerequisite for which is the extension of the tax base of local government. The issue re-emerged with Mrs Thatcher's Government, partly as a consequence of reductions in the level of the rate support grant (from 66.5 per cent in 1978–9 to 56 per cent for 1982–3). Although the Green Paper covers alternatives to domestic rating, the select committee inquiry established that its scope was much more cautious and conservative than local government would have liked. The Environment Select Committee commented in its report:

> Almost without exception the witnesses were more concerned with the autonomy of local government and the accountability of local councillors to the electorate than the domestic rating system. The Green Paper was seen as an inadequate starting point for a discussion of local government finance.[25]

Government officials indicated that by 1982 they had received 1124 responses to the Green Paper including 590 from organizations. Most representations were from district councils and rate-payer associations (154 and 108 respondents respectively). Thirty responses were received from professional organizations and trade unions, and fifty from commercial organizations. In addition, twenty individual businesses submitted replies.

Only written responses were invited. The respondents worked within the issues defined by the government. To cope with the number of replies, the Department of Environment developed a system of categorization. This categorization works within central government's conception of the issue. The consultation process did not affect definition of any of the central issues. It functioned rather like an extended exercise in qualitative market research. It had few features one could associate with a process of political consultation, negotiation and bargaining.

One can trace the efforts of departmental officers to categorize the responses through a series of five tables. Table 5.1 represents their overall summary.

Table 5.1   Responses to Green Paper – alternatives to domestic rates

Respondents	Preference					
	Retention of the domestic rating system in its present form	Retention of a reformed domestic rating system	Retention of a reformed domestic rating system or abolition	Abolition of domestic rating system	No specific preference	Totals
Political Organizations	3	15	1	13	3	35
Local Authority Associations		7				7
County Councils	2	13	1	1	4	21
District Councils in England and Wales	8	134	3	3	6	154
Local Authorities in London		16			2	18
Local Authorities in Scotland	3	21	2	1	7	34
Town and Parish Councils, Community Councils	5	31	5	7	8	56
Local Government Associated Bodies	1	9			2	12
Professional Organizations and Trade Unions	1	21	2	1	5	30
Commercial and Industrial Organizations	2	21	5	7	15	50
Private Individuals	16	122	24	311	61	534
Local Amenity, Ratepayers' and Residents' Organizations		19	1	83	5	108
Members of Parliament		7	3	4	1	15
Businesses	1	3	1	9	6	20
Other Respondents	1	10	1	3	15	30
Totals	43	450	49	443	140	1124

Source: Second Report of the Environment Committee, Local Government Finance, H.C. 217 of 1981/2, Appendices to Minutes of Evidence, 26.

Sir William Pyle's evidence on the approach to consultation in the education system touches some of the distinctive features of consultation in the two-party system. Planning is the preserve of the civil service. Planning is that stage 'when the government is formulating some of its main decisions'. Why should government do this in private? First, Sir William says, in charting a new course for policy ministers are entitled and expected to give the lead:

> Some proposals from the education interests are that they should be associ-
> ated with the planning process. There are times when I believe that our
> friends in local government would actually say that they feel they should be
> involved in the planning process before anybody else and that they should
> be partners in the confidential stages in planning, rather than purely in the
> phases when matters are open, where consultation on open proposals is
> available. . . . I do not think that the government was unreasonable in
> formulating its views first in confidence. . . . Ministers should be able to
> think their way through this in what I call a confidential phase, and I do see
> difficulties about admitting other parties to such deliberations . . . when
> there are views to be announced, consultation can be quite different.[26]

Sir William indicates how the views of interest groups could be expected to be taken into account in this confidential phase:

> In the confidential stages of the development of the decisions and the
> policies in the White Paper, a very wide array of arrangements was fol-
> lowed, whereby the Secretary of State of the day was informed about what
> people wished to see in the way of policy decisions. They were given
> innumerable occasions. . . . Mrs Thatcher had a fair idea of what line she
> wished to adopt . . . she did give a good picture of it . . . to the assembled
> representatives of the local education committees and said, there and then,
> these are the kinds of thoughts that I am thinking. If you have any reactions
> to them, please come along and tell me. The door is open. Come and discuss
> them with me. . . . Nobody took advantage of that offer.

Sir William's generally disdainful approach to consultations is implicit in the following observations:

> I certainly regarded as part of the job of the Department to try to establish
> what public opinion generally wants. I often think that in some ways this is
> the most important view that we can get. The difficulty is how in fact to
> establish it. The old problem of value judgements, measurements and
> definitions are all very much at stake here. . . . You can be sure that among
> the 150 instances in one year – when ministers meet with interest groups –
> there would be some groups that did speak for what you might call the non-
> educational stage army. They are not local authorities or the teachers. They
> will be individual pressure groups of citizens without any statutory role in
> the system at all. I would say a significant number of about 150 meetings
> would have been with people of that kind.

Sir William describes the various ways in which his department maintains its sensitivity to public opinion:

> We do get confirmation of trends that one discerns in a variety of ways. . . . We are often parents ourselves. We do not live in monastic seclusion at home, and we meet the parents of other children. One does become aware of what is stirring in people's breasts and minds, and these are articulated in one form or another through the press, gatherings and reports of speech days. I think that the letters that members of parliament write, reflect these trends . . . we have no systematic way, I must say, but the 'feel' is a very important bit of our trade. . . . I would like to think that the best policy we can adopt is a simple one of the open door.

Another device adopted by government to integrate interest groups in its deliberations is the independent commission charged with responsibility for a particular area. This development, termed tripartism, is conceived by J. J. Richardson and A. G. Jordan 'to be founded on the premise that major policies are too important to be left to Parliament'.[27] At one level tripartism involves direct negotiations on some important issues between government and the related interest groups. Joel Barnett, former Financial Secretary to the Treasury, reflects on the effects of this direct relationship in discussing the social contract implemented after Labour's victory in 1974.

> In fashioning our policies we accepted what were literally the self-imposed pressures of the TUC. Of course, any government must work closely with the TUC, but apart from the pressures that flow naturally from our historic relationships with the trade unions we went much further in the way we co-operated under the terms of the quaintly titled social contract, supposedly in trying a new relationship between government and unions. To my mind the only give and take in the contract was that the government gave and the unions took.[28]

At another level tripartism involves the direct engagement of the major producer groups on statutory boards and commissions. The CBI and the TUC both have formal representation on executive agencies such as the Manpower Services Commission, the Health and Safety Executive, the Equal Opportunities Commission, and the National Economic Development Organization. These bodies were established variously by both Tory and Labour governments. Their capacity to reach conclusions contrary to the public interest is clear in the select committee inquiries reviewed in earlier chapters (e.g. MSC Corporate Plan, review of HSE, review of CRE, proposed Anti-Discrimination Code).

The foregoing evidence reflects the distance between interest groups and the political aspects of policy making. This distance is maintained by present approaches to consultation. In turn these approaches are rooted in the conventions of the two-party system. The two-party system, true to its ethos, protects the concentration of power in the hands of ministers and departments. They determine what issues require consultation, the form of consultation, and the limits of consultation. In general, interest groups are not given a role in the strictly political aspects of policy making. That is seen as an inappropriate derogation of legitimate ministerial and departmental prerogatives.

Thus the two-party system integrates interest groups in ways that generally do not seek to transfigure their sectional concerns. If anything, this system seems likely to reinforce an interest group's commitment to its pre-existing concerns. Second, the two-party system does not create opportunities for ministers to try to establish interest group coalitions to defend the public interest in particular issues. If anything, it works in the opposite direction. It alerts those interest groups who stand to lose from a policy proposal without mobilizing those who stand to gain. Third, it does not bring to public attention constituencies concerned with emerging issues or affected positively by fundamental reappraisal of current programmes. Serious debate of public policy alternatives in particular policy areas is largely confined to departments. Yet co-operation from at least some affected interest groups is usually essential if subsequent action is to be successful. In general the presumption that political parties are the sole agents for political aspirations, and for the community's general interests, precludes structures that might recognize and accommodate a political role for interest groups.

If interest groups were mostly integrated by the parties, or if they were a relatively insignificant and impotent political force, their role would be of little political moment. The evidence suggests this is not the case. Governments of both major parties have been obliged to adopt a variety of approaches to integrate interest groups. Whether select committees have seen interest groups as a target for their efforts and whether the results of inquiries point to the potential of a plural structure to better integrate interest groups in policy making, are questions to which we now turn.

SELECT COMMITTEE OUTREACH TO INTEREST GROUPS

Outreach to interest groups by the select committees has been affected by at least two considerations. First, the pattern of outreach has varied markedly with the focus of the inquiry. Of course, all inquiries have engaged the most important interest group – the departments. The civil service has itself prepared figures on the extent of its engagement with select committees. The Leader of the House, John Biffen, gave the following account of the impact of committees on civil servants:

By February 1982 about 750 departmental memoranda had been submitted to the committees. . . . In the first three years there were about 150 ministerial appearances before the departmental committees and over 700 official witnesses. . . . It has been estimated that during 1981 officials made over 800 appearances before the committees. Over 6000 man-days were spent on the preparation of written memoranda and nearly 6000 on providing the necessary briefings.[29]

The outreach to external interest groups has been most extensive in inquiries concerned with 'strategic' issues. Inquiries arising from the budget cycle have only involved limited outreach to interest groups. For example, only two select committees heard evidence from interest groups in appraising departmental estimates in the 1981/2 session (Social Services and Foreign Affairs). The Treasury Committee has sought to engage interest groups on some of its inquiries concerned with the medium-term economic strategy. But it has not generally seen interest groups as a target for its effort. Outreach by committees concerned with current issues has been more extensive. These inquiries typically engage groups most immediately affected by the issue.

The degree of engagement of interest groups by select committees has been influenced by the attitude of parliamentarians to these bodies. The committees have not generally seen interest groups as a specific target for their work. Members have conceived committees as agents of parliament primarily concerned to increase the scrutiny and accountability of departments. This is, after all, the basic rationale for the development of the present system.

This latter consideration has influenced the way in which select committees have organized themselves to mobilize interest groups. Most individual committees have prepared a circulation list for routine notification of pending inquiries, reports and other matters the committees may wish to make public. For example, the Treasury Committee has a standard list of approximately 120 individuals and groups. Ninety of the individuals listed are media correspondents. The remaining thirty entries cover interest groups of one kind or another, public affairs consultants, think-tanks and academic units. The committee typically formulates a list of interest groups who might be interested in each inquiry. It does not deliberately project itself to interest groups. Its inquiries are notable for the engagement of leading theoreticians and its reports for their clarity of exposition of arcane technical issues. Engagement of the major domestic interest groups (e.g. producer groups, welfare groups, advocacy groups) has not been a notable feature. The Environment Committee, Home Affairs Committee and the Social Services Committee also limit their routine circulation of notices about committee inquiries and reports to media organizations. Despite this, all these committees have conducted inquiries with extensive outreach. But their engagement with interest groups is not a routine aspect of committee work. It is an ancillary, *ad hoc* aspect of each inquiry. By contrast, the Agriculture, Welsh Affairs, Transport and Education Committees engage in more deliberate outreach. The Agriculture

Committee's routine circulation list covers the following categories: national, local and agricultural press, BBC and ITV, government departments, agricultural unions (TGWU, NFU, etc.), consumer groups, agricultural attachés, local authorities, other interest groups (Country Landowners Association, Small Farmers Association, British Multiple Retailers Association, the Eggs Authority, Food Manufacturing Federation, Scottish Grocers Federation). Similarly, the Education Committee regularly circularizes some 160 organizations of whom 90 are interest groups or educational institutions. The Welsh Affairs Committee's routine mailing list comprises 240 bodies of whom 43 are councils, 96 independent interest groups and the balance media organizations. The Transport Committee regularly circularizes 40 non-media organizations with information about its activities.

Several committee chairmen expressed surprise at the response of interest groups to inquiries. The Transport Committee, for example, was surprised by the level of interest in its inquiry on transport in London (H.C. 127, 1981–2). Oral evidence was taken from 33 groups but written submissions were received from a further 74 groups. The groups giving evidence included councils and boroughs, departments, public and private transport providers, unions, business organizations and citizen groups such as Transport 2000, London Transport and Amenity Association and London Transport Passenger Committee. Similarly the Social Services Committee attracted an unexpectedly high level of response to its medical education inquiry (H.C. 31, 1980–1). This inquiry took oral evidence from 42 groups including major hospitals, the colleges and various representative bodies. But it also received 100 written submissions from individuals and local groups.

To assess interest group reaction to committees a list was compiled of all the groups giving oral evidence to the inquiries. Individuals, departments and ministers were excluded. Over 500 groups were identified. A precise number is hard to establish since the distinction between an individual and an interest group submission is not always clear. Addresses were found for 425 groups. The location of these groups throughout the UK reflects the dominance of London. Three hundred and twenty-five groups (76 per cent) had a London address. Twenty-six groups were in Scotland and five in Wales. Distribution around town and region in England was: Manchester – six; Oxford – six; Birmingham and Newcastle-upon-Tyne – four each; southern central region – six; western central – six; eastern central – five.

Most groups gave evidence to only one inquiry. However, thirty groups gave evidence to two inquiries and three to three inquiries; Oxfam and the Institute of Personnel Management appeared at four; the Association of County Councils appeared before five inquiries; the Association of Metropolitan Authorities at eight; the TUC appeared at nine inquiries and the CBI at twelve.

A questionnaire was distributed to all groups (appendix 2). Fifteen questionnaires were returned because of incorrect addresses. Forty-one respondents replied declining to participate. One hundred and twenty-seven completed questionnaires were received. Because of their frequency of appearance direct interviews were conducted with the TUC, CBI, AMA and ACC. Twenty direct interviews were also conducted with respondents to the survey to review their experience in more detail. This means detailed information was received from just over 30 per cent of the interest groups involved in select committee hearings in the 1981–2 session. A complete list of the respondent groups is at appendix 3. Ten are advisory and executive bodies associated with government, forty-nine are producer groups of one kind or another, twenty-five are service groups, ten are local or regional bodies and twenty-nine are advocacy groups on individual rights, government services or environmental issues. There are seven research groups. Three churches also completed the questionnaire.

The responses to the questionnaire suggest select committee outreach has been reasonably effective, despite its *ad hoc* character. Select committees have not generally advertised pending inquiries. Only six respondents were gathered by this means.

The weekly activities of the committees are listed in *The Times* and the *Daily Telegraph*. But this would normally be too late to allow an interest group to participate in a hearing. 81 per cent of respondents participated at the invitation of the committees and 21 per cent at their own initiative. There was overlap between these two categories because some of the groups appeared on more than one inquiry. The list of respondents who took the initiative in seeking to appear before inquiries suggests that some major groups have been overlooked or have conceived themselves to have an interest which was unrecognized by select committee staff. The groups who approached committees with a request to give evidence include the Chemical Industries Association, the National Consumer Council, British Paper and Board Industries Federation, Association for the Conservation of Energy, Chartered Institute of Building Surveyors and the Catholic Housing Aid Society. This also suggests a number of interest groups have begun monitoring the activities of the committees.

SELECT COMMITTEE IMPACT ON INTEREST GROUPS

The survey of interest groups sought to establish their experience and attitudes in four areas: first, preparation for the inquiry; second, their experience of the inquiry itself; third, their reaction to the select committee report; and finally, their overall evaluation of this procedure. A comprehensive tabulation of the results is at appendix 4.

The survey first sought to establish whether preparing for the inquiry led the interest groups to engage in some special action. Eighty-one groups or 64 per cent of respondents gathered information especially for the inquiry. There was no pattern associated with this information gathering. 45 per cent of respondents said the information concerned the issue itself and 12 per cent that it concerned their members' attitudes (figure 5.1).

Figure 5.1　Impact of inquiry on information gathering

100% = 127 respondents

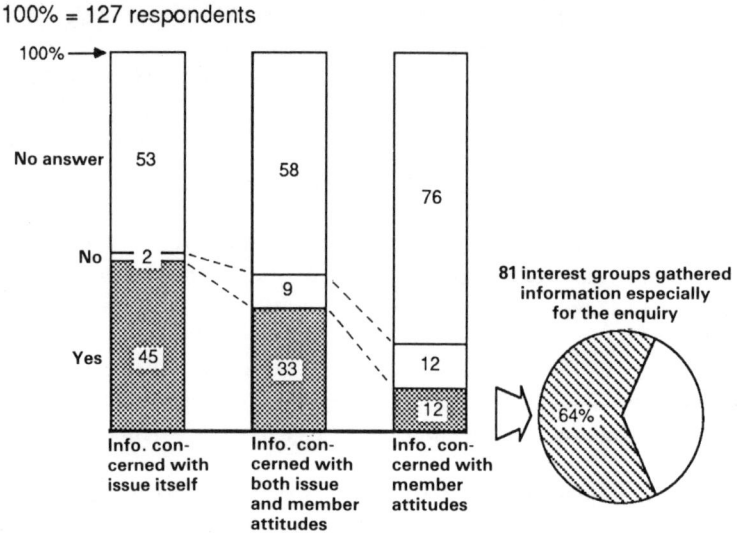

Question: Was the information gathered concerned with:
　The issue itself?
　Member attitudes?
　Both?

In gathering this information just under half of the participants (48 per cent) said they engaged in some special, non-routine consultation process. These groups included British Steel, the Law Centres Federation, Salvation Army, Association of Directors of Social Security, Geographical Association, Association of Anaesthetists, Museums and Galleries Commission, Royal College of Radiologists and the Glass and Glazing Federation. Information gathering was highly correlated with this non-routine consultation. 60 per cent of those who gathered information engaged in consultation.

The questionnaire then sought to establish what interest groups actually did in preparing for the inquiry. The results are displayed in figure 5.2.

One hundred and nine respondents (87 per cent) took one or more of those actions which involved more than recycling existing information or relying on available general knowledge. Forty-four respondents (34 per cent) said establishing a task force was an important or very important part of their preparation. Forty respondents (32 per cent) credited circularizing their members to obtain their views with a similar role. Ninety-four respondents (73 per cent) engaged in informal consultation with members who had special knowledge of the issue. 45 per cent of respondents undertook more than three actions in preparing for the inquiry. Precisely stated, 27 per cent took four actions, 15 per cent took five actions and 3 per cent took all six actions. The numbers who consulted other groups are suggestive. 45 per cent of respondents took this action. For 20 per cent it played a significant or very significant

Figure 5.2   Impact of inquiry on internal research

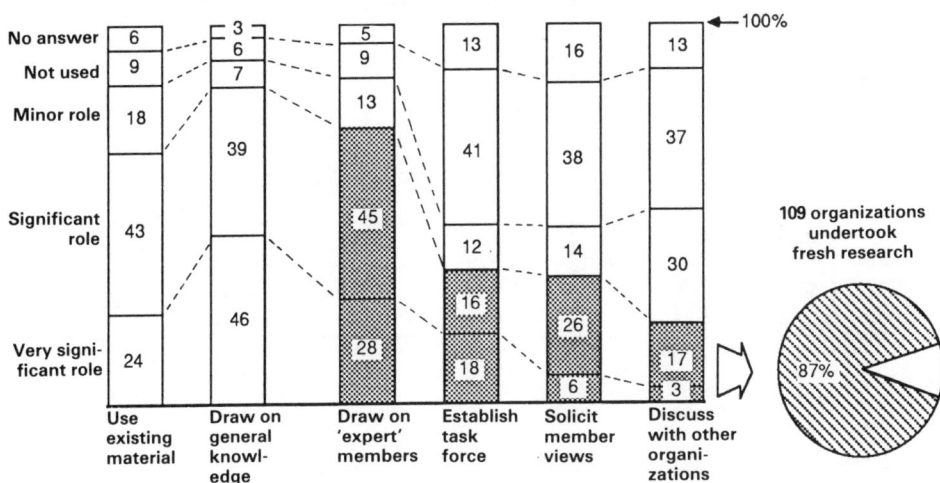

						◄—100%
No answer	6	3	5	13	16	13
Not used	9	6	9			
		7				
Minor role	18		13	41	38	37
		39				
Significant role	43		45	12	14	30
		46		16	26	
Very significant role	24		28	18	6	17 / 3

Use existing material   Draw on general knowledge   Draw on 'expert' members   Establish task force   Solicit member views   Discuss with other organizations

109 organizations undertook fresh research

87%

Question: Please indicate the role of the following actions in preparing for the inquiry. (The questionnaire offered 6 choices – establish internal task force; circularize members inviting views; consult informally with selected members with special knowledge; use material already prepared; draw on general knowledge of existing office bearers; discuss with other organizations. The questionnaire invited groups to indicate the relative importance of these actions.)

role. Finally, 92 per cent (117 respondents) prepared a written submission to support their oral evidence.

Next the questionnaire sought to establish the outcome for interest groups of attending the hearing or participating in the inquiry. The results are shown in figure 5.3. Seventy interest groups (55 per cent) experienced positive 'learning' of some kind or another and/or formed new links to other groups. The issues investigated by the select committees in nearly every case had been subject to prolonged review within the policy process. London Transport, alternatives to the domestic rate, the school curriculum, and medical education had all been subject to repeated and protracted inquiry. It is in this context that the capacity of the select committees to provide access to new information needs to be weighed.

Of the interest groups who obtained very significant or significant new information, fifty-three (41 per cent) indicated they received extra information about the issue or government or departmental attitudes. Forty-six (36 per cent) indicated they received significant or very significant new information about other interest groups. Of the fifty-three respondents who regarded new information about the issue or about government policy or about departmental attitudes as significant or very significant outcomes, ten (19 per cent) said they obtained extra information in all three areas, fifteen (28 per cent) for two of these areas and twenty-eight (56 per cent) in one area. Interest groups were also asked if the inquiry led to new or strengthened links

Figure 5.3 Impact of inquiry on interest group learning and links to other groups

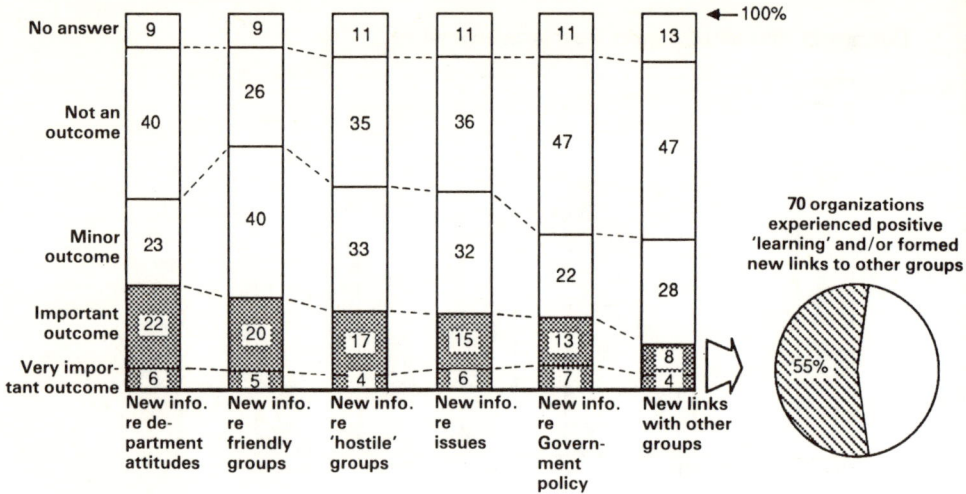

Question: Please indicate which, if any, of the following outcomes occurred as a result of the inquiry:
- We obtained new information re issue
- We obtained new information re government policy
- We obtained new information re department attitudes/judgements
- We obtained new information re friendly groups
- We obtained new information re 'hostile' groups
- We formed new or strengthened links with other groups

Figure 5.4 Reporting participation to members

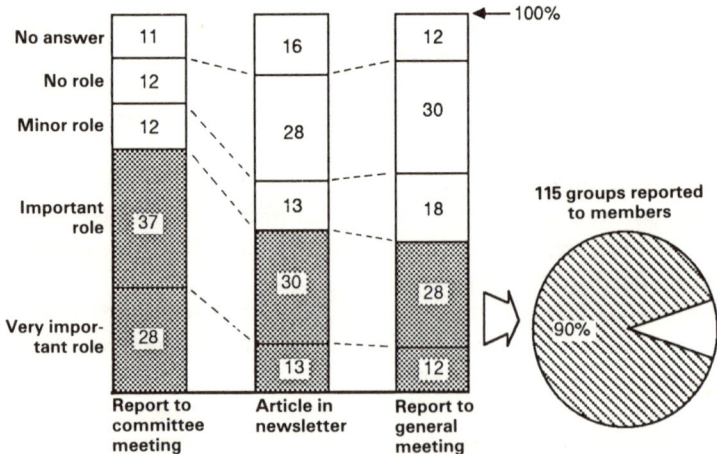

Question: Would you please indicate the role of the following actions in reporting back to members (indicating the relative importance):
- Report to committee meeting
- Article in journal/newsletter
- Report to general meeting

Figure 5.5   Interest group follow-up to committee reports

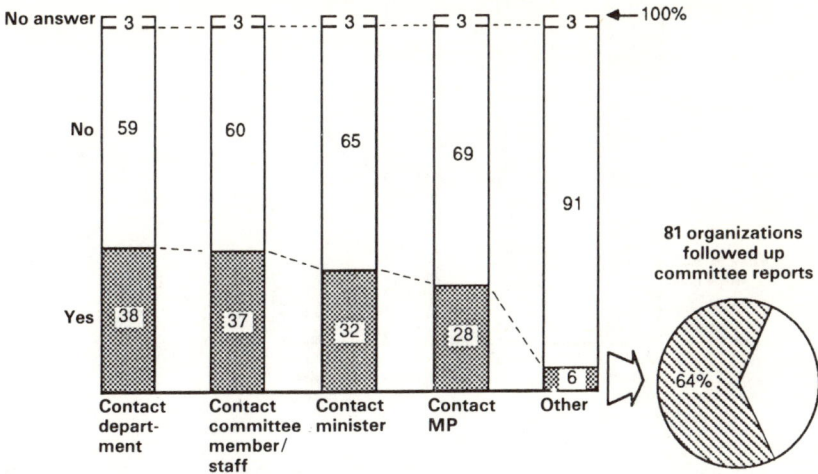

Question: Did you take any action as a result of the committee report?

with other interest groups. Fifteen groups (12 per cent) considered new or strengthened links formed with other groups to be an important or very important outcome.

The questionnaire then sought to establish whether the interest groups reported to their members on participation in the inquiry. One hundred and fifteen respondents (90 per cent) answered this question positively (figure 5.4). The most common action was a report to a committee meeting (eighty-three respondents or 65 per cent). But fifty-four respondents (43 per cent) placed articles in their organization's journal or newsletter. A further fifty respondents (40 per cent) reported on participation to special meetings of members.

The select committee findings were obtained by almost all participating interest groups (98 per cent). Eighty-one (64 per cent) took some action as a result of this report (figure 5.5). Seventeen organizations (22 per cent of those who did something and 13 per cent of total respondents) undertook all four actions. Twelve organizations (16 per cent of those who did something) undertook three actions. Twenty-one interest groups (28 per cent of those who did something) undertook two actions; and twenty-six (34 per cent) undertook one action.

Select committee findings were publicized amongst the membership of ninety-six organizations (76 per cent of respondents). This is shown in figure 5.6. It should be noted that 66 per cent (eighty-three respondents) placed a printed report in their newsletter. Thirty-six organizations (28 per cent of total respondents) gave both an oral report on findings to their committee and a written report to members in their journal. Forty-five organizations (36 per cent) did only one of these things.

Next the questionnaire sought to establish the impact of the inquiry process on the attitudes and judgements of participating interest groups. The results

Figure 5.6 Reporting Select Committee findings to members

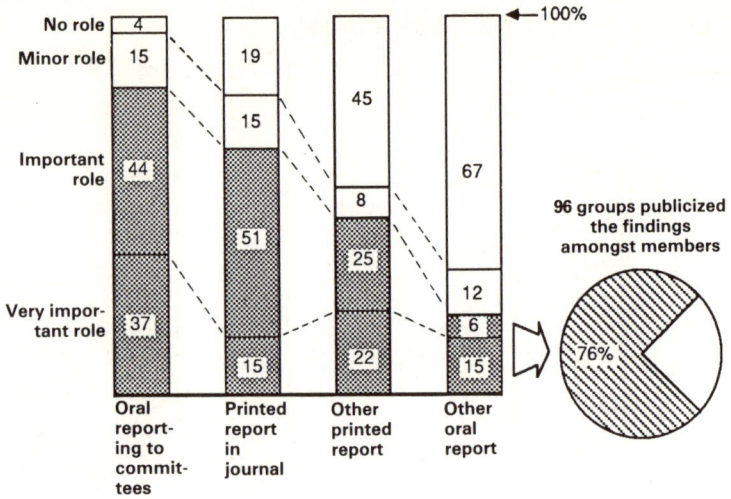

Question: Were the Select Committee findings publicized amongst your members? Please indicate method (from above choices)

Figure 5.7 Impact of inquiry on interest group attitudes

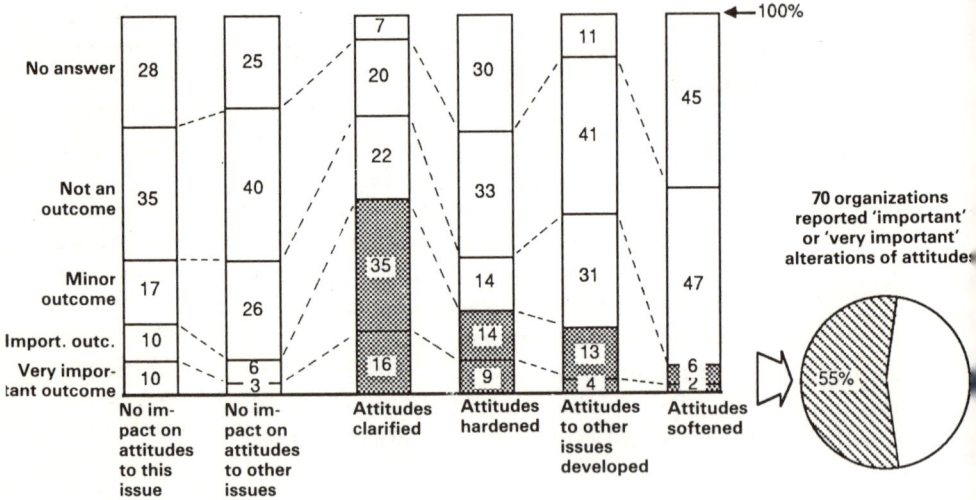

Question: Please indicate the impact of participation on your attitude:
Attitudes clarified
Attitudes hardened
Attitudes softened
Attitudes to other issues developed
No impact on attitudes to this issue
No impact on attitudes to other issues

Figure 5.8   Specially valued attributes of select committee inquiries

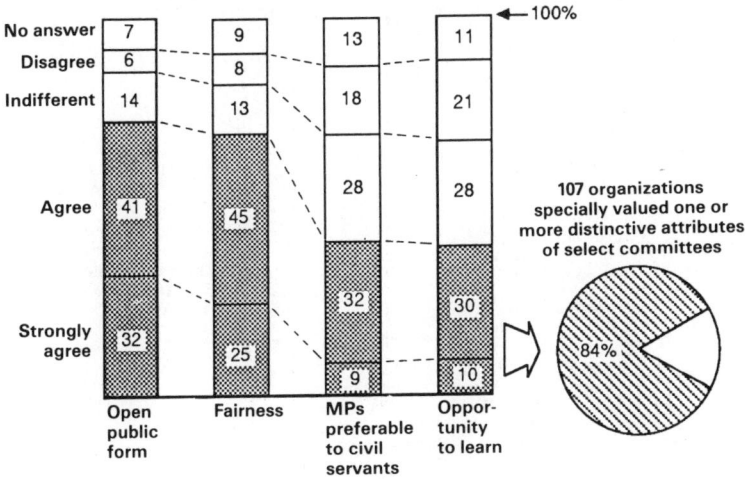

Question: How would you describe worthwhile features of a Select Committee compared with other ways of determining public policy questions?

Open and public form makes it preferable to departmental or other private approach

Select Committees are fairer

We learnt more this way

MPs are better qualified than civil servants to decide issues

are summarized in figure 5.7. Seventy organizations (55 per cent of respondents) reported 'important' or 'very important' alterations of attitude. Sixty-five interest groups (51 per cent of respondents) said clarification of their organization's position was an important or very important outcome of the whole process. The experience hardened the position of twenty-nine groups (23 per cent), softened the position of nine groups and left forty-seven groups (38 per cent) unchanged.

In assessing the experience, interest groups were asked to indicate which, if any, features of the select committee process they especially valued. They were invited to judge select committees in the context of other kinds of public investigations that they had experienced. The results are reported in figure 5.8. One hundred and seven respondents (84 per cent) agreed or agreed strongly with one or more of the suggested positive statements about select committees. These positive statements cover the public character of the select committee process, its fairness by contrast with departmental procedures, its role as a source of information, and interest group perception of the legitimacy of MPs as leaders of inquiries. The public and open form of the inquiry was most favoured. This characteristic was endorsed by ninety-three groups (73 per cent of respondents). Eighty-nine groups (70 per cent) regarded the select committee process as fairer than departmental procedures. Fifty-one groups (40 per cent) said they learnt more through this process than by

Figure 5.9   Interest group attitudes to extension of select committee powers

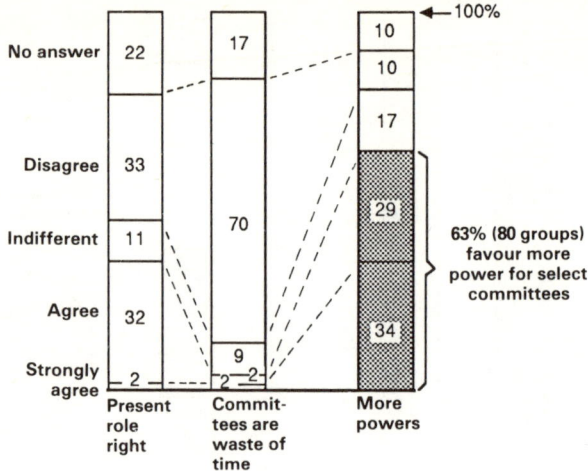

Question: Do you favour extension of the Select Committee powers (indicating strength with choices given)?

participating in a departmental inquiry or responding to an official consultation paper. Fifty-two respondents (41 per cent) regarded MPs as more legitimate arbitrators of the issue than departmental officers. Looking at the frequency of response amongst participants, sixty-nine respondents (54 per cent) strongly endorsed three or more of these statements, twenty-two (17 per cent) endorsed two statements and only sixteen (13 per cent) endorsed one statement.

Finally the questionnaire invited respondents to consider whether the role of select committees should be enlarged (figure 5.9). Eighty respondents (63 per cent) agreed or agreed strongly with this sentiment. Forty-three respondents (34 per cent) thought that their present role was about right.

Interviews with individual interest groups extended or clarified some of the points in the survey. These interviews covered major groups like the TUC and CBI and smaller groups such as the Pedestrians Association. It is clear that interest groups generally are unsure about the current or potential role of select committees. Their attitudes were influenced by their experience at particular inquiries. Some found them valuable sources of information. Some found them valuable as a source of access to policy making. The TUC, for example, used the Employment Committee to place its attitudes to Mrs Thatcher's industrial relations legislation on the public record. Arguing that the time for consultation was insufficient, the TUC had refused to enter negotiations with the government within the deadline it set for replies to its Green Paper. The select committee hearings enabled the TUC to place its views on the published record. At the same time its leaders were exposed to detailed cross-examination by MPs sympathetic to the government's purpose.

In some cases, interest groups have found select committees useful in advancing their cause. For example, the Council for the Protection of Rural England and several other environmental groups believe that the Energy

Committee has been decisive in obliging the Department of Energy to address the issue of energy conservation. Similarly, interest groups credit the same committee with an important role in moving government oil depletion policy towards a market basis. Most of those interviewed recognized that the select committees do not have a distinct and independent role in the policy process. A number of 'insider' groups were sceptical about the select committees contributing an additional, positive dimension to policy making. This applied particularly to peak groups such as the TUC and CBI. An assistant secretary of the TUC, David Lea, commented publicly:

> How do select committees relate to the polarisation of politics? What are the issues that are supposed to be considered? The lack of an industrial policy for instance, which has been a devastating experience over the last two to three years, with investment down 20%, and 3.3 million unemployed, is apparently not an issue which can be examined by select committees. If that is not their role, I am asking how far the bipartisan or the cross political approach to some subjects can hang together in the select committees, bearing in mind the very different approach as between government and opposition on these matters. . . . A select committee can agree their criticism about what the government is doing, but it always seems to me that the real question is whether one can reach agreement on a solution to the problem, not just provide an agreed criticism.[30]

Despite this scepticism, the TUC Annual Report for the 1982 Congress lists fifteen inquiries to which that organization submitted written or oral evidence. The references summarize the TUC's attitude and, where a report had been produced, the committee's findings. No other mode of interaction with government is as extensively documented in the 1982 TUC Annual Report. Eleven inquiries were treated in a similar fashion in the 1983 TUC Report. Similarly, in this year, no other mode of interaction with the policy process is so thoroughly documented.

It is instructive to note the matters that were the subject of supplemental comments by respondents to the survey. Sixty-nine supplemental comments were made about some aspect of the inquiry process. A number of comments appended to completed questionnaires confirm interest group uncertainty about the role of select committees. These respondents see little prospect of the dominant features of the present system changing. Therefore they are perplexed about the place of select committees.

A typical comment on the relevance of committees was: 'Select committees are an important point of access to the arena of public debate, and can be used to raise issues, but their effects are very limited and general given the strong opposition of the present government to the point we put.' Another group made the same point: 'There is a credibility problem vis-à-vis the degree to which the government feels bound to respond to the enquiry reports. . . . Perhaps committee powers need to be strengthened to enable them to compel government to respond within a reasonable time limit. It's all a bit cosy and polite – or seems to be!'

Interest groups participated because of the prestige of parliament. Westminster's committee corridor provides an impressive physical setting for interest groups to encounter the political process at first hand. This said, a number of groups noted that the chairman's approach holds the key to effective committee work. A number noted that they obtained additional information from the government response to the select committee report. Some criticized the approach of committees to the inquiries. They commented unfavourably on the selection of individuals and groups invited to give evidence, or about the deadline set for submission of responses, or about the vague scope of the terms of reference. Several groups sent representatives to monitor evidence provided by departments and other groups during the course of the hearing. For example the Medical Women's Federation was represented at most sessions of the medical education inquiry. But this is not a common practice. Concerning the role of MPs, one respondent answered: 'MPs are not necessarily better qualified to make judgements than civil servants, but because they are in touch with constituents they can consider other priorities than departmental ones.'

These comments are consistent with the actual impotence of select committees. Interest group uncertainty about the role of committees is also consistent with the failure of the select committees to project themselves deliberately to interest groups.

SELECT COMMITTEES AND THE INTEGRATION OF INTEREST GROUPS

The addition of an independent structure to deal with interest groups in a political context could strengthen the mobilization of consent in three potentially overlapping ways. First, policy makers could learn about interest group views before they became publicly committed to a course of action. Second, interest groups could be presented with a variety of grounds apart from agreement for accepting proposed policies. Third, ministers would be encouraged to mobilize coalitions of interest groups to defend the course of action they propose. This last outcome might be expected because select committees would confront ministers and departments with the necessity of seeking ways to manage interest group politics. These three outcomes, here distinguished for analytical purposes, would in practice occur together.

The evidence demonstrates that select committees have successfully crafted a structure whose scope covers all significant phases of policy making. It also shows that these committees have reached independent, bipartisan judgements on an impressive array of issues. They have been the vehicles for bringing new information to the attention of policy makers. Does the evidence also point to the potential of committees to better integrate interest groups in policy making? Is there evidence that committees improve interest groups' understanding of public policy issues? Is there evidence that a 'serial and remedial' process holds in prospect interest group integration on grounds other than agreement with the terms of decisions (e.g. tactical acceptance, compensation, etc.)? Is there evidence that the process promotes the formation of *ad hoc* 'encompassing' coalitions amongst interest groups?[31]

In interpreting the evidence from the survey some preliminary qualifications are important. First, with one or two exceptions, the select committees have not sought to focus their efforts on interest groups. Outreach to interest groups, while extensive in certain inquiries, has been *ad hoc* and unsystematic. Four committees have deliberately established procedures to notify at least some interest groups about their hearings and findings. But no committees have deliberately sought to cultivate interest groups. They have not seen impact on interest groups as an aspect of their activities, much less a primary aspect. A significant number of interest groups were engaged in inquiries on their own initiative.

Similarly committee chairmen have not sought to build relationships with interest groups. Many chairmen have met informally with major groups, particularly on specific inquiries. But chairmen have not seen interest groups as important targets for their efforts. Of nine chairmen interviewed, only two had sought out major interest groups to help establish the inquiry programme for their committees. The committees have seen ministers and departments as their dominant and primary concern.

Further, interest groups themselves are very uncertain about the role of committees. They welcome the access committees provide. They hold the House and its committees in very high regard. But they realize committees are impotent. Though they see committees as a new way of registering views in the political system, the precise role of the committees is not understood. The concentration of power associated with the two-party system is recognized as a fundamental obstacle to their effectiveness. The opportunities select committees might provide have not been articulated in general terms.

Despite their impotence in the current scheme of things, the results of this survey point to the potential of committees to help mobilize consent. As a normative process, mobilizing consent has both procedural and substantive dimensions.[32] Participants need to believe the system is fair in an abstract sense, that relevant evidence to the issue under review has been adduced and fairly weighed, and that the behaviour of other members of the relevant policy community will conform to the actions proposed. There is evidence of the potential of committees to contribute decisively to these outcomes. Recognition of the abstract 'fairness' of the select committee process is suggested by the characteristics most valued by participating interest groups. 74 per cent of the groups specially valued the 'visibility' or 'transparency' of the select committees and 70 per cent their 'fairness'. A further 84 per cent of responding interest groups specially valued one or another of the suggested distinctive features of the select committee process (by comparison with other methods of participating in policy development they had experienced). 65 per cent specially valued at least three of the four proposed positive characteristics of select committees.

The attractiveness of the select committee process to interest groups is also suggested by the number who favour enlargement of their role, despite the recognition that this is a forlorn hope under present constitutional arrangements: 65 per cent of the sample, and almost all the groups interviewed independently, would welcome an enlarged role for committees. Interviews suggest the prestige of parliament is an extremely potent factor. Interest groups may not have thought through the implications. But because they derive from parliament, select committees are 'instinctively' highly valued. This enthusiasm has neither been diminished nor increased by the interest group experience of the committee process. Irrespective of whether the inquiry stimulated interest groups to take action or whether they submitted pre-existing material, interest groups welcome the process.[33] Nor can it be said that this enthusiasm is in ignorance of committee findings. Almost all made it their business to establish the outcome of the select committee inquiries in which they participated. Indeed 64 per cent of the interest groups took some action as a consequence.

Next, the evidence concerning the capacity of committees to contribute to the development of interest groups' attitudes needs to be weighed. Here the findings suggest substantive bases for mobilizing consent. The process is clearly in an elemental stage. It can be observed in embryo, so to speak. Despite the relative impotence of committees, 55 per cent reported 'important' or 'very important' alterations of attitude. Only 8 per cent said their attitudes had been 'softened' by participation in the inquiry. This result is not surprising, if for no other reason than the protracted character of the process of opinion formation and the need to provide bases other than agreement for accommodation between protagonists. The most positive indicators are that 51 per cent credited the inquiry process with 'clarifying' their groups' attitude to the issue. 12 per cent said the inquiry stimulated them to form new links with other groups. 50 per cent 'consulted' other groups in preparing submissions. A further 55 per cent said the inquiry introduced them to new information – significantly, as could be expected, 75 per cent of these groups said this new information concerned government or departmental attitudes; but 65 per cent, only slightly less, said this information concerned the approach of other interest groups. 87 per cent said the inquiry caused them to undertake fresh research. Finally, as already noted, 64 per cent of the interest groups took some action as a result of the committee report. These are exactly the stimuli that, reinforced by further interactions, might produce more accommodating approaches on the part of interest groups. These results point to the potential of committees to be catalysts in opinion formation within particular policy communities and to be agents for the restoration of political trust.

The 'vertical' reach of the select committees is also suggested in the number of interest groups reporting their activities to their members. 90 per cent reported their evidence and 76 per cent reported the committees' findings to their members. Information has also been disseminated to the general public. Committee reports and deliberations have been widely reported in special interest journals and, to a lesser degree, in the national press.

This suggests attention to committees' actions amongst interest groups. It suggests that committees are capable of stimulating interest groups internally and in their relations with each other through their inquiries. It suggests the mechanisms through which attitudes might develop as a result of participation in the inquiries or dissemination of committee findings. Structures and linkages are being established spontaneously, so to speak, between interest groups and the select committees. What invites further testing is the capacity of these structures to be a 'conduit' for the shaping of behaviour. Their capacity to disseminate factual information both ways and to influence attitudes is clear. What needs to be further explored is their capacity to influence judgements about the public interest and to alter government or interest group behaviour in ways that promote this objective. The survey results suggest possibilities. Further deliberate leadership from committees – further effort deliberately aimed at interest groups – is required for a forthright judgement about committee potential.

Similarly there is little evidence so far that a 'serial and remedial' process might provide grounds other than agreement for reconciling interest groups to policy outcomes. This is hardly surprising. The role and potential of select committees would have to be much more widely understood for this to occur. What can be said is that the prestige of select committees would be extremely important in this outcome. But until the possibility – and the constitutional implications – of a serial and remedial process are more widely recognized, this will remain untested.

Similarly the potential for select committees to stimulate the formation of *ad hoc* interest group coalitions to sustain government proposals requires wider recognition amongst ministers and departments that this is an essential aspect of the management of interest group politics. There is abundant evidence that interest groups have themselves discovered the power of *ad hoc* coalitions. Ministers and departments have yet to recognize this as an essential dimension of political leadership.[34] Earlier chapters show that the committees have, without deliberate intent, placed essential information about actual and potential interest group coalitions on the public record. But until the potential of this approach to contribute to successful policy making is more widely recognized, these possibilities remain untested.

Overall, it would seem that a system to deal with interest group politics is at a rudimentary stage amongst members of parliament no less than amongst interest groups themselves. The notion that interest groups might represent a primary focus for select committee work is not recognized. Structures are well developed. But these structures could as easily remain adjuncts to the two-party system as provide the means for better integrating interest groups. Because necessary attitudes are at so rudimentary a stage amongst MPs, the impact of select committees remains ambiguous and their potential not yet adequately explored. The results of the survey provide strong grounds for further experiment. They give strong support for further development aimed specifically at building interest groups' understanding of, and engagement in, this process. But an empirical judgement that the work of select committees affirms their theoretical potential to aid integration of interest groups would be premature. Such a judgement must await further development of the system.

Chapter 6

Policy making in a multi-party parliament

A multi-party parliament can no longer be considered fanciful. Such a development would reflect that fragmentation which has been evident both in the electorate and amongst organized political groups. A multi-party parliament transforms the political requirements for policy making. Effective government in a multi-party parliament requires a political structure capable of mobilizing sufficient consent to allow policy choices to be made and realized. The executive needs to be able to win majority parliamentary support. It must also be able to mobilize interest group consent.

In the sections that follow I first review a proposed new budgetary procedure which in fact amounts to a blueprint for a plural policy-making system. Then I relate the evidence assembled in earlier chapters to the potential of such a structure to permit parliamentary consideration of government proposals and to provide a context for mobilizing interest group consent. Finally the alternatives to, and the outlook for, such a development of the policy-making system are weighed.

A PLURAL STRUCTURE OF POLICY MAKING

A detailed blueprint for a more plural policy-making system has been worked out in the context of the budget and public expenditure cycle. New budgetary procedures have been suggested which, if fully implemented, would transform the policy-making system.[1] The present 'collectivist' two-party system would be replaced by a more plural structure. The keystone for such a plural reconstruction would be an enlarged role for parliament in the budget process. This would be achieved through some version of a two-stage budget process. Under such a procedure bipartisan parliamentary select committees would have the right to advance scrutiny of government revenue and expenditure proposals. They would review its actual spending and borrowing programmes as they unfold. They would have the right to challenge the executive on the floor of parliament if their judgement of the public interest on any of these matters differed from that of the government.

Such powers would decisively alter relations between select committees, ministers, parliament, departments, and interest groups. These proposals would result in a substantial flow of power from the executive and civil service to parliament. The regime of concentrated central power would be decisively broken. Parliamentary select committees would acquire a role secondary to, but complementing, that of ministers in the planning and scrutiny of departmental expenditure. We shall first review this proposed change in procedure and then consider how executive–legislative relations might work in practice.

A two-stage budget process

The adequacy of existing budget arrangements has been called into question since the mid-1970s. This criticism has been cast in technical terms. The needs of economic policy making have preoccupied critics. The former Chancellor, Sir Geoffrey Howe, whilst in Opposition, criticized the secrecy surrounding budget policy making:

> The budget is shrouded in secrecy until the Chancellor unveils his master plan. He presents it as a fiscal *fait accompli* receptive to neither the benefit nor opportunity of prior examination or constructive comment. . . . The Treasurer plays the part of a sort of economic Mt. Sinai . . . the archaic ritual by which parliament decides on it is about as appropriate to a modern democracy as tally sticks to the international money market.[2]

This concern was pursued and amplified in a report from the Institute for Fiscal Studies in 1978. This report is crucial. It directed attention towards the possibility of a new structure. It provided a powerful technical argument justifying such a step. The IFS report concludes with an indictment of present procedures:

> The conclusion of this study is that the economic framework used for the formulation of budgetary policy, the control system for public expenditure, and parliamentary procedure interlock. The present procedure with no medium term budget constraint and with different time horizons for expenditure and taxation is adapted to a post war economic approach in terms of short run claims on real resources which has been found to be defective and which has been largely abandoned. Only when they are linked coherently to a new economic framework can attempts to reform the control system and procedure be expected to be successful. What appears to be needed therefore is a complete and impartial review of the whole budgetary system including the economic framework, the expenditure system, and parliamentary procedure.[3]

This report was followed by the appointment of an unofficial task force by the Institute for Fiscal Studies chaired by the former Head of the Civil Service,

Lord Armstrong. The Armstrong Committee reported in July 1980. It recommended a two-stage budget process for Britain. It envisaged the Chancellor offering in November each year a detailed draft of his expenditure and taxation plans. Over the ensuing four months these would be the subject of parliamentary review and public discussion. On the basis of these reviews, the Chancellor would bring down the government's formal budget in March.[4]

This proposal entered the parliamentary process in 1981. In that year the Procedure Committee on the Supply Process invited the Treasury Committee to investigate proposals for budgetary reform. The Treasury Committee took evidence from members of the Armstrong Committee and from the Chancellor about the principle of a two-stage budget process. It took evidence from revenue departments − Board of Internal Revenue and Customs and Excise − and from three major spending departments − Environment, Health and Social Security and Defence − about its practicality. The Committee also sought evidence from affected interest groups. The evidence is all on the public record. It provides a comprehensive survey of the grounds for, and the practicality of, such a procedure.

International comparisons are carefully documented.[5] The committee contrasts current British practices with those adopted in other EEC countries (such as Germany, Holland and France), and the United States and Canada. All these countries follow a two-stage budget process. The period for public discussion and debate extends up to eleven months.

In evidence, the Treasury objected to public discussion of revenue proposals because of the risk of forestalling. The committee assessed these difficulties by taking evidence from the government's revenue-collecting agencies and from a range of liquor, tobacco, and other commercial groups most likely to be affected. It concluded that Britain, like other countries where revenue proposals are publicly discussed before implementation, should be able to manage the problem.

Although not canvassed in the report (and mostly unremarked by subsequent commentators), there is no gainsaying the revolutionary character of what is at stake. The most significant transformation would be at the political level. Sir Leo Pliatzky, a former Second Permanent Secretary to the Treasury, gave evidence on the constitutional impact of a two-stage budget process:

[A two-stage budget process] would entail not merely reform but a revolution in relationships within the cabinet and between the executive and the parliament. There is at present a dichotomy between the system for collective cabinet decision taking on public expenditure and the arrangements on the taxation side, under which there is a greater or lesser degree of discussion in cabinet of broad budgetary strategy but specific decisions are taken by Treasury ministers after reference to the Prime Minister. . . . [Adoption of the proposals] would entail conceding more to parliament than has so far been conceded to Cabinet.[6]

The committee reviews the arguments for and against open debate. It weighs Treasury caution about the risks to fiscal prudence, against the need for publicity and public discussion. The following comments of Professor Neild (a member of the Armstrong inquiry) illustrate what is at stake in this disagreement.

> *Mr. Meacher:* Taking up a point which the chairman made rather more politely, would you agree that the real reason behind the tradition of budget secrecy is the preservation of power in the hands of the Treasury ministers *vis-à-vis* their colleges in the Cabinet, and senior civil servants *vis-à-vis* anyone else rather than any sustainable economic rationale.
> *Professor Neild:* Yes I would agree with that. I have often wondered how well founded is that belief that it gives them so much power. It seems to me a very open question. It is assumed it does. It is believed that because I get a secret document and he does not that I have power in some sense. But it is not clear that at the end of the day I am going actually to look more powerful because I very possibly will not make a good decision.[7]

The Treasury Committee report outlines the procedures required by a two-stage budget process. A 'green budget' would be published in November. This green budget would include preliminary departmental expenditure proposals, general revenue requirements and options for meeting these revenue needs. These expenditure and revenue proposals would be advanced in the context of the medium-term economic strategy. Treasury objected particularly to providing information about revenue needs beyond aggregate requirements. The committee, after reviewing its arguments, endorsed the Armstrong proposals that 'the taxation plans . . . should include an indication of government provisions for income and capital rates and allowances and the major indirect tax rates, as well as discussions and projections of any current tax issues.'[8]

In the period between November and early February, departmental select committees would review the green budget proposals. They could, if they so chose, take evidence from affected interests. Final proposals for departmental expenditure would be made available in January after they had been settled by Cabinet. Over this same period, the Treasury Committee would review the overall budgetary strategy. It would report to the House in January. This report would be the basis for a debate about the proposed medium-term financial strategy. This debate would be based on an amendable motion. The various select committees would report their findings on departmental expenditure proposals to the house in mid-February. In March the Chancellor would, as now, present his budget to parliament.

The select committees would immediately review the government's proposals in the light of their own findings. They would decide whether to recommend alternatives to the House. They could, if they so desired, take further evidence from departments or interest groups. Proposals for change from select committees would take the form of amendments to the estimates.

At the same time, the Treasury Committee would examine any new revenue proposals. These would be embodied in a new Finance Bill. If it was unhappy with government proposals it would so report before debate on the Bill. As numerous witnesses pointed out, the government would presumably be able to whip its majority to defeat any proposed amendments. Nevertheless, the reformers claim, the mere possibility of being forced to such an action would exercise a salutary impact on the policy-making process.

Against Treasury reservations, various former ministers and Treasury officials indicate that, providing the need for review in the light of later developments is accepted, there is no reason why detailed economic forecasts and assessments should not be published in November. The government already gets such information to help it finalize its November expenditure decisions.[9]

The Treasury Committee proposals were in the first instance submitted to the select committee reviewing overall financial procedures. This committee reported in May 1983. It does not follow the Treasury Committee's proposals precisely but, taken together, the new financial procedures it suggests would transfigure parliament's role. The report suggests procedures to give parliament a role in the scrutiny and control of longer term borrowing and of public expenditure as a whole, including that part of public expenditure not now covered by the supply process. Control of borrowing would be achieved through Treasury Committee scrutiny of the monthly estimates of outcomes against forecast. This committee would have right of access to the House if the figures gave it cause for concern. In addition, the government's annual borrowing requirement would be the subject of a separate resolution. This resolution would come forward for endorsement during the budgetary process. Control of non-supply expenditure would be achieved, first by making the nationalized industries' external financing limit subject to approval by the House, and second by making provisional Rate Support Grant Orders subject to approval by the House. Public expenditure as a whole would be monitored by the Treasury Committee in the same way as public borrowing. The Treasury Committee would report to the House any deviation from forecast quarterly spending which caused it concern.

The report also suggests reforms to the budget process. It broadly follows Treasury Committee (and the Armstrong group) proposals in relation to revenue. The report proposes splitting the Finance Bill in two. A 'major' Bill dealing with proposed changes in the rates of tax, and a 'minor' Taxes Management Bill covering changes to taxation schedules and procedures. New taxes would be introduced through separate legislation. The report also suggests a January House debate of the government's proposed medium-term financial strategy. This would follow review by the Treasury Committee of the Chancellor's Autumn Statement. It attenuates somewhat the role proposed by the Treasury Committee for departmental select committees in review of individual estimates. But this weakening of the role of select committees in the context of the budget cycle is balanced by a proposal to strengthen their role in the context of the expenditure planning cycle of individual departments. Here the report suggests that any major capital project included in the estimates which has not previously been endorsed by the relevant select committee, would require explicit approval from the House.

Table 6.1, which is taken from the report,[10] sets out the role envisaged for select committees and for the House at the various stages of the financial process.

This report was debated in the Commons on 6 December 1983. The government spokesman, the Financial Secretary to the Treasury, conceded no new powers to the House. The debate began at 9.40 p.m. Despite the timing, it attracted some hundred members to the chamber. The government's negative approach was criticized by all twelve backbench participants. One Labour member, Dr Jeremy Bray, spoke explicitly of the possibilities of later backbench disaffection. He pointed to the opportunities presented by the new estimates process for the backbench to assert itself against the executive. Several members spoke indirectly of the need for a new rationale for the role of backbenchers to cover their bipartisan work in select committees. Both Edward du Cann and Dr Jeremy Bray alluded to this. But its essence was stated by another Tory, Anthony Beaumont-Dark:

> If Parliament is to be anything except a talking shop, the House must have amendable Motions and be able to put pressure on Government. Hon. Members are meant to be the balance as Parliamentarians, not just the voting fodder, which is how Government clearly regard all Members of Parliament. The House has to carve out for Parliament and for the electorate something worthwhile to act as a true balance between the tyrannies of government and freedom of the Members of Parliament.[11]

The further development of parliament's role in this area is now in the hands of members themselves. There are historic precedents for such a development.[12] A programme for reform exists. A number of influential backbenchers are committed to its realization. How, if at all, the proposals might be converted to actuality will depend on a number of factors, not least on unfolding exigencies. I return to this question in the last section. I want now to sketch some of the likely broader characteristics of a policy-making system in which select committees share powers and political initiative with ministers and in which votes on the floor of the House determine policy outcomes.

A plural structure in practice

What would be the leading characteristics of a system in which parliament ceases to be dominated by a majority party and select committees spearhead

Table 6.1 Proposed timetable of financial business

	November	*Christmas Recess* December	January	February	*Easter Recess* March	April	May	*Whitsun Recess* June	July
Papers presented to the House	Autumn Statement Winter Supp. Ests. and Votes on Account Taxes Management Bill Public Expenditure Quarterly Profile		Public Expenditure White Paper Appropriation Accounts Public Expenditure Quarterly Profile	Spring Supp. Ests. and Excess Votes	Financial Statement Budget Resolutions Main Estimates Borrowing Order	Finance Bill			Summer Supp. Ests. Public Expenditure Quarterly Profile
Consideration by Select Committees — Departmental Committees		(Autumn Statement esp. Nationalized Industries' EFLs) Winter Supp. Ests.		Spring Supp. Ests.	Public Expenditure			White Paper Main Estimates	
Treasury Committee	Autumn Statement Public Expenditure Quarterly Profile		Public Expenditure Quarterly Profile	Public Expenditure White Paper		Budget Borrowing Order	Public Expenditure Quarterly Profile		
				Borrowing Monthly Statements (throughout Session)					
PAC				Excess Votes					
				Appropriation Accounts (throughout Session)					

(continued)

187

Table 6.1—continued

	November	December	January *(Christmas Recess)*	February	March	April *(Easter Recess)*	May	June *(Whitsun Recess)*	July
Month:									
Consideration by Standing Committees		Taxes Management Bill (up to 16 days)						Finance Bill (3–4 days)	
Consideration by the House (excluding *formal* consideration of Estimates under the guillotines)	Taxes Management Bill (2nd Reading)		Estimates Day (possible) Autumn Statement and Nationalized Industries' EFLs (1–2 days)	Taxes Management Bill (Report) (2 days)	Estimates Day (possible) Public Expenditure Borrowing White Paper Order Budget (4 days)	Finance Bill (2nd Reading)	Finance Bill (certain clauses CWH) (2 days)	Finance Bill (Report) (2 days)	Estimates Days (possible) Long-term expenditure projects (possible)

Source: Select Committee on Procedure (Finance), H.C. 24, 1982/3, table B.

the renewal of parliament's deliberative role? It would be composed of two sub-systems: one primarily concerned with party and electoral politics; and one primarily concerned with interest group politics. The former sub-system would be dominated by political parties. Parties would remain the channel for mass mobilization of the electorate. Parties would continue to champion competing definitions of general interests. The largest party or party coalition would constitute the executive. The Prime Minister and the Cabinet would continue as the principal initiators of policy. The second sub-system would be concerned with parliamentarians and interest groups. It would be mediated by select committees. Multipartisan select committees would provide a context for interaction between the executive and the legislature as well as between the executive and interest groups. Contention that is now often concealed from public view would be brought into the open.

Reconciling these two sub-systems would require redefinition of the conventions which underwrite the present two-party structure. First, the confidence convention would need to be reformulated. The practice of the Callaghan government in its last years provides a precedent.[13] A government need not regard loss of a floor vote as tantamount to a loss of confidence. It would itself determine which matters are vital to its programme. It would itself determine when to treat a floor defeat as an issue of confidence. The opportunity would be available to minority parties or to individual members to move motions of dissent from current policies. Only if they (or the government) specifically proposed a confidence motion would the government's life be at stake.

Second, the conventions of ministerial responsibility and collective Cabinet responsibility would also be modified.[14] This would allow the convention of civil service independence from politics to be reworked.[15] This doctrine has served the cause of prudent government in the past. This convention allows departments to distinguish policy making into political and technical components regarding activities under the former head as the province of ministers and activities under the latter head as within their own purview. The fact that this distinction is often honoured as much in the breach as in the observance, does not alter its significance in the current scheme of things.[16] In a more plural system, civil servants would presumably be free to speak before committees about all matters not subject to national security or to immediate Cabinet or ministerial attention – in other words about all matters outside the government's projected programme. More importantly, they could also accept responsibilities to counsel ministers about the politics of policy making as it bears upon interest groups.

As a consequence of these developments there is likely to be a realignment of the role of the executive. More 'presidential' arrangements could be expected to emerge. Such a development has been anticipated by several former Cabinet ministers, notably Edmund Dell and David Owen.[17] Dell notes the problems caused for the present system by the dilution of the concept of ministerial responsibility: 'It is now a doctrine that a minister cannot be held blameworthy for those activities of his department of which he has no knowledge, however responsible he may be constitutionally.'[18] Dell also argues that government is ill-served by the doctrine of collective Cabinet responsibility. 'Who is responsible for what, if everyone is responsible for everything? What is collective responsibility? The truth is that its meaning is rather obscure. . . . It exerts too great a pressure to agree, to fudge issues, to find smooth formulae, to conceal what the real issues are.'[19]

Dell sees weakness at the centre of British politics. He sees the need to reinforce the power of the centre, particularly that of the Prime Minister and the Chancellor.

> What I am suggesting is rather more presidential and rather less prime-ministerial than is the theory of our constitution. The theory of our constitution – and the practice of cabinet government – disperses and even confuses responsibilities. What is needed is to focus responsibility much more clearly in all departments of government, but above all in respect of economic management and the control of public expenditure.[20]

Mrs Thatcher is reported to have been considering establishing a Prime Minister's Department in Britain. She is reported to have contemplated the appointment of a Chief of Staff with Cabinet rank. This individual would be responsible for translating her political priorities into action, tending the programme, and acting as general 'go-between' with ministers and officials.

Strengthening the role of central government, with individual ministers more dependent on the Prime Minister and with the latter having responsibility for defining the scope and purposes of the government, is consistent with the move to a more plural structure of policy making. Dell himself remarks on the need to match a more presidential executive with an enhanced capacity for multipartisanship in the House. 'If Parliament was a body with only a moderately strong inclination to consider issues on their merit, the risks of greater openness might be more readily accepted by Governments.' (p. 31)

A more plural British system would have different political 'tension' points and perhaps somewhat different political dynamics from the established American system. In the United States, the President and congressional committees work within distinct institutional settings. Cabinet officers have no independent political standing. Departments are relatively weak. They enjoy no pre-eminence in policy advice. There is no official Opposition to champion unorganized but national interests. Much longer term policy thinking takes place outside of government in the Washington 'think-tanks'.[21]

In Britain the situation would be reversed. Even in a more 'presidential' setting, British ministers would have independent political standing. Even with the further growth of think-tanks, British departments would have few rivals in policy-making experience or expertise. Ministers and select committee members would continue to sit together in the House of Commons. The

Opposition or minority parties would remain visible and influential champions for unorganized interests. Further, the influence of party in the US is modified by the different electoral timetables to which the Senate, the Presidency and the House work, and by the differing constituencies to which they are obligated. In the British case there would be less variation. Members of the executive and members of the select committees would sit together in the Commons. Both would work to the same electoral timetable. Government, Opposition and minority party members would continue to meet in separate party rooms. The executive and members of select committees would be dependent on common constituencies.

At Westminster, both ministers and select committees would have a common arena – the parliament – before which fundamental differences would be debated. The executive would be sensitive to the publicity that a select committee challenge would attract. Government members of select committees would need strong grounds to challenge their colleagues. Finally, the Opposition or minority parties would continue to champion the cause of large numbers of otherwise unorganized citizens adversely affected by government policies.

The foregoing summarizes some of the likely characteristics of a new system in practice. Our next task is to see if this system will work.

WILL A PLURAL SYSTEM WORK?

The need to look afresh at the political requirements for policy making arises from fragmentation of the political environment. A multi-party parliament would reflect the dissolution of encompassing general interests within the electorate. The congeries of interest groups clustered around each policy area reflect the widening role of government, the spread of participative impulses and of the arts of organization.[22] These developments frame the quest for a basis for common action. The policy-making task is twofold: first, to provide structures to permit the executive to gauge parliamentary reaction to its proposals; and second, to mobilize consent amongst the ubiquitous interest groups. Does the evidence gathered in earlier chapters suggest the select committees are capable of fulfilling these requirements?

Mobilizing parliamentary support

The select committees, in the period we have considered, have had very limited powers of political initiative. They have had guaranteed access to only three days of parliamentary time. They have operated in the 'culture' of the two-party system which denies an independent role to backbenchers. Indeed their early success led to a (predictable) effort by the whips to muzzle committees.[23] The evidence cannot therefore be expected to yield definitive conclusions. But it can be weighed against the requirements that select committees would need to satisfy if parliament's role in policy making were to be developed. The requirements are threefold. First, a select committee structure would be required to allow parliamentary intervention in key phases of policy making. Second, committees would need to be able to reach independent, timely, bipartisan judgements on contested issues. Third, committees would have to be able to stimulate the development of backbench, departmental and executive attitudes. The evidence gathered in earlier chapters supports the conclusion that select committees have demonstrated their effectiveness, albeit in varying degrees, in these three areas.

A comprehensive structure that has intervened in all cycles and phases of policy making has been crafted. There is evidence of successful committee intervention in each of the major current policy-making sub-systems – one concerning the budget process and the other concerning current government proposals. There is also strong evidence of effective committee intervention in each phase of these processes. In addition, committee reports provide strong evidence of the potential of the committees to add two new political capacities to policy making. First, an extended political capacity for fundamental scrutiny and review of programmes in a setting dominated by concern for the public interest. Second, a new capacity to lead departments, ministers and interest groups in the appraisal of emerging issues in the context of the public interest. In this latter role the work of select committees complements and augments that of political parties.

In these inquiries, the select committees have shown a capacity for independent and timely bipartisan judgement. The level of bipartisanship that has been achieved on the committees has been noted in preceding chapters. It is remarkably high in each band of inquiries. Nor can it be said that committees have avoided difficult issues. Further, as noted in earlier chapters, there is little evidence that committees have been 'captured' by their interest group 'clients' or that they have been advocates for increased public expenditure regardless of surrounding macro-economic considerations. The evidence suggests a contrary finding. The select committees have generally adhered to the common strategy of expenditure restraint championed differentially by the parties.

There is some evidence of the ability of committees to stimulate backbench, executive and departmental attitudes. This is the area where lack of formal powers most inhibits existing committees. There have been so few debates on specific committee reports (only six in the parliamentary session reviewed here), that the ability of committees to influence the judgement of the House has been little tested. Committee reports have been highlighted on the Notice Paper when relevant debates are scheduled. But these do not provide reasonable evidence since the terms of debate are set by the executive. Further, all the established habits and conventions inhibiting backbencher independence are at work on the Commons floor. This said, there are some very significant examples of committee work. The development of a parliamentary view on the powers of the Auditor General was stimulated by Treasury Committee and Public Accounts Committee inquiries. Clearly other considerations apart from these inquiries – and other actors apart from committee members – became involved as the issue unfolded. But the inquiries made two essential contributions. They provided a channel through which the evidence could be gathered, weighed and assembled into a comprehensive and documented case which was distributed to all members. They also provided a core group of convinced backbenchers who could in turn solicit the support of colleagues. Similar processes are evident in the unfolding of the 'SUS' issue and in the patriation of the Canadian Constitution, to cite two other equally significant examples.

Committee ability to influence the backbench and the executive is best attested in these episodes since they ended in floor debates and policy change. But capacity for more subtle forms of influence should be noted as pointers to committee potential. The nuclear power inquiry, the Wytch Farm Field sale price, the proposed Youth Training Programme, amongst numerous possible examples, all provide evidence of important modifications to the executive approach, introduced partly as a consequence of committee findings. In these cases committee influence arose from a variety of factors – the evidence committees marshalled, the unanimity and clarity of reports, the pressure members were able to apply privately over several parliamentary sessions as the issue unfolded. Committee capacity to mobilize and ventilate backbencher concerns in a constructive fashion is also evident in inquiries such as those staged by the Defence and Foreign Affairs Committees after the Falklands war or the Employment Committee's hearings on the executive decision to bar unions at GCHQ (in Mrs Thatcher's second term).

Further, not one but several committees exemplify in their total activity the capacity of committees to be energetic and consistent decision-making instruments. The Treasury Committee is most frequently cited. Its reports have been notable for their clarity and timeliness. The committee has pursued the logic of its own findings in its approach to subsequent inquiries, in its examination of witnesses and in its emphasis on issues in parallel inquiries. Earlier chapters showed equally enterprising and consistent approaches by the Education, Energy and Social Services Committees to cite only three examples.

It is harder to demonstrate positive impact on departments. The judgements cited earlier about the contribution of the Treasury Committee to the quality of economic appraisals in the Treasury are relevant. Civil servants are on record as welcoming, albeit cautiously, the opportunity to explain and defend their approaches in public. The quick response of some other departments to committee reports and the careful documenting by the civil service of the costs involved in responding to committee requests for information, suggest they have not been without impact. But the practices of the two-party system are so strong – and so alien from those that would prevail in a more plural system –

that the evidence available, positive though it is, calls for judicious assessment. That select committees can cover all phases and aspects of policy making and that they can produce agreed reports that are timely and well argued is beyond doubt. Their ability to contribute to the formation of a parliamentary view in a way that would complement effective policy making is clearly demonstrated in a few specific cases. That evidence is significant but as yet insufficient for strong general conclusions.

Mobilizing interest group consent

Evidence concerning the ability of select committees to provide a context for the mobilization of interest group consent also needs to be weighed in the light of the stage of development of the select committee system. As we saw in earlier chapters, outreach to interest groups has been extensive. Select committee inquiries have been effective in stimulating interest group attention to issues. Interest groups have learnt new information from inquiries. They value the access provided by select committees. They hold parliament in very high esteem. They value the fairness of the select committee process and they acknowledge the legitimacy of the committees. The survey of interest groups shows that committees, in stimulating interest group attention to issues, have stimulated interest group attention to each other. *Ad hoc* coalitions have been formed to press a case on particular issues. The survey shows that participation in select committee inquiries has become an important, if little understood, dimension of interest group interaction with government. Taken together the evidence on interest group impact is suggestive. But to properly gauge the potential of committees to provide a context for mobilizing interest group consent, the wider possibilities, tested by the inquiries only in a preliminary way, need to be weighed.

One model of one part of this process can be derived from Charles Lindblom.[24] In effect, Lindblom invites us to look to committees as catalysts for improved public choice. In a fragmented polity, this outcome might be expected from the pressures for accommodation amongst protagonists as they engage in a public search for collective values. Ideally the inquiry process opens the way for reformulation of an issue in more 'expansive' terms.[25] In this way the process wins the support of protagonists in bringing the public interest to light.

In practice agreement is likely to be insufficiently widespread to provide a basis for political action. Lindblom invites us to consider the variety of ways other than agreement in which a plural structure opens up possibilities for accommodation between participants. He explores the way in which open, accessible inquiry procedures encourage adjustment between partisans who differ in some basic values, or in their perception of some relevant facts, or both. In this process the politics of policy making receive priority.

In such a system, Lindblom invites us to note the variety of pressures that would stimulate participants to re-express their sectional concerns in terms of the public interest. In practice the engagement of interest groups would be facilitated by the select committees. Presentations to the select committees require interest groups to justify their sectional aspirations in terms of the public interest.[26] Knowledge of the departmental position and the possibility of overturning it, might be expected to stimulate effort to build a better case.[27] At present interest groups are often not privy to departmental thinking and they do not share the privileged access to political power that the two-party system provides to the civil service. Publication of departmental evidence before select committees means outside groups will be able to formulate their views in the context of departmental arguments. A select committee has the power and status to oblige a department to declare its hand. Interest groups will have vital information about the stage and direction of government thinking. Departmental arguments will provide a standard which interest groups will not generally be able to ignore. Departments have the analytic resources. They have a professional concern for the public interest. The publication of their case before a body with independent power might be expected to stimulate interest groups to research their own case more deeply and to work harder to demonstrate the validity of the interpretation of the public interest they favour.

Select committee inquiries might be expected to encourage interest groups to build contingent alliances with each other.[28] This too could be expected to moderate their approach. The best way for an interest group to demonstrate the moral and political force of its preferred values would be to show that the course of action it favours is widely shared. The attempt to build alliances with others means an interest group would pay more attention to re-expressing its sectional concerns in terms acceptable to potential allies.

This 'structural' pressure for agreement between groups builds in motives to find agreement. It discourages disclosure by any one group of its 'bedrock' social preferences or values.[29] Participants learn that conflict over 'bedrock' values need not be a barrier to settling differences. They recognize there is a range of ways in which their basic demands can be met.

In seeking alliances participants might cast appeals in terms of the criteria of others.[30] They might limit their own claims by becoming aware of others' retaliatory capacity. They may become aware of possibilities of agreement based on some other basis — for example compensation. They may decide that the opportunity to mount a later challenge as more evidence unfolds warrants acceptance of a current decision with which they disagree.

Additionally, within individual interest groups the pressure to build alliances constrains the scope of argument towards shared values.[31] It directs interest groups to frame their own positions in the context of values shared with other protagonists. Even zealous partisans might come to recognize the virtues of moderation through a process that provides so many apparent rewards for its skilful practice.

The impact of select committees on interest groups arises from the fact that the former are agents of parliament. The fact that select committees would have independent access to political initiative is critical. Policy making would be converted from a remote and monolithic apparatus, seemingly designed for large, irreversible decisions into a 'serial and remedial' process.[32] This makes policy making potentially more flexible and accessible.

A second – prudential – ground for looking to select committees as a context for mobilizing interest group consent arises from the likely impact of a more plural structure on the approach of ministers and the civil service.[33] Ministers and civil servants have a professional concern for the public interest. Their pre-eminent role – which would be maintained even in a more plural structure – means that these professional custodians of the public interest are likely to be most advantaged in practice. The select committees would moderate and qualify centralized and concentrated state power once embodied in the monarch and now institutionalized in the executive. In the process, the select committees could create new opportunities for the skilful deployment of central power. If select committees are to become agents with independent powers of political initiative, they could be expected to confront ministers and departments with the necessity of attending to interest group politics. Ministers and departments could be stimulated to adopt a variety of new approaches. They would be confronted with the need to manage interest group politics in a new context.

In seeking to build public support on any contested issue ministers and/or departments would be confronted with the necessity of publicly associating major interest groups with the government's stand. For example interest groups might issue press releases in support of ministers' proposals. They might carry favourable articles in their journals.[34] They might sponsor direct mail campaigns targeted to particular groups. They might mobilize their members to campaign for the government (e.g. leaflet distribution, joint advertising). Their representatives might appear on public platforms or on the media with ministers. They could give evidence favouring the government's approach to select committee inquiries. They might lobby members of other parties privately.

Equally, where opposition is spearheaded by a coalition of hostile interest groups ministers and/or departments would be 'induced' to recognize the merit of forging informal coalitions of interest groups to support their case. These outcomes would all require more attention by the civil service to the politics of policy making. They require projection of information about emerging issues to interest groups well in advance of a decision being required by government. They require advance negotiation of government proposals and their modification if unanticipated but relevant considerations come forward. They require development of a much deeper understanding of the process of opinion formation. Departments would need to interest themselves in this process both in relation to national opinion and amongst potentially friendly or hostile interest groups. Departments would need to monitor interest group views and be ready to counsel ministers on opportunities for networking, coalition building or other action necessary to the successful management of the politics of policy making.[35]

Select committee inquiries would be catalysts in the development of a successful capacity to conduct interest group politics amongst ministers and departments. Inquiries place on the public record the evidence of hostile groups. Inquiries provide an opportunity for advantaged groups and other advocates to be engaged. If interest groups do not come forward of their own accord, ministers or departments may want to take the initiative in having 'friendly' groups called to give evidence. Inquiries provide an opportunity for departments and ministers to assess the terms on which interest groups might be persuaded to switch camps. There is abundant American evidence of the apparently disparate coalitions that can be assembled to support proposed reforms.[36] Because evidence sessions would be conducted before final decisions are taken by the government, final choices would be made with adequate information about likely interest group reactions. Because the select committees would be composed of members from the various parties, the government would have an opportunity to assess the likely position of these parties. All this information is invaluable if political decisions are to be taken which are sensitive to the politics of policy making. Select committees have demonstrated the capacity to aid ministers in all these tasks.[37]

In sum, an independent political structure to deal with interest groups would draw such groups into a different phase of debate – political debate. At best, such a structure offers to draw interest groups into deeper reflection about the connection between their sectional aspirations and the public interest. At the least, interest groups would be exposed to a new range of influences and a new range of pressures. In the process ministers and departments would be exposed to a variety of new influences. They would be provided with a range of new opportunities to give leadership in policy making. These consequences would arise from the existence of machinery through which interest group claims could be made and prosecuted and through which government could be called to justify proposed policy initiatives in detail and in public. This machinery would exist in a political context. Ministers would remain pre-eminent. But select committees would share the power of political initiative now concentrated in their hands.

The foregoing analysis suggests the grounds for looking to a plural structure to better mobilize interest group consent. The risks too must be acknowledged. The danger in a more plural structure is that fragmentation now manifest at the sub-political level would simply be transferred to the political level. This process would be accompanied by a diminution in the formal powers of the central authorities. Government would thus, perversely, be even less equipped to assert its authority than at present. Some appraisals of American developments point to these hazards.[38] The most recent evidence points strongly in the opposite direction.[39] The separation of powers in the United States means that its experience must be used cautiously as a harbinger for likely British outcomes. There is, nevertheless, no gainsaying that a more interdependent polity, with the electoral monopoly of the major parties ended and with more interest groups claiming the right to participate in policy making, complicates the policy-making task.

It complicates it in the sense that the authority of existing office holders is more qualified and compromised. It complicates it in a second sense: the range of values competing for incorporation in the public interest − and the range of issues competing for a place on the public agenda − is potentially expanded. More interdependence in a society with a high valuation of equality is an explosive mix. More equality creates more opportunities for more widespread disagreement. Interdependence creates the power to prosecute that disagreement. A multi-party parliament institutionalizes these possibilities. A prudent liberal, Frank Knight, observes: 'One primary function of social institutions is to prevent the raising of [insoluble problems].'[40] Whether a plural system would breach this principle − or renew it in a manner appropriate to the fragmentation of contemporary society − remains an open question.

A multi-party parliament would bring policy making into closer and more complex relationships with public opinion. Public opinion would play a more immediate and more intricate role in policy making. Some may doubt the prudence of public opinion. Some may judge that the potential for politicization of a range of economic and social decisions − now distanced from the public agenda − is unacceptable. The present collectivist system differs from the more plural system that has been considered here in two fundamental respects. First, formal powers of political initiative would be more dispersed. Second, the range of organizations recognized as legitimate political champions of citizen interests would be increased. There is no doubt that the *formal* powers of the central authorities are stronger in the present party system than they would be in a more plural system. The issue at stake is: would the *effective* power of the central authorities be strengthened in a more plural policy-making system?[41]

Perhaps ministers and departments will give ground on some issues. Perhaps interest groups will be willing to accept a contrary outcome on the basis of their respect for parliament. Perhaps they will give way in the face of public opinion mobilized by ministers and their interest group allies. Perhaps they will accept a contrary decision because they accept the fairness of a 'serial and remedial' process or because they see the opportunity to renew their case on another occasion, or for some other reason (e.g. compensation), or for some combination of reasons. These must remain possibilities. The system we have examined is insufficiently developed for these possibilities to be clearly vindicated empirically.

THE OUTLOOK FOR REFORM

Past sections have reviewed a detailed blueprint for a more plural policy-making structure and weighed its potential to overcome immobilism in policy making. In this final section I want to assess the likelihood of a plural reconstruction actually occurring. First, alternatives to the development of a more plural policy-making structure will be considered, then the political outlook will be weighed.

Alternatives to a plural policy-making structure

The renewal of parliament's deliberative role is only one possibility in the development of policy-making structures. There are three major alternatives. The first alternative, currently being pursued by Mrs Thatcher's government, involves a reassertion of centralism.[42] There is no reason, in principle, in a multi-party parliament, for the executive not to try to conduct its affairs according to practices carried forward from the two-party system. Mrs Thatcher's current efforts provide evidence for judging how well this would work. In most domestic policy areas – local government, education, transport, health – Mrs Thatcher's government has abandoned moves towards decentralized power. In the pursuit of efficiency and expenditure control, she has moved to reassert the authority of central government. Early in 1984 the government obtained 'rate capping' legislation (in the face of substantial Tory opposition) which allows environment ministers to intervene directly with local authorities judged by central government to be 'over-spenders'. A number of metropolitan authorities have been abolished – including the GLC. Some former GLC responsibilities – for example relating to London Transport – have been restored to central departments. Similarly in education, the government proposes to provide some funds as 'earmarked grants' direct to local authorities rather than through the general rate support grant. DES proposes to intervene on curriculum matters. Some education responsibilities have been transferred to the MSC. The government has appointed an executive responsible for the Health Service. It seeks by this means to assert central control against regional authorities and to try to limit consultant prerogatives. The cash management system is being developed through the financial management initiative, one consequence of which will be expanded Treasury influence over departmental spending and programme planning. Finally, advisers closely associated with the Prime Minister are on record arguing the merits of a Prime Minister's Department to strengthen central influence.[43]

These moves aim to eliminate opposition to central directives. Mrs Thatcher will deploy her own formidable determination, her ministers, and the capacity of the civil service to attain her objectives. Such efforts in the past have been thwarted by interest group power. They have also been thwarted by the intellectual incapacity of central government to formulate adequate system-wide policies. This bodes ill for the present attempt.[44] But centralism is historically deeply rooted. Its durability and familiarity means it cannot be discounted. Nevertheless a multi-party parliament compounds the difficulties that would confront a centralist approach. In such a context, a centralist approach could be expected to foment contention. The pursuit of electoral advantage, operating without any modifying influences, could be expected to produce this result. An institutional basis to regularize negotiation and power-sharing between the parties seems essential to avoid this outcome.

The second option deals with interest group integration but not intra-parliamentary negotiations. This is the approach of the left 'Campaign Group' of Labour MPs. The Campaign Group conceives political parties continuing as the leading element in shaping public opinion. Under the radical version of this strategy, party not parliament would become the principal element modifying ministerial power.[45] The independent legitimacy of interest groups other than trade unions would not be accepted or recognized. The Campaign Group concedes a legitimate role only to the trade unions as the industrial wing of the working class. The Campaign Group envisages party committees being appointed. These would function as a 'departmental cabinet' advising ministers and reviewing departmental proposals. These committees would also be responsible for liaison with outside groups, particularly the trade unions. Indeed the Campaign Group's pamphlet on constitutional reform envisages individual trade unions appointing liaison officers to deal with these intra-parliamentary committees.

Participation within the Labour Party would be strengthened by requiring annual elections to Cabinet (and the Shadow Cabinet) by the conference electoral college. The Campaign Group envisages the parliamentary Labour Party acquiring a right of advance consultation on all proposed Cabinet and Shadow Cabinet decisions. The votes of PLP members on these matters would be recorded and available to their constituency Labour parties at pre-selection. The PLP would also be involved in development of the manifesto. The Campaign Group would withdraw remaining prime ministerial prerogatives concerning the timing of elections. It would end prime ministerial patronage by making all public appointments subject to party and parliamentary approval. It proposes four-year parliaments, abolition of the House of Lords, and a strong Freedom of Information Act. These proposals envisage a radical extension of participation, but within the bounds of party. This approach to participation assumes that the economic classes remain pre-eminent in determining political attachments and political identity. Unlike liberal approaches, this analysis fails to recognize interest groups as legitimate political actors or independent protagonists in determining the public interest. Further, it does not begin to address the practical problems of government in a multi-party house.

The third approach involves an extended role for parties in the integration of interest groups and the development of corporatist arrangements to consolidate interest group integration. This is the practice in some European countries which are seen to have achieved more successful interest group integration than the UK. For example, the late John Mackintosh proposed turning the House of Lords into an Economic and Social Council on the Dutch model.[46]

There is scope for extending consultative arrangements and for developing the consultative apparatus in Britain. The agenda of issues subject to tripartite negotiation could be widened. Philippe Schmitter classifies Britain as medium/weak in the present degree of its corporatism.[47] More formal arrangements to determine income shares would be the keystone of a reassertion of corporatism. The Austrian Joint Commission on Wages and Prices is a model of the kind of institutional apparatus that could be created. At the same time the rights and obligations of participating organizations might be more clearly spelt out in law. Austria, Sweden and Holland all provide examples of this development.

Paralleling these moves, the symbiosis between interest organizations and the party system could be developed. In Austria, for example, interest group leaders frequently enter parliament under the aegis of one or another of the parties. Institutional co-ordination between interest groups and policy makers could be widened. There is no British equivalent of the Dutch Economic and Social Council.

In step with this development of institutional arrangements the consultative agenda might also be widened. European experience suggests a corporatist apparatus can lead to pressure for interest group (particularly union) involvement not only in tripartite determination of wages and working conditions but also in fiscal matters, welfare and social policy, and investment and plant closure decisions.[48]

There are three principal differences between the development of a plural political structure and this corporatist approach. First the former structure offers access to many interests not just those designated by government. It does not try to constrain, through legislation or in any other way, the number of organizations with access to the process. On the contrary, multiple participants are essential. Their public interaction, through the process Lindblom describes as partisan mutual adjustment, can be expected to moderate their behaviour and in the process advance the public interest.

Second, a policy-making role for select committees obliges departments and ministers to treat with interest groups publicly. This could be expected to act as a 'forcing device' stimulating the former to engage in the tactics required for the successful management of interest group politics. In a corporatist apparatus interest-group/department interactions would continue to be private and distanced from final decision making. Departments and ministers lack any incentive to accord interest groups political status and to treat with them as with other political entities. There is considerable evidence that these private arrangements have been successfully exploited by interest groups in the past to pursue their sectional aspirations at the expense of the public interest and to thwart unwanted policy proposals.[49]

Finally, the corporatist model takes for granted what is at stake when interest groups are granted access to the political aspects of policy making. A more plural policy structure, based on select committees, admits interest groups to a direct role in determining the public interest. It attaches prime importance to the determination of this value. It makes this determination visible and public. By contrast, the corporatist model presumes common interests can be best determined 'synoptically', to follow Lindblom's phrase. Reinforced by cultural norms favouring hierarchy and respect for state power, corporatism looks to central outcomes and peak groups to define general interests and impose this determination on their members. Where such restraining cultural norms erode, the practical no less than the intellectual difficulties in a 'synoptic' approach become manifest. The erosion of collectivist attachments – implicit in Beer's analysis of the fragmentation that has accompanied the rise of interest group power, and Särlvik and Crewe's analysis of party decomposition[50] – suggests the great difficulties that might be expected to accompany further development of a corporatist approach in Britain. Even if interest group consent could be mobilized through corporatist approaches, the problem of regularizing negotiation and power sharing between the parties would remain. One conceivable arrangement would be for minority parties to join in a majority coalition which would seek to manage interest groups through an extension of corporatist arrangements. The evidence already adduced on tripartism, suggests the difficulties that would be associated with this approach. But it would involve a less sharp break from present assumptions and practices. This option might not work, but it is perhaps likely to have most immediate appeal.

The political outlook

With the partial exception of Dr David Owen, the rationale for and possible form of a role for parliamentary select committees in buttressing the executive and in providing a context for the integration of interest groups, has not been articulated by political leaders, by parliamentarians or by those bodies – principally think-tanks – most immediately involved in proposing policy reforms. What has been articulated – indeed what has become widely accepted – is a rationale for parliamentary reform based on recovery of parliament's historic role in the supply process. In practice this focuses parliamentarians on scrutiny of government policy proposals, programmes, and expenditure. Key protagonists have determined that an effective role for parliament in these areas requires that select committees have the power to challenge the executive. Support for this view is however still confined to a relatively small group of backbench MPs.

The notion that select committees might contribute essential additional capacities to the politics of policy making is not widely recognized. Dr Owen is the only influential protagonist for the view that select committees should have an enlarged role in policy making. But he has not specifically linked this to their potential to be the catalysts for reconciling interest groups with policy making in ways that serve the public interest. Nor has he publicly endorsed a select committee structure as a way of institutionalizing power sharing in a multi-party parliament. Protagonists for a two-stage budget process have argued for more public discussion. They have not based their case on the primacy of the need to integrate interest groups. They have not identified the failure to mobilize consent as the central challenge to statecraft. Their arguments do not reflect a grasp of the possibilities and conditions for improved 'partisan mutual adjustment'. They have not urged the merit of structures which would position ministers and departments to better manage interest group politics. Nor have they advocated a two-stage budget as a way of conducting multi-party politics.

A formidable array of antagonists might be expected to resist reform in the direction of more plural policy-making arrangements. The strength of the centralist tendency cannot be overestimated. Perhaps the strongest continuing strand in Tory belief concerns the necessity to maintain effective central authority. To see more dispersal of the power of political initiative as the best buttress of effective central authority requires a considerable imaginative leap. This leap could be expected to be particularly difficult for individuals conditioned over a lifetime to value symbols celebrating concentrated power. Long years in government and opposition will have reinforced these attachments.

In the Labour Party an attachment to concentrated power is fortified by class allegiance. Marxist analysis sustains the class focus of the contemporary left. Many contemporary Marxists do not question the pre-eminence of party. Both the Tory concern for strong central authority and the Labour concern for class solidarity are hostile to plural policy-making approaches. Both groups will rightly see in such a development a fundamental limitation upon the power of the centre. Just such a limitation is a traditional concern of liberalism.

At a practical level, the attitude of the Tory Party in the late 1970s to parliamentary reform reflected the commitment of Mrs Thatcher's first Leader of the House, Norman St John Stevas. None of his successors share his commitment. Mrs Thatcher is not herself sympathetic to parliamentary reform.[51] Perhaps she has been too long a minister. No other leading Tories are explicitly sympathetic.

The Labour Party leadership has been preoccupied with policies and party structures, but not with policy-making structures.[52] There is no sign that Neil Kinnock plans to reverse these preoccupations. The major reformist impulses influencing the Labour Party propose reduced ministerial and departmental prerogatives through an enlarged role for the party rather than for parliament.

None of the major think-tanks or research groups has addressed the issue of the relationship between the policy-making structure, a multi-party parliament and the management of interest group politics.[53] We have seen the role played by the Study of Parliament Group in stimulating the first phase of parliamentary reform. This group has been less active in exploring the rationale for continuing procedural reform. This means there is no research group actively investigating the case for extended select committee powers or seeking to project these possibilities on to the political agenda. At the very least some intellectual protagonists need to emerge before this development has the chance of going further.

The magnitude of the change involved in moving towards independent powers of political initiative for select committees points to the difficulty such a development is likely to encounter. Ministerial and public service prerogatives would be substantially modified. The approach of ministers and departments to policy making would need to be recast. A political system to handle interest group politics would oblige ministers to attend to a new range of tasks. The approach of departments would become more visible, and more subject to informed (and uninformed) criticism. The present system marshals the ambitions of those aspiring to political power and regulates their interaction. Those who see their ambitions well served by the present structure of power might be expected to resist change most.

The foregoing considerations create numerous defenders of the present structure. But perhaps the most implacable defence lies in established habits and attitudes – the practised and proven ways of doing things. This is the defence voiced by a senior Treasury officer in his evidence during the Budget Inquiry: 'The whole concept of open government, consultation, is very much a thing of our time. It may be . . . there is a correlation between increasing failure of things to happen and open government. It may not be a very fashionable thing for ministers to say they think they can perhaps take decisions best by themselves.'[54]

On the other hand there are a number of forces, at various levels of the political system, likely to favour reform. A blueprint exists at the parliamentary level. This is being advocated by a determined group of backbench reformers.[55] These reformers come from both major parties and the Liberals. The government has rejected all the proposed changes to financial procedures. But through the new estimates days procedure, committees have the opportunity to keep their proposals before ministers, departments and their fellow parliamentarians. They have already taken steps in this direction. Their inquiries indicate a continuing willingness to tackle politically sensitive subjects.[56] This will keep the work of the committees in the public eye.

Apart from parliament the SDP is, as we have seen, most committed to a programme of reform of policy making. Dr David Owen has committed himself to an enlarged role for parliament in policy making. As we saw in the first chapter he envisages committees playing a key role. But he has not specifically identified the need for a political structure to deal with interest groups. The possible reconstruction reviewed here is consistent with Alliance policies and dispositions. Indeed, in its effects on access, information sharing, accountability and participation, a plural policy-making structure is the logical summation of Alliance policies and dispositions. But the Alliance has yet to see this possibility with clarity and in its full implications. Nevertheless, in the immediate future, the prospects for change in the policy-making structure would seem to be bound up with the fate of the Alliance. An essential precondition for the reconstruction reviewed here seems to be a multi-party parliament. Only that context seems likely to provide the political momentum necessary for such fundamental constitutional change. In addressing the practical problems of reconciling a minority executive to a parliamentary majority, the potential role of committees is bound to come into focus.

At its broadest, the argument for reconstruction of the policy-making system draws on the liberal vision of modernity. According to this view, modern egalitarian society is built on, and propelled by, two principles which are inherently in tension − rationalism and voluntarism. Rationalism values technology and scientific enquiry and embodies the promise to conquer nature for man's benefit (or at least for his distraction). Voluntarism values widespread participation in political life and embodies the democratic promise to found authority on consent − perhaps even to advance individual moral development through political engagement. The technocratic impulse created the post-war welfare state and managed economy. It underwrites and legitimizes corporatism. In the creation of the post-war state in Britain, the voluntarist impulse was contained and moderated by the dominant 'cultures' of class solidarity and deference. During the 1960s, these 'cultures' were challenged and gravely damaged. On this analysis, the task now is to devise participatory arrangements, building on the promise of voluntarism, which can harness popular support to larger national interests and needs.

Whether parliamentary select committees suggest a way of meeting this need is the issue considered in earlier chapters. As already indicated, the results so far suggest that the full potential of select committees is yet to be tested. There are indicators that point to their capacity to mobilize consent. There are promising indicators of their potential to contribute to the restoration of political authority. A role for select committees as catalysts in the integration of interest groups draws on liberal doctrine about the structure of regimes and about the role of interest groups. Liberalism, broadly understood, is the principal resurgent current in contemporary politics.[57] Whether it has the power to break through traditional Tory centralism or traditional Socialist collectivism remains to be seen.

I conclude with a cautious assessment of the prospects for political reconstruction. The necessity, perhaps even the desirability, of such a development is clear.[58] Parliament has already moved some distance down this path. However, the decisive constitutional issue, giving committees access to the voting power of the House as a right, remains to be confronted. For this to occur a fragmented House would seem to be prerequisite.[59] Liberalism, whose highest promise is the recovery of political authority through the development of citizenship to a new level of actualization, may be the strongest, but is by no means the only, system of political morality competing for the allegiance of the partisans. Other currents to the left and right of liberalism are surging through British political life. The present study of the development of a plural policy-making structure shows that amongst decisive participants critical decisions have still to be confronted. Political leaders still need to come to terms with the logic of present tendencies. A liberal reconstruction is clearly in prospect. A number of decisive steps, not least a growth in consciousness – a conviction of promise and possibility – will be necessary to bring this about.

Appendix 1.1

Green Papers and Consultation Papers produced by the Departments of Health and Social Security, Education and Science, and the Environment 1979–1983

Health and Welfare

Structure and Management of NHS

Income during Initial Sickness

Industrial Injuries and Compensation

Future Pattern of Hospital Provisions in England and Wales

Self-Employed and National Insurance

Maternity Benefits

Strategy for Social Security Operations

Patients' Money in Long Stay Hospitals

Community Health Councils

Compensating Employers for Statutory Sick Pay

Care in the Community

Registration under Residential Homes Act

Death Grant

Education

View of the Curriculum

Framework for School Curriculum

Examinations 16–18

Postgraduate Certificate of Education in the Public Sector

Higher Education in England Outside the Universities

Review of the Schools Council

Science Education

Teacher Training

Foreign Languages in the School Curriculum

Local Government

Streamlining the Cities

Local Authority Direct Labour

Publication of Financial Information by Local Authorities

Urban Development Corporation

Local Authority Housing Subsidy Scheme

Transfer of GLC Housing

Planning Appeal System

Proposals for an Audit Commission

Source: List supplied by Office of Public Information, House of Commons.

Appendix 1.2

Green Papers involving additional regulations 1979–1983

Health and Safety Executive

Manmade Mineral Fibres

Work with Asbestos

First Aid at Work

Dangerous Pathogens

Homeworkers

Amendments to Scheduled Works and Noxious Gases

Consumer Goods Containing Radio-Active Substances

Poisonous Substances

Petroleum Spirit Licences

Notification of New Substances

Petroleum Spirit Regulators

Asbestos Insulation and Coating

Protection of Hearing at Work

Manual Handling of Loads

Dangerous Substances Road Conveyance

Other departments and agencies

Building Controls

Regulation of Private Security Industry

Fire Hazards in Furniture

Lorries, People and the Environment

Conservation and the Countryside

Lotteries and Amusement Act Regulations

Tenants Charter

Commuters Charter

Welfare of Cattle

Elimination of Sex Discrimination (EOC)

Preserves Regulations

Motorcycle Driving Test

Safety at Sea

MSC New Training Initiative

Disclosure of Interests and Shares

Carriage of Passengers in Wheelchairs on Public Sector Vehicles

Employment of Disabled

Welfare of Ducks

Welfare of Rabbits

Poultry at Time of Slaughter

Facilities Shared by Cyclists and Pedestrians

Selling by Telephone

Source: List supplied by Office of Public Information, House of Commons.

Appendix 1.3

Government agencies producing Green Papers 1979–1983

Office of Fair Trading

Countryside Review Committee

Manpower Services Commission

Health and Safety Executive

Supplementary Benefit Commission

Countryside Commission

National Radiological Protection Board

Law Commission

Farm Animal Welfare Council

Forestry Commission

Equal Opportunities Commission

Source: Information supplied by Office of Public Information, House of Commons.

Appendix 2

Witness reaction to participation in select committee inquiries

1 How did your organization learn of the inquiry? *(Please tick the appropriate box)*

through press advertisements   [   ]
by invitation from Select Committee   [   ]
through general reports or gossip   [   ]
other (please specify)

2 Did your organization gather information especially for the inquiry?

	Yes	*No*
	[ ]	[ ]

3 Was this information concerned with:

	Yes	*No*
the issue itself?	[ ]	[ ]
member attitudes?	[ ]	[ ]
both the issue and member attitudes?	[ ]	[ ]
other (please specify)		

4 In determining your organization's position, did you engage in some special non-routine, consultation process with all or some segment of your membership?

	Yes	*No*
	[ ]	[ ]

5 Would you please indicate the role (if any) of the following actions, and their relative importance, in your preparation for the inquiry.

	Very significant role	Significant role	Minor role	Not used
establish internal task force	[ ]	[ ]	[ ]	[ ]
circularize members/ member groups inviting their views	[ ]	[ ]	[ ]	[ ]
consult informally with selected members with special knowledge	[ ]	[ ]	[ ]	[ ]
use material already prepared for dept or other inquiry	[ ]	[ ]	[ ]	[ ]
draw on general knowledge of issue and member views of existing office bearers	[ ]	[ ]	[ ]	[ ]
discuss issue with other organizations	[ ]	[ ]	[ ]	[ ]
other (please specify)				

_____

_____

6 Did you prepare a written submission?

	Yes	No
	[ ]	[ ]

7 The following list indicates various outcomes that may have occurred as a result of attending the hearing – or of participation in the inquiry process in general. Would you please indicate which, if any, describe your organization's experience, and their relative importance.

	Very important outcome	Important outcome	Minor outcome	Not an outcome
We obtained new information about the issue itself	[ ]	[ ]	[ ]	[ ]
We obtained new information about government policy	[ ]	[ ]	[ ]	[ ]
We obtained new information about departmental attitudes/ judgements	[ ]	[ ]	[ ]	[ ]

	Very significant role	Significant role	Minor role	Not used
We obtained new information about the attitudes of other groups friendly to our position	[ ]	[ ]	[ ]	[ ]
We obtained new information about other interest groups hostile to our position	[ ]	[ ]	[ ]	[ ]
We formed new or strengthened links with other groups sharing our concern for the issue	[ ]	[ ]	[ ]	[ ]

Some other outcomes (please specify)

_____

_____

_____

_____

8 Would you please indicate the role (if any) of the following actions in reporting back to members on your participation in the inquiry and their relative importance.

	Very important role	Important role	Minor role	No role
Individual report to Committee meeting	[ ]	[ ]	[ ]	[ ]
Article in your house journal/ newsletter	[ ]	[ ]	[ ]	[ ]
Report to meetings of members	[ ]	[ ]	[ ]	[ ]

other (please specify)

_____

_____

9 Did you obtain a copy or a summary of the Select Committee report?

Yes   [ ]
No   [ ]

10 Did you take any of the following actions as a result of the Committee report? Please tick if the answer is 'Yes'.

Contact any members of the Committee or its staff [ ]
Contact another MP [ ]
Contact a minister [ ]
Contact a department [ ]
Other (please specify) [ ]

11 Were the Select Committee findings publicized amongst your members?

Yes [ ]
No [ ]

12 If yes, would you please indicate the role, if any, of the following actions and their relative importance.

	Very important role	*Important role*	*Minor role*	*No role*
oral report to Committee	[ ]	[ ]	[ ]	[ ]
printed report in journal/ newsletter	[ ]	[ ]	[ ]	[ ]
some other form of oral report (please specify)	[ ]	[ ]	[ ]	[ ]
some other form of printed report (please specify)	[ ]	[ ]	[ ]	[ ]

13 Were the Select Committee findings generally favourable to your organization's position?

Yes [ ]
No [ ]

14 If they were unfavourable, would you please tick if you agree with one or more of the following statements.

The Select Committee findings were generally fair and reasonable [ ]

The Select Committee findings would be acceptable, if they could be enforced on all parties [ ]

The Select Committee findings would be acceptable, if we could reopen the issue as subsequent events demonstrated the error of the original decision [ ]

15 How would you assess the overall outcome of the Select Committee's inquiry and reporting process? Would you please answer the following questions about aspects of your experience.

	Very important outcome	Important outcome	Minor outcome	Not an outcome
Did your participation in the inquiry help to clarify your organization's position on this issue?	[ ]	[ ]	[ ]	[ ]
Did your experience of the inquiry:				
– harden your organization's position on this issue?	[ ]	[ ]	[ ]	[ ]
– soften your organization's position on this issue?	[ ]	[ ]	[ ]	[ ]
– not affect your organization's position on this issue?	[ ]	[ ]	[ ]	[ ]
Did your experience of the inquiry help develop your organization's attitudes towards other issues?	[ ]	[ ]	[ ]	[ ]
Would you say your participation had no effect on your attitude on this, or any other issue?	[ ]	[ ]	[ ]	[ ]

Some other outcome (please specify)

_____

_____

_____

16 How would you describe the worthwhile features of a Select Committee inquiry compared to other ways of determining public policy questions? Please check any of the following statements you agree with in terms of the indicated scale.

	Strongly agree	Agree	Indifferent	Disagree
The open and public form of a Select Committee inquiry makes it preferable to a departmental inquiry or some other more private approach to policy development	[ ]	[ ]	[ ]	[ ]

	Strongly agree	Agree	Indifferent	Disagree
Select Committees provide a fairer procedure for analysing public policy issues than a departmental procedure	[ ]	[ ]	[ ]	[ ]
Our organization learned more about a controversial issue through participating in the Select Committee inquiry than by making written responses to a government task force or Green Paper	[ ]	[ ]	[ ]	[ ]
Members of parliament are better qualified to judge the public interest on particular matters that ministers are too busy to handle personally, and that would otherwise be determined mostly by civil servants or advisory commissions	[ ]	[ ]	[ ]	[ ]
Some other statements about the good or bad aspects of the Select Committee procedure compared to other methods of investigating controversial or medium-term issues	[ ]	[ ]	[ ]	[ ]

_____

_____

_____

17 What would your attitude be to an extension of Select Committee powers? Please answer the following questions in terms of the indicated scale.

	Strongly agree	Agree	Indifferent	Disagree
Would you welcome Select Committees having a greater chance of influencing the political process?	[ ]	[ ]	[ ]	[ ]
Is their present role about right?	[ ]	[ ]	[ ]	[ ]
Do you think a parliamentary inquiry is a waste of time?	[ ]	[ ]	[ ]	[ ]

18 This questionnaire seeks to assess your experience of a Select Committee Inquiry, your attitude to the outcome of this inquiry, and to an extension of the role of Select Committees in general. If there are other points relevant to these matters not covered in earlier questions please indicate your views:

_____

_____

_____

_____

NAME OF RESPONDENT (for circulation of results only): _____

NAME OF ORGANIZATION: _____

ADDRESS: _____

_____ Postcode: _____

NUMBER OF MEMBERS: _____

INDIVIDUAL: _____ CORPORATE: _____

DO YOU PUBLISH A NEWSLETTER/JOURNAL?   Yes [   ]   No [   ]

Appendix 3

Interest groups interviewed or completing formal questionnaire

Advisory Commissions	Members	Journal/ Newsletter
National Consumer Council		x
National Water Council	10 water authorities	x
Commission for Local Administration in England		x
Schools Council for Curriculum and Exams		x
Welsh Consumer Council		x
Post Office Users National Council	19	
Museums and Galleries Commission	14	x
Scottish Community Educational Council	20 members	x
Transport Users Consultative Committee	16 members	
Council for Museums and Galleries in Scotland	150 corp.	

Producer Groups and Individual Firms	Members	Newsletter
British Steel		x
Chemical Industries Association	30 corp. members	x
Abbey National Building Society		x
Unilever PLC		
British Paper and Board Industries Federation	50 corp. members	x
UK Atomic Energy Authority		x
Edinburgh Chamber of Commerce	1,137 corp. members	x
Committee of London Clearing Banks	6 corp. members	
Cadogan Estates		x
Wales TUC	650,000	x
TGWU	1.8 million	x
British Actors Equity	31,000	x
J. Sainsbury	50,000 employees	x
Transport Salaried Staffs Association	58,881	x
Scottish Landowners Federation	4,500	x

Producer Groups and Individual Firms	Members	Newsletter
Britoil	2,800 employees	x
Society of Pensions Consultants	134 corp. members	x
Brewers Society	87 corp. members	x
National Farmers Union	110,000	x
Tobacco Advisory Council	10 corp. members	
National Coal Board		
Freight Transport Association	14,000	x
Wine and Spirit Association	1,000	x
Electronic Engineers Association	50 corp. members	
Building Societies Association	173 corp. members	x
General Electric Company		
Society of British Aerospace Companies	312 corp. members	x
Iron and Steel Trades Federation	100,000	x
Society of West End Theatres		
Gin Rectifier and Distillers Association	15	x
Chartered Institute of Building Surveyors	11,000	x
Sand and Gravel Association		
H. Sallinger and Company		
Rating and Valuation Association	5,000	x
National Federation of Self-Employed	45,000	x
British Gas		
Federation of Shipbuilding and Engineering Unions	2.4 million	x
British Property Federation		
British Shipbuilders	62,500 employees	x
Lloyds Bank Ltd		x
British Veterinary Association	8,000	x
Country Landowners Association	50,000	x
Leatherhead Foods RA		
Glass and Glazing Federation	360 members	x
Timbers Growers UK	3,500 members	x
Ford Motor Company		
Managerial, Professional and Staff Liaison Groups		
TUC		
CBI		

Service Groups	Members	Journal
Royal Academy of Arts	30,000 friends	x
Association of Directors of Social Security	200	x
City and Guilds Institute of London		x
Institute of Professional Civil Servants	87,000	x
National Association of Careers and Guidance Teachers	1,000	x
British Post-Graduate Medical Federation		x
University of Stirling		x

Service Groups	Members	Journal
British Medical Association	75,000	x
Geographical Association	7,000	x
Language Teaching Centre, York	10	x
British Film Institute	400	x
British Museum		
Modern Languages Association	2,500 200 corp.	x
University of London		
Brunel University		
Association of Anaesthetists	4,800	x
Chartered Institute of Finance and Accountancy	9,000	x
Association of Teachers of Russian	550 ind. 150 corp.	x
Police Superintendents Association	2,500	x
Institute of Rent Officers		
Royal College of Psychiatry	6,700	x
Royal College of Radiologists	2,000	x
Royal Shakespeare Theatre		x
Traverse Theatre Club	2,400	x
English National Opera		

Local/Regional Government	Members	Journal
London Borough of Hillingdon		
City of Birmingham		
Essex County Council		
Kyle and Carrick District Council		
Torfaen Borough Council		
Association of District Councils	333	x
London Borough of Southwark		
London Borough of Hounslow		
Association of County Councils	44 member councils (30 million pop.)	x
Association of Metropolitan Authorities		

Rights/Service/Environment Advocacy Groups	Members	Journal
Law Centres Federation	46 corp. members	x
Help the Aged	400 branches	x
National Union of Students	1,200,000	
Society for Co-operative Dwellings		
Joint Council for Welfare of Immigrants	350 corp.	x
Pedestrians Association	740 ind. 60 corp.	x
Royal British Legion	530,000 219,000 (assoc.)	x

Rights/Service/Environment Advocacy Groups	Members	Journal
Greater London Tenants Association	600 ind. 300 corp.	x
Paddington Federation of Tenants and Residents Association	60 groups (i.e. 1,500 ind.)	x
National Secular Society	20 affiliated groups (400 + members)	x
National Association Community Relations Council		x
Christian Education Movement	8,500	x
UK Council on Overseas Student Affairs	419 corp. members 100 ind./50 corp. assoc.	x
Medical Women's Federation	2,200	x
Justice		
National Federation of Old Age Pensioner Associations		
Age Concern	2,300 local groups (approx. 120,000 inds.)	x
London Transport Passenger Committee	30 cttees	
Railway Development Society	1,000	x
Mail Users Association	150 corp. members	x
Society for General Microbiology	3,400	x

Advocacy Groups	Members	Journal
Centre for World Development Education		
Oxfam	330,000 groups 600 staff	x
Catholic Housing Aid Society	20 corp. members	
Voluntary Service Overseas		
SHAC		x
Council for the Protection of Rural England	30,000	x
Ecology Party	6,000	x
Association for the Conservation of Energy	16 corp. members	x

Other	Members	Journal
Salvation Army	2,500	x
Free Church Federal Council		x
General Synod Board of Education	21 members Synod 650	x

Think-Tanks/Research Centres	Members	Journal
Department of Applied Economics, Cambridge	9	
North East London Polytechnic		
Fulmer Research Institute		x

Think-Tanks/Research Centres	Members	Journal
West India Committee	2,500 ind.	x
	1,500 corp.	
Institute for Fiscal Studies		
Adam Smith Institute		
Centre for Policy Studies		

Appendix 4

Question one

Response possible	Tick	No tick
Q1A Advertisement	6 (4.7%)	121 (95.3%)
Q1B Invitation	104 (81.9%)	23 (18.1%)
Q1C Gossip	26 (20.5%)	101 (79.5%)
Q1D Other	5 (3.9%)	119 (96.1%)

Question two

Response possible	Yes	No	No answer
Q2 Special information	81 (63.8%)	42 (33.1%)	4 (3.1%)

Question three

Response possible	Yes	No	No answer
Q3A Issue itself	57 (44.9%)	2 (1.6%)	68 (53.5%)
Q3B Attitudes of members	15 (11.8%)	15 (11.8%)	97 (76.4%)
Q3C Both	42 (33.1%)	11 (8.7%)	74 (58.2%)

Question four

Response possible	Yes	No	No answer
Q4 Consultation process	61 (48.0%)	61 (48.0%)	5 (3.9%)

Question five

109 organizations (87.2% of total respondents) responded 'Very Significant Role' or 'Significant Role' to subsections A, B, C or F in question five.

Response possible	No answer	Very significant role	Significant role	Minor role	Not used
Q5A Task force	16 (12.6%)	23 (18.5%)	21 (16.5%)	15 (11.8%)	52 (40.6%)
Q5B Invite views	20 (15.9%)	8 (6.5%)	33 (26.0%)	17 (13.6%)	49 (38.0%)
Q5C Spec. knowlge	6 (4.7%)	37 (28.3%)	57 (44.5%)	23 (12.6%)	11 (8.7%)
Q5D Old info. used	8 (6.3%)	31 (24.4%)	54 (42.5%)	23 (18.1%)	11 (8.7%)
Q5E Gen. knowlge	4 (3.1%)	58 (45.7%)	49 (38.6%)	9 (7.1%)	7 (5.5%)
Q5F Other orgs	16 (12.6%)	4 (3.1%)	22 (12.3%)	38 (29.9%)	47 (37.1%)

Question six

Response possible	Yes	No	No answer
Q6 Written submission	117 (91.9%)	7 (5.6%)	3 (2.4%)

Question seven

70 organizations (55% of total respondents) reported a 'Very Important outcome' or 'Important outcome' to at least one of the sub-questions in question 7.

Response possible	No answer	Very important outcome	Important outcome	Minor outcome	Not an outcome
Q7A New info.	14 (11.0%)	8 (6.3%)	19 (15.0%)	41 (32.3%)	45 (35.4%)
Q7B Gov. policy	14 (11.0%)	9 (7.1%)	16 (12.6%)	28 (22.0%)	60 (47.3%)
Q7C Dept attds	11 (8.7%)	8 (6.3%)	28 (22.0%)	29 (22.8%)	51 (40.2%)
Q7D Attd others	11 (8.7%)	7 (5.5%)	25 (19.7%)	51 (40.1%)	33 (26.0%)
Q7E New info.	14 (11.0%)	5 (3.9%)	22 (17.3%)	42 (33.1%)	44 (34.7%)
Q7F New links	16 (12.7%)	5 (3.9%)	10 (7.9%)	36 (28.3%)	60 (47.2%)

Question eight

Response possible	No answer	Very important role	Important role	Minor role	No role
Q8A Indiv.	14 (11.0%)	36 (28.3%)	47 (37.1%)	15 (11.8%)	15 (11.8%)
Q8B Article	20 (15.7%)	16 (12.6%)	38 (30.0%)	17 (13.4%)	36 (28.3%)
Q8C Meetings	15 (11.8%)	15 (11.8%)	35 (27.6%)	23 (18.1%)	39 (30.7%)

Question nine

Response possible	Yes	No	No answer
Q9 Copy of committee report	123 (97.6%)	3 (2.4%)	1 (0.8%)

Question ten

81 organizations (64% of total respondents) responded positively, i.e. ticked at least one sub-question in response to question 10.

Response possible	Yes	No	No answer
Contact action taken			
Q10A Member staff	44 (37.0%)	76 (59.8%)	4 (3.2%)
Q10B Printed report	36 (28.3%)	87 (68.5%)	4 (3.2%)
Q10C Minister	41 (32.3%)	82 (64.6%)	4 (3.2%)
Q10D Department	48 (37.8%)	75 (59.1%)	4 (3.2%)
Q10E Other	8 (6.3%)	115 (90.6%)	4 (3.2%)

Question eleven

Response possible	Yes	No	No answer
Q11 Findings publicized	96 (75.6%)	21 (16.5%)	10 (7.9%)

Question twelve

This question only completed if 'YES' answered to question 11.

Response possible	Very important role	Important role	Minor role	No role
Q12A Oral report	30 (37.0%)	36 (44.4%)	12 (14.8%)	3 (3.7%)
Q12B Printed report	12 (15.4%)	39 (50.0%)	12 (15.4%)	15 (19.2%)
Q12C Other oral form	5 (14.7%)	2 (5.9%)	4 (11.8%)	23 (67.6%)
Q12D Other printed report	8 (22.2%)	9 (25.0%)	3 (8.3%)	16 (44.5%)

Question thirteen

Response possible	Yes	No	No answer
Q13 Favourable findings?	90 (70.9%)	26 (20.5%)	11 (8.7%)

Question fourteen

Responses were only analysed if respondent answered 'NO' to question 13.

Response possible	Yes	No
Q14A Fair/reasonable?	4 (15.4%)	23 (88.5%)
Q14B Acceptable if enforced?	4 (15.4%)	22 (84.6%)
Q14C Acceptable if error?	6 (23.1%)	20 (76.9%)

Question fifteen

70 organizations (55% of total respondents) reported a 'Very Important outcome' or 'Important outcome' to sub-sections A, B, C or E in question 15.

Response possible	No answer	Very important outcome	Important outcome	Minor outcome	Not an outcome
Q15A Clarification?	9 (7.1%)	21 (16.5%)	44 (34.7%)	28 (22.0%)	25 (19.7%)
Q15B Harden posn?	38 (29.9%)	12 (9.4%)	17 (13.4%)	18 (14.2%)	42 (33.1%)
Q15C Soften posn?	58 (45.7%)	0 (0.0%)	2 (1.6%)	7 (5.5%)	60 (47.2%)
Q15D Unaffect posn?	36 (28.3%)	12 (9.4%)	13 (10.2%)	22 (17.3%)	44 (34.8%)
Q15E Dev. attitudes?	14 (11.0%)	5 (3.9%)	17 (13.4%)	39 (30.7%)	52 (41.0%)
Q15F Par. no effect?	32 (25.2%)	3 (2.4%)	8 (6.3%)	33 (26.0%)	51 (40.1%)

Question sixteen

107 organizations (84% of total respondents) 'Strongly Agreed' or 'Agreed' to at least one of the sub-questions in question 16.

Response possible	No answer	Strongly agree	Agree	Indifferent	Disagree
Q16A Open/public	9 (7.1%)	41 (32.3%)	52 (40.9%)	17 (13.4%)	8 (6.3%)
Q16B Fairer proced.	11 (8.7%)	32 (25.2%)	57 (44.9%)	17 (13.4%)	10 (7.8%)
Q16C Learning	14 (11.0%)	13 (10.2%)	38 (29.9%)	35 (27.6%)	27 (21.3%)
Q16D MP vs minister	16 (12.6%)	11 (8.7%)	41 (32.3%)	36 (28.3%)	23 (18.1%)
Q16E Good? bad?	103 (81.1%)	6 (4.7%)	6 (4.7%)	10 (7.9%)	2 (1.6%)

Question seventeen

Response possible	No answer	Strongly agree	Agree	Indifferent	Disagree
Q17A Influence	13 (10.2%)	43 (34.0%)	37 (29.1%)	21 (16.5%)	13 (10.2%)
Q17B Role right?	28 (22.0%)	2 (1.6%)	41 (32.3%)	14 (11.0%)	42 (33.1%)
Q17C Waste of time	22 (17.3%)	2 (1.6%)	3 (2.4%)	11 (8.7%)	89 (70.1%)

Notes

INTRODUCTION

1   See, for example, *The Economist*, 29 June 1985, 50, for an analysis of '120 seats which the Alliance in a very good year indeed, might hope to add to its present 24'.

2   For a comprehensive discussion of these possibilities, their historical precedents and their constitutional complexity see Vernon Bogdanor, *Multi-Party Politics and the Constitution* (Cambridge University Press, Cambridge, 1983); David Butler, *Governing Without a Majority* (Collins, London, 1983).

3   The most significant political proponent for an enlarged role for parliament in policy making is Dr David Owen. His views will be considered in detail in chapter 1. His intentions are clear but his approach remains generalized. He does not link the enlarged role he envisages for parliament to the maintenance of a minority executive, nor does he acknowledge (except in a generalized way) the possibility that committees might make a key political contribution to policy making – for example, in providing a context which would permit interest groups' consent to be mobilized. For an analysis that attributes policy-making vicissitudes to the structure of the two-party system see S. A. Walkland and A. M. Gamble, *The British Party System and Economic Policy, 1945–1983* (Clarendon Press, Oxford, 1983), 152–70.

4   *The Federalist Papers* provides perhaps the most sober argument for the protection of liberty through political structures that mobilize interests and set them to check each other. Madison's observations concerning the best means of protection against powerful interests are worth recalling:

> It is of great importance not only to guard the society against the oppression of its rulers, but to guard one part of the society against the injustice of the other part. Different interests necessarily exist in different classes of citizens. If a majority be united by a common interest, the rights of the minority will be insecure. There are but two methods of providing against this evil: the one by creating a will in the community independent of the majority – that is, of the society itself; the other, by comprehending in the society so many separate descriptions of citizens as will render an unjust combination of a majority of the whole very improbable, if not impracticable. Whilst all authority will be derived from and dependent on the society, the society itself will be broken into so many parts, interests and classes of citizens, that the rights of individuals, or of the

minority will be in little danger from interest combinations of the majority. In a free government the security for civil rights consists in the multiplicity of interests. The degree of security will depend on the number of interests. . . . In a society under the forms of which the stronger faction can readily unite and oppress the weaker, anarchy may . . . be truly said to reign.

(*The Federalist Papers*, no. 51, Modern Library College Edition, New York, 1961, 339)

5 See for example, Gavin Drewry, 'The new select committees – a constitutional non-event?', and Ann Robinson, 'Monitoring the economy – the work of the Treasury and Civil Service Committee', in Dilys Hill (ed.), *Parliamentary Select Committees in Action: A Symposium* (Strathclyde Papers on Government and Politics, 24, 1984); also Nevil Johnson, 'An academic's view', in Dermot Englefield (ed.), *The Commons Select Committees – Catalysts for Progress?* (Longman, Harlow, 1984); also David Lowe, 'Legislative oversight and the House of Commons new committee system' (paper delivered to 1981 meeting of the American Political Science Association); and J. A. G. Griffith, 'The Constitution and the Commons', in *Parliament and the Executive* (Royal Institute of Public Administration, London, 1982).

6 Samuel Beer, *Britain Against Itself* (W. W. Norton, New York, 1982). Samuel Brittan, *The Role and Limits of Government* (Maurice Temple Smith, London, 1983); also 'The unradical British right', *Australian Financial Review*, 27 November 1984. J. J. Richardson and A. G. Jordan, *Governing Under Pressure: The Policy Process in a Post-Parliamentary Democracy* (Martin Robertson, Oxford, 1979). Michael Moran, *The Politics of Industrial Relations: The Origins, Life and Death of the 1971 Industrial Relations Act* (Macmillan, London, 1977). Wyn Grant, *The Political Economy of Industrial Policy* (Butterworth, London, 1982). Joel Barnett, *Inside the Treasury* (André Deutsch, London, 1982). Mancur Olson, *The Rise and Decline of Nations* (Yale University Press, New Haven, 1983). Franz Lehner and Klaus Schubert, 'Party government and the political control of public policy', *European Journal of Political Research*, 12, 1984, 131–46. James Douglas, 'The overloaded Crown', *British Journal of Political Science*, 6, 1976, 483–506. Colin Crouch, 'New thinking on pluralism', *Political Quarterly*, 54, 1983, 363–74.

7 For a brief, cautionary account of the role of select committees in the 1850s, see Asa Briggs, *Victorian People* (Pelican Books, Middlesex, 1982), esp. 80–90; also Norman Gash, *Politics in the Age of Peel* (Longman, London, 1953); J. K. Grainger, *Character and Style in English Politics* (Cambridge University Press, Cambridge, 1979).

8 Walter Bagehot, 'Parliamentary reform', in Norman St John Stevas (ed.), *Collected Works of Walter Bagehot* (*The Economist*, London, 1974), VI, p. 195.

9 Walter Bagehot, *The English Constitution*, Dolphin Books edn (Doubleday, New York), 173.

10 ibid., 174.

11 ibid., 172.

12 For radically different versions of this argument see Sir Douglas Wass, 'The 1983 Reith Lectures', *The Listener*, 24 November 1983, 19–25; 8 December 1983, 21–7; 15 December 1983, 12–17. David Owen, 'We have had enough of conservatism with a small "c"', *Political Quarterly*, 55 (1), 1984, 17–23; also 'Agenda for

competition with compassion', *Economic Affairs*, 4 (1), 1984, 26–34. Douglas Ashford, *Policy and Politics in Britain: The Limits of Consensus* (Basil Blackwell, Oxford, 1981). Sir John Hoskyns, 'Conservatism is not enough', *Political Quarterly*, 55 (1), 1984, 3–17; and his 'Whitehall and Westminster: an outsider's view', *Fiscal Studies*, 3 (3), 1932, 162–73.

13   Select Committee on Procedure (Finance) H.C. 24, Session 1982–3.

CHAPTER 1: DEVELOPMENT OF THE SELECT COMMITTEE SYSTEM

1   The Conservative Manifesto (Conservative Central Office, April 1979). For Norman St John Stevas's account of this development see N. St John Stevas, 'Government by discussion', in J. R. Nethercote (ed.), *Parliament and Bureaucracy* (Hale & Iremonger, Sydney, 1982).

2   H.C. Debates, 25 June 1979, col. 35.

3   Sydney and Beatrice Webb, *A Constitution for the Socialist Commonwealth of Great Britain* (Cambridge University Press, Cambridge, 1975).

4   Harold Laski, *A Grammar of Politics* (George Allen & Unwin, London, 1948).

5   Sir Winston Churchill, *Parliamentary Government and the Economic Problem, Romanes Lectures* (Clarendon Press, Oxford, 1930).

6   L. S. Amery, *Thoughts on the Constitution* (Oxford University Press, London, 1964; first published 1951).

7   Bernard Crick, *Reform of Parliament* (Anchor Books, New York, 1965).

8   ibid., 79.

9   Bernard Crick, 'Whither parliamentary reform?', in A. H. Hanson and Bernard Crick (eds), *The Commons in Transition* (Fontana/Collins, London, 1970).

10   Andrew Hill and Anthony Whichelow, *What's Wrong with Parliament?* (Penguin Books, London, 1964).

11   S. A. Walkland, 'The politics of parliamentary reform', *Parliamentary Affairs*, 29 (2), 1976, 190–210.

12   First Report from the Select Committee on Procedure, H.C. 588 of 1977–8, III.

13   *The Economist*, 5 November 1977, 11–16.

14   ibid.

15   S. A. Walkland and Michael Ryle, *The Commons Today* (Fontana, London, 1981).

16   Lord Hailsham, 'Elective dictatorship', *The Listener*, 21 October 1976.

17   Roy Jenkins, *British Government and Politics: Some Reflections*, The Royal Institution, London, 24 November 1977. See also Lord Crowther Hunt, 'Whitehall – the balance of power', *The Listener*, 6 January 1977, 10–11.

18   H.C. Debates, 25 June 1979, cols 83–4.

19   See, for example, Fourth Report of the Select Committee on Procedure, H.C. 303 of 1964–5.

20   Scrutiny of Public Expenditure and Administration, H.C. 410 of 1968–9.

21   Members of the Study of Parliament Group, 'Specialist committees in the British parliament: the experience of a decade, *Political and Economic Planning*, XLII, June 1976.

22   H. Heclo and A. Wildavsky, *The Private Government of Public Money*, 2nd edn (Macmillan, London, 1981), xxi.

23 For an appraisal of the work of the Expenditure Committee see: Ann Robinson, *Parliament and Public Spending* (Heinemann, London, 1978); Heclo and Wildavsky, op. cit., ch. 5.

24 First Report from the Select Committee on Procedure, H.C. 588 of 1977–8, I.

25 St John Stevas, op. cit. Also interviews with MPs.

26 First Report from the Select Committee on Procedure (Supply), H.C. 118 of 1980–1, 203a.

27 Enoch Powell, 'The menu and the bill', *The House Magazine*, 5 March 1982.

28 First report from the Select Committee on Procedure, H.C. 588 of 1977–8, II, 136. See also Edward du Cann, *Parliament and the Purse Strings*, The Conservative Political Centre, May 1977; and 'Parliamentary select committees and democracy', *Public Money*, June 1981.

29 First Report from the Select Committee on Procedure (Supply), H.C. 118 of 1980–1, Minutes of Evidence, 6 July 1982, 100–15.

30 At least five debates on procedure took place during Mrs Thatcher's first term. The references are as follows: H.C. Debates, 25 June 1979, cols 33–257; H.C. Debates, 16 January 1981, cols 1262–1323; H.C. Debates, 15 February 1982, cols 67–118; H.C. Debates, 19 July 1982, cols 117–80; H.C. Debates, 6 December 1983, cols 245–91.

31 The reports debated are listed in a written answer to a parliamentary question by the Leader of the House, H.C. Debates, 29 July 1983, cols 643–4. In addition to the three reports debated on specific motions, three reports were debated on the Adjournment. Thirteen reports have been noted on the Order Paper as relevant to a debate.

32 See note 30 above.

33 Interviews with MPs, January 1984.

34 Gavin Drewry, 'The National Audit Act – half a loaf?' *Public Law*, winter 1983, 532; *The Economist*, 4 December 1982, 28; Robert Sheldon, MP, 'Public sector auditing and the United Kingdom Committee of Public Accounts in 1984', *The Parliamentarian*, spring 1984, 91–8.

35 *The Times*, 10 January 1984; data supplied by Dr O'Higgins.

36 First Report from the Select Committee on Procedure, H.C. 588 of 1977–8, II.

37 H.C. Debates, 25 June 1979, cols 176–7.

38 See Ivor Crewe and Bo Särlvik, *Decade of Dealignment: The Conservative Victory of 1979 and Electoral Trends in the 1970s* (Cambridge University Press, Cambridge, 1983).

39 See speech by the Financial Secretary to the Treasury, John More, H.C. Debates, 6 December 1983, cols 261–4 and 290–3; or evidence by Leon Brittan to Select Committee on Procedure (Finance) – H.C. 24 of 1982–3, VI.

40 Personal interviews with MPs, January 1984.

41 See, for example, interview with Michael Meadowcroft, MP, *Marxism Today*, February 1984, 14–20.

42 David Owen, *Face the Future* (Cape, London, 1981).

43 ibid., 55.

44 ibid., 280.

45 ibid., assembled from 293, 296, 315 and 317.

46 David Owen, 'We have had enough of conservatism with a small "c"', *Political Quarterly*, 55 (1), 1984, 17–23.

47 Shirley Williams, *Politics is for People* (Harvard University Press, Cambridge, Mass., 1981), 185, 188.

48 Norman St John Stevas in 'Government by discussion', op. cit.

49 First Report from the Select Committee on Procedure (Supply), H.C. 118 of 1980–1.

50 H.C. Debates, 19 July 1982, cols 117–80.

51 H.C. Debates, 14 March 1983, cols 21–61.

52 First Report from the Select Committee on Procedure (Supply), H.C. 118 of 1980–1, I, para. 39.

53 Fourteenth Report from the Expenditure Committee, H.C. 661 of 1977–8. The most recent, most thorough and most suggestive review of these issues is by Andrew Likierman and Peter Vass, *Structure and Form of Government Expenditure Reports: Proposals for Reform* (Association of Certified Accountants and London Business School, 1984).

54 Third Report from the Public Accounts Committee, H.C. 232 of 1978–9; Thirteenth Report from the Public Accounts Committee, H.C. 570 of 1979–80; Treasury comments are in evidence to this latter inquiry and in Cmnd. 8067, Treasury Minute on the Eighth to Thirteenth Report from the Committee of Public Accounts, 1979–80.

55 H.C. Debates, 19 July 1982, cols 152–3.

56 Sixth Report from the Treasury and Civil Service Committee, H.C. 325 of 1980–1.

57 First Report from the Select Committee on Procedure (Finance), H.C. 24 of 1982–3, I, xiv–xvii.

58 Cmnd. 8616, 1982.

59 The Structure and Form of Financial Documents Presented to Parliament, H.C. 110 of 1983–4.

60 First Special Draft from the Committee of Public Accounts, The Role of the Comptroller and Auditor General, H.C. 115 of 1980–1, para. 1.3.

61 ibid., para. 1.6.

62 For a fuller account of this development see Gavin Drewry, op. cit.

63 Bruce George and Barbara Evans, 'Parliamentary reform – the internal view', in David Judge (ed.), *The Politics of Parliamentary Reform* (Heinemann Educational Books, London, 1983).

CHAPTER 2: ECONOMIC POLICY MAKING AND THE BUDGET CYCLE

1 The most recent comprehensive study of the budget process from an economic perspective is contained in R. R. Neild and T. Ward, *The Measurement and Reform of the Budgetary Process* (Heinemann Educational Books, London, 1978). A similar study from a political perspective is Hugh Heclo and Aaron Wildavsky, *The Private Government of Public Money*, 2nd edn (Macmillan, London, 1981). See also Douglas Ashford, 'Economic policy making', in *Policy and Politics in Britain* (Basil Blackwell, Oxford, 1981), 97–136; Sir Leo Pliatzky, *Getting and Spending* (Basil Blackwell, Oxford, 1982).

2 Hugo Young and Ann Sloman (*But Chancellor: An Enquiry into the Treasury*,

BBC Publications, London, 1984) quote David Kemp, a Treasury Under-Secretary: 'The Budget is the great annual moment towards which every kind of interest group, from licensed victuallers to pensioners, through building societies, child poverty people, stockbrokers and even actors and theatre managers, directs its lobby for change favourable to itself.'

3   A comprehensive account of the current budget process is to be found in the evidence collected by the Treasury Committee in the course of its inquiry on Budgetary Reform, H.C. 137 of 1981–2. For a discussion of the problems of central control see, for example, Ann Robinson, 'The myth of central control', *The Listener*, 17 June 1982, 9–10; also Ann Robinson and Bengt-Christer Ysander, *Public Budgeting Under Uncertainty: Three Studies*, The Industrial Institute of Economic and Social Research, Stockholm, 1983; for a theoretical discussion see Charles E. Lindblom, 'Decision making in taxation and expenditures', in *Public Finances: Needs Sources and Utilisation*, National Bureau of Economic Research Conference Series 12 (Princeton University Press, Princeton, 1961).

4   Sarah Hogg, in 'Stop this Spending Punch-Up', *The Times*, London, 15 February 1984, comments:

> Judged as the consequence of five years' struggle over public spending, the 1983/84 results are less impressive. And with the ink hardly dry on this White Paper, the Chancellor will be engaged in a new round of quarrels with his spending colleagues over the figures for 1985–86. It is a system designed to yield minimum cuts for maximum political effort, and to distribute these cuts between departments in a manner which is a random one at best, and politically distorted at worst.

For a similar view see Joel Barnett, *Inside the Treasury* (André Deutsch, London, 1982), 59.

Mrs Thatcher's public expenditure spending totals more in real terms every year from 1979 to 1983–4 as the following table illustrates:

Rise in public spending

Annual change in planning totals of public expenditure

	In cash terms %	In cost terms (after inflation) %
1979–80	+17.0	+0.1
1980–81	+20.5	+1.5
1981–82	+13.0	+2.8
1982–83	+8.3	+1.6
1983–84 est.	+6.1	+1.1
1984–85 plans	+5.0	0.0
1985–86 plans	+4.5	—
1986–87 plans	+3.5	—

Adjusted for inflation as measured by the GDP deflator. Derived from Cmnd. 9143. (*The Times*, London, 17 February 1984.)

The Economist, 26 November 1983, notes:

> The Thatcher government came into office in 1979 determined to cut public spending as a proportion of gross domestic product. The Tories wanted to reverse a long-established trend: public spending had totalled 33% of GNP in 1959, 39% in 1969. In 1978–79, the last fiscal year of the Labour government, the ratio had risen to 41%. Judged by its own ambitions, the first Thatcher term was a failure. In 1982–83, the year before the 1983 general election public spending had risen to 44% of GNP.

See also Samuel Brittan, 'The unradical British right', *Australian Financial Review*, 27 November 1984, 13.

5   For an account of this process during the Callaghan government, see Joel Barnett, *Inside the Treasury* (André Deutsch, London, 1982), 40–4, and 59–67; see also Simon Jenkins, 'The "Star Chamber", PESC and the Cabinet', *Political Quarterly*, 56 (2), April 1985, 113–21.

6   This presumption was reflected in evidence before the Treasury Committee, by Sir Anthony Rawlinson (a Permanent Secretary of the Treasury). He justified the disclosure of plans in cash, but not cost or prices terms, as follows:

> The resources which under present policy, are regarded as crucial, are financial resources . . . the cash planning system fits into this . . . ministers wish to establish figures in cost and price terms which do not represent their decisions or their policies and which might be misinterpreted both inside and outside the Government machine as having some status of decisions which they did not have.   (H.C. 316, 1981–2, Q 445)

This argument reflects the fear of Treasury and the Chancellor and perhaps the Prime Minister that any alternative approach (requiring the provision of more information) would weaken the primacy of the drive to cut spending. On this view, the purpose of the public dimension of policy making is to signal an intention through an edict. The authority of the signaller is presumed to be sufficiently legitimized by the preceding election.

7   Barnett, op. cit., 63:

> A group that had to be treated seriously was the Parliamentary Labour Party. The Chancellor went to talk to them both before and after the Budget. He also frequently met the Economic and Finance Group and the Tribune Group of backbenchers, as well as having small groups in for drinks from time to time. The problem was that they never came up with a coherent package, except the Tribune Group, who would demand more of everything, making it all the easier to ignore them. It was relatively easy to fathom general dislikes – they disapproved of doing anything for the higher-paid or companies and frowned on cuts in public expenditure. It was less easy to know what the Party as a whole really wanted, because of the great differences of opinion among those who spoke.

8   ibid., 78, 134–7, and 170–4.

9   The total staff of Treasury concerned with expenditure surveillance amounts to 250 people (Young and Sloman, op. cit., 43); 10 people appraise DHSS expenditure (ibid., 49); 3 people maintain oversight of the Department of Transport and the Roads Programme (ibid., 53).

10　*The Times*, 18 July 1983:

Nationalized industries, 1981–82

	Turnover £m.	Capital employed £m.	Workforce 000s	% change in workforce since 1979–80
Electricity industry	8,057	32,605	147	−8
British Telecom	5,708	16,099	246	+2
British Gas	5,235	10,955	105	0
National Coal Board	4,727	5,891	279	−5
British Steel	3,443	2,502	104	−38
BL	3,072	1,521	83 (1)	−31
British Rail	2,899	2,746	227	−7
Post Office	2,636	1,347	183	0
British Airways	2,241	1,338	43 (2)	−24
Rolls-Royce	1,493	992	45	−23
British Shipbuilders	1,026	655	67	−18
S Scotland Electricity Board	716	2,817	13	−5
National Bus Company	618	508	53	−16
British Airports Authority	277	852	7	−7
N Scotland Hydro Electric	270	1,981	4	−3
Civil Aviation Authority	206	162	7	−2
Scottish Transport Group	152	157	11	−17
British Waterways Board	16	50	3	−2
Total	42,792	83,178	1,627	—

(1) UK only; overseas approximately 22,000.
(2) Reportedly 37,500 as at March 1983.

11　British Steel, H.C. 336 I and II and H.C. 444, 1980–1; British Leyland, H.C. 294, 1980–1.

12　Committee–Commission relations are reviewed in David Lowe, 'Legislative oversight and the House of Commons' new committee system, paper delivered at the 1981 meeting of the American Political Science Association.

13　First Report from the Treasury and Civil Service Committee, Provision for Civil Service Pay Increases in the 1980–1 Estimates, H.C. 371 of 1979–80.

14　See, for example, Budgetary Reform, H.C. 137 of 1981–2, para. 2.12. The committee can also draw on the 'Green Budget' produced annually by the Institute for Fiscal Studies which contains forecasts of the major variables and suggested policy approaches. This annual study is modelled on the (more comprehensive) annual publication of the Brookings Institution in Washington. See for example, *Budget Options in 1984*, Institute for Fiscal Studies Report, Series No. 7, 1984.

15　Edward du Cann lost the Chairmanship of the Treasury Committee after the 1983 elections. He continued as Chairman of the 1922 Committee until November 1984.

16　The full list of economist and central bank respondents is:

Bank of England
London Discount Market Association
United States Federal Reserve System
Banque Nationale Suisse
Osterreichische Nationalbank

Bank of Canada
Committee of London Clearing Banks
Deutsche Bundesbank
Banque de France
Nederlandsche Bank

Professor D. E. W. Laidler

Professor M. Friedman

Professor J. Williamson

Professor R. Dornbusch

Lord Croham

Professor F. Hahn

Professor Lord Kaldor

Professor A. P. Minford

Sir Alec Cairncross

Professor Willem Buiter

Professor D. Hendry

Professor A. Rose

Professor N. Thygesen

Professor James Tobin

Professor M. Artis

Dr M. Beenstock

National Institute of Economic and
Social Research

17   Eighth Report from the Treasury and Civil Service Committee, Financing the Nationalized Industries, H.C. 348 of 1980–1, para. 7.1.

18   Personal interviews with individuals concerned. For a more reflective and balanced assessment of the virtues of – and the lessons from – this inquiry, see A. B. Atkinson, 'Taxation and social security: reflections on advising a House of Commons select committee', Policy and Politics, 12 (2), 1984, 107–18.

19   The Structure of Personal Income Taxation and Income Support, H.C. 20 of 1982–3, Minutes of Evidence ii.

20   ibid., H.C. 386 of 1982–3, para. 7.3.

21   For a careful review of the contribution of select committees to earlier tax reform efforts, see Ann Robinson and Cedric Sandford, Tax Policy Making in the United Kingdom: A Study of Rationality, Ideology and Politics (Heinemann Educational Books, London, 1983), esp. chs 6–17.

22   See David Lowe, op. cit.

23   Third Report from the Treasury and Civil Service Committee, Monetary Control, H.C. 713 of 1979–80, para. 11.7.

24   ibid., para. 11.16.

25   ibid., para. 11.26.

26   Eighth Report from the Treasury and Civil Service Committee, Financing the Nationalized Industries, H.C. 348 of 1980–1, para. 7.1.

27   M. R. Garner, 'The financing of the nationalized industries', Public Administration, 59, winter 1981, 471.

28   The Treasury Committee reports on each budgetary announcement have usually included a section commenting on the difficulties caused by inadequate information. See, for example, 'The Government's Economic Policy': Autumn Statement, Treasury and Civil Service Committee, H.C. 49 of 1982–3.

   The Procedure Committee (Finance) Report, H.C. 24, Session 1982–3, recommends that the Treasury and Civil Service Committee further review the financial information available to parliament. This review was carried out in the 1983–4 session (The Structure and Form of Financial Documents presented to Parliament, H.C. 110 of 1983/4).

   See also John Hills, 'A co-operative and constructive relationship? The Treasury response to its Select Committee 1979–82', Fiscal Studies, 4 (1), March 1983, 3–9.

   An appraisal of current practice and some suggestions for reform are in Andrew Likierman and Peter Vass, Structure and Form of Government Expenditure Reports: Proposals for Reform (Association of Certified Accountants and London Business School, 1984).

29   The Government's Expenditure Plans 1982–3 to 1984–5, H.C. 316 of 1981–2, para. 10.

30   The 1982 Budget, H.C. 270 of 1981−2, para. 12.

31   ibid., para. 24.

32   ibid., para. 37.

33   Second Report from the Select Committee on Energy, Department of Energy Estimates for 1981−2, H.C. 231 of 1981−2, para. 33.

34   Supplementary Estimates (Class II Vote 12), H.C. 226 of 1981−2.

35   See, for example, his scrupulous study, *The Politics of the National Health Service* (Longman, Harlow, 1983).

36   For details of the DHSS approach to Strategic Planning, see Public Expenditure on Social Services, H.C. 324 of 1980−1. See also Third Report from the Social Services Committee, H.C. 702 of 1979−80 and the government's reply, Cmnd. 8086 of 1979−80. In a government whose public rhetoric suggested spending contraction and privatization in the Health and Social Services area, it is interesting to note the studies completed or planned by the Policy Strategy Unit from 1979 to the end of 1982.

Studies have been undertaken in the following areas:
   (i) Financing of Ophthalmic Services
   (ii) The Dental Estimates Board
   (iii) Prescription charges
   (iv) Voluntary bodies in the field of alcohol misuse (with the National Council for Voluntary Organizations)
   (v) Benefits for the unemployed
   (vi) Effects of social and economic change on benefits and services
   (vii) Elderly people
   (viii) Ethnic minorities
   (ix) Unemployment and health
Studies are currently in hand in the following areas:
   (i) Financial provision for those in residential accommodation
   (ii) Purchase of care by personal social services authorities
   (iii) Benefits and services for disabled people
   (iv) Scientific and Technical Services
   (v) Interaction of changes in benefits, taxes and charges
   (vi) NHS residential accommodation
   (vii) Response to social and economic change
   (viii) Benefits and services for poor families with children
(Social Services Expenditure, H.C. 324 of 1980−1, Evidence Session, 12 May 1981.)

37   *The Economist*, 12 February 1983, 23−4. For a survey of earlier developments, see edition of 6 March 1982, 39−45. For an appraisal of the government's privatization strategy see Samuel Brittan, 'The politics and economics of privatisation', *Political Quarterly*, 55 (2), 109−28.

38   Concorde, H.C. 193 of 1981−2.

39   *The Economist*, 29 June 1982, 29−30.

40   Interviews with committee members.

41   For an assessment of the debate about financing nationalized industries see Samuel Brittan, op. cit.

42   See, for example, 'The government view' by the Leader of the House, John Biffen, and 'A civil servant's view' by Peter Kemp in Dermot Englefield (ed.), *The Commons Select Committees − Catalysts for Progress?* (Longman, Harlow,

1984); P. Mosley, 'The Treasury Committee and the making of economic policy', *Political Quarterly*, 52 (3), July–September 1981, 348–55.

43 Peter Kemp, 'A civil servant's view', in Englefield, op. cit., 55–9. (Peter Kemp is a Treasury Deputy Secretary.)

> Contrary to a popular view, civil servants often actually rather enjoy appearing in front of a select committee. I do myself. We want to try to be helpful to the committee. We are not allowed to disclose political advice given to ministers, but we do have views and it would be quite wrong had we not. The committees must be interested in these views. The committees help to draw back the veil of anonymity covering the civil service. This may be a good thing or it may be a bad thing, but it is certainly an effect of the committees that we should note. There really is an effect on Whitehall and, on balance, probably a beneficial effect.

44 See, for example, Ann Davies, *Reformed Select Committees: The First Year* (Outer Circle Policy Unit, London, 1980).

45 Education Committee proceedings have been extensively reported in the *Times Educational Supplement* and *Times Higher Education Supplement*. The extent of this coverage is illustrated by the twenty-one references in the *TES* to Christopher Price in his capacity as chairman: 1981–14, 30 Jan.; 20, 27 Feb.; 13 March; 10, 17, 24 April; 1, 8 May; 10 July; 23 Oct.; 1982–1 Jan.; 8 April; 12 May; 2, 9, 30 July; 24 Sep.; 1, 20 Oct.

46 Barnett, op. cit., 21.

47 David Lea, 'A trade unionist view', in Englefield, op. cit., 51–4.

48 Transcript of programme broadcast on BBC Radio 4 on 25 January 1984, reviewing Sir Douglas Wass's 1983 Reith Lectures.

49 First Report of the Liaison Committee, H.C. 92 of 1982–3; also H.C. 363 of 1984–5.

50 In an assessment of the Treasury Committee contribution, Paul Mosley (op. cit., 355) comments:

> It would be hard to overstate the improvement in public awareness of the inner processes of economic policy-making that has occurred in recent years: it was only 10 years ago that a Treasury Permanent Secretary was forced to admit that: 'No Government has so far been prepared to display to Parliament or to the public the actual processes by which it reaches decisions [in the field of public expenditure]'. Now that all this has changed, it is however clear, thanks to the work of the Treasury Committee, that the process of policy choice within the Treasury departs very far from the model of a 'rational economic man' who chooses, from a range of possible policies, that with the greatest surplus of benefits over costs. Rather, once an approach had been worked out to the intellectual dilemma posed by 'stagflation' . . . it was assumed very nearly *a priori* that the approach was the correct one, and the process of scanning the options stopped. . . . The public already has good cause to thank the Treasury Committee's latest report for showing them in more detail than ever before what is going on in central economic policy-making; if the report also forces researchers inside and outside the Treasury to think more creatively about alternatives to present macro-economic policies and their implications, it will have reason to be doubly grateful.

CHAPTER 3: CURRENT ISSUES AND THE GOVERNMENT PROGRAMME

1 Terry Ward, 'Cash planning', *Public Administration*, 61 (1), 1983, 85–90; P. K. Else and G. P. Marshall, 'The unplanning of public expenditure: recent problems in expenditure planning and the consequences of cash limits', *Public Administration*, 59, autumn 1981, 253–79. For an alternative view on cash limits see Sir Leo Pliatzky, *Getting and Spending* (Basil Blackwell, Oxford, 1982).

2 Recent developments affecting the doctrine of ministerial responsibility are reviewed in Philip Norton, *The Constitution in Flux* (Martin Robertson, Oxford, 1982), ch. 2; An account of the deficiencies of the doctrine in current practice and its use to constrain civil service evidence before select committees can be found in David Judge, 'Ministerial responsibility', *The House Magazine*, 26 November 1982, 4–6.

3 There are currently ninety-one All-Party Issue Groups. At least seventeen of these groups have a part-time secretary or research officer seconded from an external advocacy or commercial group. See Grant Jordan, 'Parliament under pressure', *Political Quarterly*, 56 (2), April 1985.

4 The Green Papers issued by the first Thatcher government in the Health, Education and Welfare area are listed in appendix 1. For a discussion of the current interest group/department/minister policy-making structure see J. J. Richardson and A. G. Jordan, *Governing Under Pressure* (Martin Robertson, Oxford, 1979), ch. 3.

5 The Procedure Committee which preceded the establishment of the departmental committee system (First Report from the Select Committee on Procedure, H.C. 588 of 1977–8, I) considered what role these committees might play in considering legislative proposals. The report recommended against departmental select committees replacing standing committees. It concluded:

> If government legislation were regularly referred to specialised select committees, the party leadership would have a natural and proper interest influencing the proceedings of these committees and many of the characteristics which select committees now possess would be lost.   (para. 2.13)

Most committees have heeded this warning. Pre-legislative inquiries were not common practice either in the 1981–2 session or in earlier or subsequent sessions. Prima facie, it is not clear why examination of government legislative proposals by committees carries more political hazards than examination of departmental estimates.

6 Trade Unions (Legal Immunities), H.C. 282 of 1980–1, Evidence 8 April 1981, Q. 707.

7 Department of Energy Estimates for 1981–2, H.C. 231 of 1981–2.

8 Turks and Caicos Islands, H.C. 26 of 1980–1.

9 Public and Private Funding of the Arts, H.C. 49 of 1981–2.

10 Funding and Organization of Courses in Higher Education, H.C. 787 of 1979–80.

11 H.C. Debates, 5 December 1980, cols 532–97.

12 Higher Education Funding, Minutes of Evidence, H.C. 293 of 1982–3.

13 Christopher Price's reflections on his experience and his advice to members of the

new committees established after the 1983 election is to be found in *The House Magazine*, 15 July 1983, 13.

14 See David Lowe, 'Legislative oversight and the House of Commons new committee system', paper delivered to 1981 meeting of the American Political Science Association.

15 Michael O'Higgins (the Committee's special adviser) reviews its work in 'Privatisation and social security', *The Political Quarterly*, 55 (2), 1984, 133–5.

16 J. Barry Jones, 'Limited power and potential influence: the Committee on Welsh Affairs and the policy process', in Dilys Hill (ed.), *Parliamentary Select Committees in Action: A Symposium* (Strathclyde Papers on Government and Politics, 24, 1984), 65.

17 Dr Jeremy Bray, H.C. Debates, 19 July 1982, cols 152–3.

18 The PAC report is fully reported in *The Times*, 23 March 1982, 3.

19 For a negative reaction to this proposal see *The Economist*, 26 June 1982, 29.

20 H.C. Debates, 14 March 1983, cols 21–61.

21 For a penetrating study of the necessity of integrating the system of functional representation with the system of parliamentary representation if effective policy development is to occur see Michael Moran, *The Politics of Industrial Relations: The Origins, Life and Death of the 1971 Industrial Relations Act* (Macmillan, London, 1977).

22 See, for example, cross-examination of CRE representatives on 17 March 1982 by Greville Janner (Lab.) and John Gorst (Cons.), H.C. 273 of 1981–2.

23 Ann Davies, *Reformed Select Committees: The First Year* (Outer Circle Policy Unit, London, 1980), 51.

24 Fourth Report from the Home Affairs Committee, H.C. 744 of 1979–80.

25 Information from interviews with responsible officials.

26 First Report from the Liaison Committee, H.C. 92 of 1982–3, 79.

27 Bruce George and Michael Woodward, 'The Foreign Affairs Committee and the patriation of the Canadian Constitution', in Dilys Hill (ed.), op. cit., 130.

28 *The Times*, 12 May 1984.

29 For coverage of the Education Committee by the *Times Educational Supplement*, see chapter 2, n. 45.

30 See, for example, *Commercial Motor*, 18 June 1983.

31 First Report from the Liaison Committee, H.C. 92 of 1982–3, 129.

32 Summarized in Christopher Price, op. cit.

33 *The Times*, 15 May 1982, records the result of a Liaison Committee meeting which reviewed what action, if any, committees might take against newspapers publishing leaks of their reports. Needless to say, the Liaison Committee decided to take no action.

34 A summary and (equivocal) appraisal of this argument is provided by J. A. G. Griffith, 'The Constitution and the Commons', in *Parliament and the Executive*, Royal Institute of Public Administration, London, 1982.

CHAPTER 4: STRATEGIC POLICY MAKING

1 Samuel Brittan, 'The unradical British right', *Australian Financial Review*, 27 November 1984.

2 Sir John Hoskyns quoted in *The Economist*, 12 November 1983, 33.

3 Christopher Pollitt, 'The Central Policy Review Staff 1970–1974', *Public Admin-istration*, 52, winter 1974, 375–91; Sir Kenneth Berrill, 'The role of the Central Policy Review Staff', *Management Service in Government*, 32 (3), 1977, 121–6; Lord Rothschild, 'A useful exercise with interest', *The Times*, 2 July 1983.

4 See, for example, Ronald Butt, 'A thinking centre for government', *The Times*, 26 January 1984. See also articles on 'The Whitehall machine' by Sir Leo Pliatzky, 'We have had enough of conservatism with a small "c"' by Dr David Owen and 'Conservatism is not enough' by Sir John Hoskyns, *Political Quarterly*, 55 (1), 1984, 3–29; James McDonald and G. K. Fry, 'Policy Planning Units – ten years on', *Public Administration*, 58, winter 1980, 421–37; Andrew Gray and Bill Jenkins, 'Policy analysis in British central government: the experience of PAR', *Public Administration*, 60, winter 1982, 429–50; Frank Stacey, *British Govern-ment 1966–1975: Years of Reform* (Oxford University Press, Oxford, 1975).

5 Samuel H. Beer, *British Politics in the Collectivist Age* (Vintage Books, New York, 1969) 347. A succinct appraisal of the extent to which current practice deviates from this ideal is in Franz Lehner and Klaus Schubert, 'Party government and the political control of public policy', *European Journal of Political Research*, 12, 1984, 131–46.

6 For a discussion of the concentration of political power in the two-party system and its origin in the cultural premises of Old Tory politics see Beer, ibid., 277–301.

7 Bernard Crick, *Reform of Parliament* (Anchor Books, New York, 1965).

8 On relations between departments and ministers see R. H. S. Crossman, *Inside View* (Cape, London, 1972), 22.

> If we think of the civil servants as marine animals and politicians as fishermen operating on the surface, we shall have some idea of the relation between the two. The civil servants take a long view. They know that the boat-loads of politicians now anchored above them are certain to be changed within five years. They also know that any ideological crusade to carry out the mandate will be blunted by failure, electoral unpopularity, and sheer exhaustion. So they are prepared to concede quite a lot under the first impact of an election victory. But when that is over, they resume their quiet defence of entrenched departmental positions and policies against political change.

Joel Barnett, *Inside the Treasury* (André Deutsch, London, 1982), 21:

> Another tactic employed by officials is delay. This may occur when officials find themselves unhappy with a decision being contemplated by a Minister, or more frequently a ministerial request for further information that seems likely to lead to a decision with which they strongly disagree. In such cases they may well decide the best approach is to 'play it long'. The Minister, bogged down with so many other concerns, may forget it long enough for the particular issue to die, or the Minister himself may 'die', in the ministerial sense, by moving on to another post. . . . Another area where officials were quite brilliant was in the different ways they had of 'fudging' figures, particularly on expenditure decisions.

A report in *The Times*, 28 April 1984, 2, with quotes from Norman Strauss:

> Mrs Margaret Thatcher has fallen into the hands of cautious and conventional

advisors. It is time for her to trust her instincts, break free and think the unthinkable. Mrs Thatcher must go back to leadership isolation and trust more to her own instincts for change, than to this pusillanimous plethora of pedantic paternalism. He said: 'When isolated with her back against the wall, with survival at stake, she leads. When closeted in comfort, she merely follows.'

Mr. Strauss recommended 'a truly innovative culture-bursting prime minister's department' to help Mrs. Thatcher think the unthinkable and break the grip of Whitehall departments which behave as if they were pressure groups.

See also Samuel H. Beer, 'British pressure groups revisited: pluralistic stagnation from the 50s to the 70s', *Public Administration Bulletin* (32), April 1980, 13.

9   For example, Joel Barnett notes that despite Mrs Thatcher's vehement opposition to the Capital Transfer Tax he introduced in 1975, it continues unrepealed by her government (op. cit., 56–7).

10   See Tony Benn, H.C. Debates, 25 June 1979, cols 81–3.
Barnett, op cit., 20–1, writes:

I try to explain in this book how 'the system' can defeat Ministers like myself who stayed rather a long time by modern standards. The sheer volume of decisions, many of them extremely complex, means that by the time even a fairly modest analysis of a problem is done, and the various options considered, you find yourself coming up against time constraints. Consequently, Ministers often find themselves making hasty decisions, either late at night or in an odd moment during a day full of meetings. It does not follow that the decisions would necessarily be better made in more leisurely fashion, but there can be little doubt that some bad decisions were made in this way.

See also Wyn Grant and Stephen Wilks, 'British industrial policy: structural change, policy inertia', *Journal of Public Policy*, 3 (1), February 1983, 13–28.

11   Joel Barnett, op. cit., 40:

On complex issues, Cabinet Committees are just about the worst possible way of arriving at sensible decisions. Ministers would come to the meetings with long briefs prepared by officials who had been members of the appropriate Official Committee which 'shadowed' the Ministerial Committee. In fact, 'shadowed' is an inappropriate term, for the Official Committee, after carrying out the detailed analytical work intended only to set out options for Ministers, usually left their Ministers no doubt whatsoever as to which was the best option – the one they recommended. In most cases, the Ministers not directly involved had either read the brief late the previous night, or started to do so as the argument proceeded. More often than not, as I have said, they would follow the line of the brief.

The Times, 3 April 1984, lists the 25 Standing Cabinet Committees and 110 *ad hoc* Cabinet groups established by the Thatcher government.

12   For a full description of ministerial engagements over a twelve-month period see Tony Benn, 'The nine lives of a Cabinet Minister,' *The Guardian*, 11 February 1978. In summary, in 1977 Tony Benn was engaged in the following activities:

(i) Work as a constituency MP: 50 public engagements; 12 major speeches; 16

advice sessions to constituents; 5000 letters received and sent; 29 party functions attended.

(ii) MP in the House of Commons: attended 149 days; voted on 126 occasions; attended 12 meetings parliamentary Labour Party; spoke to 14 party committees.

(iii) Secretary of State for Energy: introduced 3 bills on nuclear power, coal industry and oil industry; spoke in 8 debates; made 5 parliamentary statements; answered 171 written and 57 oral questions; gave leadership to 4 ministers and a department of 1363, and to NCB, Gas Corporation, electricity industry, Atomic Energy Authority, BNOC.

(iv) Cabinet minister: attended 42 meetings and 106 committee meetings. Received 1800 Cabinet papers. Submitted 4 papers to Cabinet and 45 to committees.

(v) Miscellaneous: 19 overseas trips; 15 NEC meetings; 47 NEC committee meetings; 113 miscellaneous speeches at 65 locations in UK; 83 radio and 57 TV broadcasts; 34 press conferences; 30 interviews with journalists.

13 For an account of ministerial turnover in the first Thatcher government see *The Economist*, 22 October 1983, 26. It records that in the first Thatcher government there were three Energy Secretaries, four Transport Secretaries and five Trade Secretaries.

14 'Thatcher's think tank takes aim at the Welfare State', *The Economist*, 18 September 1982; *The Times*, 25 January 1984, reports Mrs Thatcher in the following terms:

> Mrs Margaret Thatcher has used the relative freedom of a foreign newspaper interview to disclose deep anxiety about the scale of welfare spending and its effect on individual responsibility. Britain faced a 'time bomb' over social security spending she told Mr. R. W. Apple, the London correspondent of The New York Times, and she said she would not sit by and 'do nothing' about the cost of pensions and the National Health Service. . . . Mrs Thatcher says she wants to bring before the British people the consequences of present social security arrangements before it is too late. She said she needed another parliamentary term for that.
>
> Mrs Thatcher, relying on the work of her 10 Downing Street policy unit, appears convinced that Britain is an aging society in which paying for health care and pensions for the elderly constitutes an open call on public finance.

15 The subsequent White Paper on Public Expenditure suggested that existing programmes could be maintained unchanged. This was affirmed orally by the Prime Minister. *The Times*, 24 March 1984.

The Economist, 7 January 1984, reflects on Mrs Thatcher's performance in the following terms:

> Mrs. Thatcher has correctly read a Tory mood which seemed to require of her the language of radicalism but the measures of moderation. . . . Mr. Nigel Lawson's budget is already emitting a cacophony of conflicting signals as he searches for meagre fare to offer backbenchers furious at the hint that Britain's as yet unreformed personal taxes might be going up. The social services secretary, Mr. Norman Fowler, has less than a year to stave off further treasury

pressure – and left-wing Tory revolt – on the long-term fate of the health and social security budget. On the European community, the foreign office had last month to request the whips to suppress a backbench revolt against an increase in the community's 'own resources', as the prime minister prepared to about-turn on the subject as part of a possible EEC budget deal. All these are areas of policy in which Mrs. Thatcher, despite five years of leadership, has failed to grasp basic strategic issues since her political intuition has apparently told her they might be politically unpopular.

16 'Reform of Social Security', Cmnd. 9517, 9578, 9519; 'Housing Benefit Review', Cmnd. 9520.

17 Samuel H. Beer, *Britain Against Itself* (W. W. Norton, New York, 1982). See also references in footnote 5, chapter 5.

18 See, for example, Leo Panitch, 'The development of corporatism in liberal democracy', in Philippe C. Schmitter and Gerhard Lehmbruch (eds), *Trends Towards Corporatist Intermediation* (Sage Publications, Beverly Hills, 1979).

19 Beer, op. cit.

20 Hugh Heclo and Aaron Wildavsky, *The Private Government of Public Money*, 2nd edn (Macmillan, London, 1981).

21 R. L. Borthwick, 'The Defence Committee: can it hope to affect policy?', in Dilys M. Hill (ed.), *Parliamentary Select Committees in Action: A Symposium* (Strathclyde Papers on Government and Politics, 24), 145.

22 Government Reply to the Education Committee Report on Bio-technology, H.C. 208 of 1982–3, Annex 2.

23 For a review of the difficulties confronting organizations in this task see A. Wildavsky, *Speaking Truth to Power: The Art and Craft of Policy Analysis* (Little, Brown & Co., Boston, 1979), especially ch. 9, 'The self-evaluating organization'.

24 Efficiency and Effectiveness in the Civil Service, H.C. 236 of 1981–2, Q. 512.

25 Andrew Likierman, 'Management information for ministers: the MINIS system in the Department of the Environment', *Public Administration*, 60 (2), 1982, 127–63.

26 Cmnd. 8616 of 1981–2.

27 The Civil Service, H.C. 535 of 1976–7; Response to Government Observations on Committee Report on the Civil Service, H.C. 576 of 1977–8.

28 For a discussion of how this dilemma was handled by the Callaghan Cabinet in 1978 see Barnett, op. cit., 43.

29 See report of a speech by CEGB chairman, Sir Walter Marshall, *The Guardian*, 7 February 1984.

30 'Previous Recommendations of the Committee', Fourth Report of the Defence Committee, H.C. 55 of 1982–3.

31 See report of comments by Bruce George, MP, *The Times*, 7 September 1981, 2. Other comments were expressed in interviews with committee members.

32 The House of Commons debate is reported in *The Times*, 2 February 1982, 4.

33 Beer, op.cit., 211–13.

34 Medical Education, H.C. 31 of 1980–1, xlvii.

35 ibid., para. 58.

36 First Report from the Transport Committee, The Roads Programme, H.C. 27 of 1980–1, I, paras 60–3.

37 Secondary School Curriculum and Exams, H.C. 116 of 1981–2, xix.

38 See *New Society*, 12 January 1984, for a report of Sir Keith Joseph's Sheffield speech which endorsed moves from 'norm reference' to 'criterion reference' exams. See also *The Economist*, 4 February 1984, 36, concerning later government decisions to give the MSC a bigger role in college-based vocational training and to give central government control of a small proportion of the education budget.

39 See *The Economist*, 14 April 1984, 68, for further appraisal of this issue. No action has been taken. For an analysis of the government's policy towards council house sales see George Boyne, 'The privatisation of public housing', *Political Quarterly*, 55 (2), 1984, 180–7.

40 Public Transport in London, Cmnd. 9004. Government proposals for the re-allocation of responsibilities for highways and traffic management were set out in a Consultation Paper issued by the Department of Transport, October 1983.

41 *The Times*, 12 August 1981.

42 Interviews with conservation interest groups.

43 The Secretary of State's Parliamentary Statement is reported by *The Times*, 3 April 1984, 4. The Green Papers published in May 1985 as a result of this inquiry have already been noted.

44 *Daily Telegraph*, 3 February 1984.

45 Sir Douglas Wass in his 1983 Reith Lecture proposes a permanent Royal Commission to attend to forward planning. *The Listener*, 15 December 1983, 15–17.

46 See, for example, *The Times*, 26 January 1984. This report concludes: 'The rejection of some of the select committee's more adventurous contentions is hardly likely to surprise art circles, who are somewhat surprised that the select committee report was so favourable.'

CHAPTER 5: SELECT COMMITTEES AND INTEREST GROUPS

1 S. Brittan, 'The economic contradictions of democracy', *British Journal of Political Science*, 5 (1975), 129–59.

2 Mancur Olson, *The Logic of Collective Action* (Harvard University Press, Cambridge, Mass., 1965).

3 Joseph A. Schumpeter, *Capitalism, Socialism and Democracy* (Harper Colophon Books, New York, 1976), esp. chs xxii and xxiii.

4 James Douglas, review article, 'The overloaded crown', *British Journal of Political Science*, 6 (1976), 483–505.

5 Samuel Beer, *Britain Against Itself* (W. W. Norton, New York, 1982); J. J. Richardson and A. G. Jordan, *Governing Under Pressure* (Martin Robertson, Oxford, 1979). The various neo-liberal and neo-Marxist analyses are succinctly summarized and critically appraised in Anthony Birch, 'Overload, ungovernability and delegitimation: the theories and the British case', *British Journal of Political Science*, 14 (1984), 135–60.

   The following is by no means a comprehensive list of other recent analyses of interest groups: David Marsh (ed.), *Pressure Politics: Interest Groups in Britain* (Junction Books, London, 1983); P. Whiteley and S. Winyard, 'The origins of the new poverty lobby', *Political Studies*, 32, 1984, 32–54; and 'Influencing social policy: the effectiveness of the poverty lobby in Britain', *Journal of Social Policy*, 12 (1), 1983, 1–27; Joyce Gelb, 'Feminism in Britain: the politics of isolation', paper delivered to the 1984 annual meeting of the American Political Science Association; Andrew Blowers, 'Master of fate or victim of circumstance: the exercise of corporate power in environmental policy making', *Policy and Politics*, 11 (4), 1983, 393–415; M. A. McCarthy, 'Trade unions, the family lobby and the Callaghan Government – the case of child benefits', *Policy and Politics*, 11 (4), 1983, 461–85; Jock Bruce-Gardyne and Nigel Lawson, *The Power Game* (Archon Books, Hamden, Connecticut, 1976); Claus Offe, 'Ungovernability: the renaissance of Conservative theories of crisis', in *Contradictions of the Welfare State* (Hutchinson, London, 1984); J. T. Winkler, 'Corporatism', *Archiv European Sociology*, 17, 1976, 100–36; David Marsh and Wyn Grant, 'Tri-partism: reality or myth', *Government and Opposition*, 12, 1977, 194–211; Alan Cawson, 'Pluralism, corporatism and the role of the state', *Government and Opposition*, 13 (2), 1978, 178–98; Colin Crouch, 'Pluralism and corporatism: a rejoinder', *Political Studies*, 31, 1983, 452–60; Leo Panitch, 'Recent theorisations of corporatism: reflections on a growth industry', *British Journal of Sociology*, 31 (2), 1980, 159–84; Philippe C. Schmitter and G. Lehmbruch (eds), *Trends Towards Corporatist Intermediation* (Sage Publications, Beverly Hills, 1979), also *Patterns of Corporatist Policy Making* (Sage Publications, Beverly Hills, 1980); Colin Crouch (ed.), *State and Economy in Contemporary Capitalism* (Croom Helm, London, 1979); see also Suzanne Berger (ed.), *Organising Interests in Western Europe* (Cambridge University Press, Cambridge, 1981). For a US survey see Jeffrey M. Berry, *The Interest Group Society* (Little, Brown & Co., Boston, 1984).

6   Birch, op. cit., 145.

7   Beer, op. cit.

8   Wyn Grant, 'Insider groups, outsider groups and interest group strategies in Britain', University of Warwick, *Working Paper* (19), May 1978.

9   See report in *The Times*, 20 February 1984, concerning Ramblers Association action protesting against BR plans to close the Settle to Carlisle line.

10   Minutes of Evidence, Social Services Committee, 3 March 1982, H.C. 26 of 1981–2, xiii.

11   *The Economist*, 3 December 1983, 61; 21 January 1984, 21; and 11 February 1984, 26–7.

12   See, for example, *The Times*, 20 February 1984, for a report of a Low Pay Unit study which characterizes fringe benefits as an 'inefficient and inequitable way of rewarding people [which] should be brought under tight control'.

13   *The Times*, 13 January 1984.

14   *The Guardian*, 17 February 1984.

15   *The Times*, 21 February 1984.

16   Report of the 114th Annual Trades Union Congress, Brighton, 6–10 September 1982.

17   For a study of this process in one policy area see Stuart Haywood and David J. Hunter, 'Consultative process in health policy in the United Kingdom: a view from the centre', *Public Administration*, 69, summer 1982, 143–62.

18   *The Times*, 8 February 1984.

19   Treasury evidence to Treasury Select Committee, 25 January 1983, H.C. 24 of 1982–3, v, 232.

20 John Kay and C. Sandler, 'The taxation of husband and wife: a view of the debate on the Green Paper', *Fiscal Studies*, 3 (3), 1982, 174–5.

21 Treasury evidence, op. cit.

22 Tenth Report from the Expenditure Committee, Policy Making in the Department of Education and Science, H.C. 621 of 1975–6. Evidence session 10 November 1975, 15.

23 ibid.

24 Evidence session 15 December 1975, 103.

25 Second Report from the Environment Committee, H.C. 217 of 1981–2.

26 Tenth Report from the Expenditure Committee, op. cit., H.C. 621 of 1975–6. Evidence session 19 January 1976.

27 Richardson and Jordan, op. cit., ch. 3.

28 Joel Barnett, *Inside the Treasury* (André Deutsch, London, 1982), 49.

29 John Biffen, 'The government view', in Dermot Englefield (ed.), *The Commons Select Committees: Catalysts for Progress?* (Longman, Harlow, 1984).

30 David Lea, 'A trade unionist view', in Englefield, op. cit.

31 On 'encompassing' organizations see, for example, Colin Crouch, 'New thinking on pluralism', *Political Quarterly*, 54, 1983, 363–74.

32 Beer, op. cit., 211–12.

33 Chi Square tests revealed no significant correlations between positive and negative respondents to Questions 2 and 4 and Question 16, parts (b), (c), (d) or (e).

34 For a discussion of the potential of this approach (albeit in an American context) see Martha Derthick and Paul Quirk, *The Politics of Deregulation*, The Brookings Institution, Washington, 1985.

CHAPTER 6: POLICY MAKING IN A MULTI-PARTY PARLIAMENT

1 Treasury Committee, The Form of the Estimates, H.C. 325 of 1980–1; Budgetary Reform, H.C. 137 of 1981–2; Select Committee on Procedure (Supply), H.C. 118 of 1980–1; Select Committee on Procedure (Finance), H.C. 24 of 1982–3.

2 Quoted in *The Economist*, 14 August 1982, 12. This speech is extensively quoted in *Politics and Industry – The Great Mismatch*, Hansard Society, London, 1980.

3 R. R. Neild and T. Ward, *The Measurement and Reform of the Budgetary Process* (Institute for Fiscal Studies, Heinemann Educational Books, London, 1978).

4 *The Economist*, 26 July 1980.

5 Budgetary Reform, H.C. 137 of 1981–2, Annex 2, Budgetary Practice in Other Countries, xxxii–xli.

6 ibid., 163, para. 2.

7 ibid., 21, Q. 63.

8 ibid., xviii, paras 2–31.

9 See for example, evidence by Joel Barnett and Sir Leo Pliatzky to Select Committee on Procedure (Supply), H.C. 325 of 1980–1.

10 Select Committee on Procedure (Finance), H.C. 24 of 1982–3, I, table B.

11 H.C. Debates, 6 December 1983, col. 285.

12 Professor Samuel Beer (*British Politics in the Collectivist Age*, Vintage Books,

New York, 1969, 15) cites parliamentarism as the decisive distinction between the 'Old Tory' and the 'Old Whig' regimes:

> Whether in making laws or controlling the ministry, the House of Commons now had the role – consistently denied it by the Old Tory monarchs – of representing the community as a whole as well as its several parts. Now the members for Bristol, in Burke's famous words, were not only 'members for a rich commercial city', but also 'for the nation which however is itself a part of a great empire extended by our virtue and fortune to the farthest limits of the East and of the West'. Hence, parliament was not 'a congress of ambassadors from different and hostile interests, which interests each must maintain as an agent and advocate against other agents and advocates'. It was rather a 'deliberative assembly of one nation with one interest, that of the whole – where not local prejudices ought to guide but the general good resulting from the general reason of the whole'.
>
> What we may call the parliamentarism of the Old Whig conception consisted, first, in this notion of the Member of Parliament as the representative of the whole community as well as of its component interests. He performed this function in Parliament with his fellows by deliberating on the great questions of state. That is the second element in Old Whig parliamentarism: deliberation. It is, so to speak, a thought rather than a will theory of how the general good is arrived at. As Burke said to his constituents: 'If government were a matter of will upon any side, yours without question, ought to be superior. But government and legislation are matters of reason and judgement and not of inclination.' While a member ought to give 'great weight' to the wishes of his constituents he ought never to sacrifice to them 'his unbiased opinion, his mature judgement, his enlightened conscience.'

13 Geoffrey Marshall, 'What are constitutional conventions?' *Parliamentary Affairs*, 38 (1), winter 1985, 33–9; John E. Schwarz, 'Exploring a new role in policy making: the British House of Commons in the 1970s', *American Political Science Review*, 74 (1), 23–37. Also Samuel H. Beer, 'Votes of confidence in Britain', *George Washington Law Review*, 43 (2), 365–71.

14 Philip Norton, *The Constitution in Flux* (Martin Robertson, Oxford, 1982), chs 1 and 2. Also John P. Mackintosh, *The British Cabinet*, 3rd edn, (Stevens & Sons, London, 1977), ch. 1.

15 To deal with existing select committees, the civil service has prepared a 'Memorandum of guidance for officials appearing before select committees'. The Liaison Committee comments:

> Anything which qualifies a committee's ability to find things out must be of concern to the House; the memorandum for instance tells civil servants not to disclose the advice given to Ministers, or details of consultation between Ministers, or inter-departmental exchanges. The Liaison Committee and the individual committees naturally gave close attention to the revised version of the Memorandum which was issued in May 1980, and they found that it was on the whole slightly less restrictive than its predecessor. It is a fair statement of a not very satisfactory situation.
>
> (First Report of Liaison Committee, H.C. 92 of 1982–3, para. 46)

Individual reports probing committees' powers to obtain information include: 'The Provision of Information to Select Committee by Government Departments', Education, Science and Arts Committee, H.C. 606 of 1979–80; Welsh Affairs Committee, H.C. 64 of 1981–2, Q. 1448–1501. Transport Committee and CPRS report on railway electrification (H.C. 371 of 1981–2).

16 For a list of twenty-two important leaks from the Thatcher government in the 1979–83 period see *The Times*, 31 March 1984.

17 David Owen, *Face the Future* (Cape, London, 1981); Edmund Dell, 'Some reflections on Cabinet government by a former practitioner', *Public Administration Bulletin* (32), April 1980, 17–33.

18 Dell, op. cit., 23.

19 ibid., 23.

20 ibid., 25.

21 In passing, the new role of think-tanks as a conduit for the transmission of ideas into political life is worth noting. Mrs Thatcher's programme draws heavily on the work of the Centre for Policy Studies and, more generally, on the persistent advocacy of the Institute for Economic Affairs. The challenge to present budget arrangements originally emerged from the Institute for Fiscal Studies. The role of think-tanks is an organizational development of some significance in British politics. Think-tanks were originally invented to serve the needs of the egalitarian, fragmented politics of the United States. They reflect the fluid cultural base of American politics. They reflect the weakness of her parties, the porousness of her policy-making structures, and the need for special organizations to draw ideologues and intellectuals into partisan debate. Britain has witnessed a flowering of think-tanks over the past eight years. The Conservative neo-liberal programme continues to be formulated not in the Conservative research department but in the Centre for Policy Studies. At least three other neo-liberal think-tanks have been established (the Social Affairs Unit, the Adam Smith Institute, the Institute of Directors Research Unit). Political and Economic Planning has achieved new financial security as the Policy Studies Institute. The Trade Policy Research Centre has been established. Social Science Research Council funds have been used to create a number of applied policy research centres located within universities.

For a discussion of the role of 'think-tanks' see my *An Australian Think Tank?* (University of New South Wales Press, Sydney, 1981). Also James Q. Wilson, 'Policy intellectuals and public policy', *Public Interest*, 64, summer 1981, 31–46.

22 'In democratic countries knowledge of how to combine is the mother of all other forms of knowledge; on its progress depends that of all the others.' A. de Tocqueville, *Democracy in America* (Anchor Books, New York, 1969), 517.

23 *The Times*, 13 June 1984 (editorial).

24 Charles Lindblom, *The Intelligence of Democracy* (The Free Press, New York, 1965).

25 Lindblom, op. cit., especially ch. 14, 'Social agreement'. The normative basis of this argument can be traced to J.-J. Rousseau, *The Social Contract*. A prudential version (which indeed proceeds from a normative basis the opposite of Rousseau's) is to be found in Aristotle's *Politics*, book 3, ch. 1.

26 ibid., ch. 18, 'The public interest and group interests'.

27 ibid., 220–1.

28 ibid., 210–11. Lindblom's third principle is: 'The need for allies is an especially powerful motivation towards agreement in partisan mutual adjustment.'
29 ibid., 209.
30 ibid., 208.
31 ibid., 211.
32 ibid., 216.
33 For a fuller exposition of the possibilities summarized in the following paragraphs see my 'The assets test: a case study in the politics of expenditure control', *Australian Journal of Public Administration*, 44 (3), September 1985, 197–223.
34 For example, the main independent social work magazine *Community Care* gave full coverage to the Social Services Committee's weekly evidence sessions on children in care between November 1982 and April 1983. The survey of interest groups participating in select committee inquiries (reported in chapter 5) established that 43 per cent of respondents (N = 127) placed articles in their newsletters or journals on their participation in the inquiry; 76 per cent reported the committee's findings.
35 Renee Loth, 'Coalition, communication and consensus', *John F. Kennedy School of Government Bulletin*, spring 1984. This article describes the deliberate programme of outreach to Bay State interest groups followed by the staff of Governor Michael Dukakis gaining legislative endorsement for a new, broad-based tax proposal. For a discussion of the role of a parallel function in private sector management – public affairs management – see publication series of Public Affairs Division, *The Conference Board*, New York. For studies that explore the membership and patterns of power within particular policy communities see David Marsh (ed.), *Pressure Politics: Interest Groups in Britain* (Junction Books, London, 1983); L. J. Sharpe, 'Central co-ordination and the policy network', *Political Studies*, 33, 1985, 361–87.
36 Thomas G. Moore in an unpublished paper on 'Airline deregulation in the United States' (Australian Graduate School of Management Workshop, 24 May 1984), points to the creative possibilities in coalition building. He lists the following interest groups as, amongst others, members of the Ad Hoc Committee on Airline Deregulation: American Conservative Union, Americans for Democratic Action, Common Cause, Congress Watch, Libertarian Advocate, National Consumers Congress, National Taxpayers Union, Public Interest Economics Centre, Sears Roebuck and Co., American Association of Retired Persons.
37 Stephen Breyer in 'Analyzing regulatory failure: mismatches, less restrictive alternatives, and reform', *Harvard Law Review*, 92 (3), 605–9, points to the key role of congressional committee hearings in achieving airline deregulation. He cites three benefits from such hearings:

> First they acted as a catalyst in forcing other agencies of government to focus upon the problem and develop a policy position. . . .
>
> The hearings provided the opportunity for those urging reform to contact a wide range of executive and administrative officials; the hearings helped develop a network of persons throughout the government who would influence policy and help each other in the movement for reform. The hearings also acted as a catalyst with respect to the regulated industry. The threat of hearings forced each airline to reassess its position, to develop new information, and to put its own bureaucracy to work to develop and assess alternatives. . . .

Second, the hearings served to gather the detailed factual information used to write a comprehensive report. The report did not need to produce empirical information that would definitively resolve every issue, but it had to be comprehensive. . . .

The empirical effort had to determine who is actually being helped or hurt by the programme in order to evaluate the arguments made in its favour. . . .

Each of the many major objections to reform had to be treated in a similar manner. While the hearings could not definitively answer all the questions raised, they could investigate them in detail, marshall the relevant information, and base policy recommendations on that work.

The third function served by the hearings was as a drama, which helped mobilize public and political support for regulatory reform. To analogize a legislative hearing to a judicial or fact-finding hearing is to miss an essential difference: the legislative hearing has an educational objective and a political purpose. A congressional hearing moves on a more dramatic or educational oral level which should illustrate the issues in a way that is both comprehensible and interesting to the general public. . . .

It is crucial to understand that both the oral, dramatic level and the written detailed factual level of the hearings are needed. . . .

The experience suggests that Congress, and more particularly a congressional committee, is an effective institution for bringing about major individual programmes of substantive regulatory reform.

38   Hugh Heclo, 'Issue networks and the executive establishment', in Anthony King (ed.), *The New American Political System*, American Enterprise Institute, Washington, 1978; S. Huntington, 'The democratic distemper', *Public Interest* (41), 1975, 9–38 and *American Politics: The Promise of Disharmony* (Harvard University Press, Cambridge, Mass., 1982). Hugh Heclo's reflections are reviewed perceptively by Grant Jordan, who finds more power at the centre than Heclo allows ('Iron triangles, woolly corporatism and elastic nets: images of the policy process', *Journal of Public Policy*, 1 (1), 1981, 95–123).

39   Martha Derthick and Paul Quirk, *The Politics of Deregulation* (The Brookings Institution, Washington, 1985); Arthur Maass, *Congress and the Common Good* (Basic Books, New York, 1983).

40   Frank H. Knight, 'The planful act: the possibilities and limitations of collective rationality', in *Freedom and Reform: Essays in Economics and Social Philosophy* (Liberty Press, Indianapolis, 1982) 399.

41   James Q. Wilson, writing of when the departmental select committees were established in 1979, comments:

It is ironic to note the stirrings among British politicians who would like to see their system, which stifles the backbench member of Commons, changed into something more 'American'. They may suppose that they can combine the advantages of strong party government with the advantages of powerful legislative committees and more autonomous legislators, but I suspect they are wrong.

('American politics, then and now', *Commentary*, 67 (2) February 1979, 46)

42   Martin Birch, 'Mrs. Thatcher's approach to leadership in government: 1979–June 1983', *Parliamentary Affairs*, 36 (4), 1983, 339–416; Peter Riddell, *The Thatcher*

Government (Martin Robertson, Oxford, 1983); Geoffrey K. Fry, 'The development of the Thatcher Government's "Grand Strategy" for the civil service: a public policy perspective', *Public Administration*, 62, autumn 1984, 322–35.

43 Norman Strauss, article in *The Times*, 28 April 1984; Sir John Hoskyns, 'Conservatism is not enough', *Political Quarterly*, 55 (1), 1984, 3–17.

44 For appraisals of Mrs Thatcher's achievements see Rob Ellis, 'Fiscal policy: rhetoric and reality', *Economic Affairs*, April–June 1985; Anthony King, 'Governmental responses to budget scarcity', *Policy Studies Journal*, 13 (3), March 1985, 476–93.

45 *Parliamentary Democracy and the Labour Movement*, published by the Campaign Group of Labour MPs.

46 'Reshaping Britain, a programme of social and economic reform', *Political and Economic Planning*, 1974, ch. V.

47 Philippe Schmitter and Gerhard Lehmbruch (eds), *Trends Towards Corporatist Intermediation* (Sage Publications, Beverly Hills, 1979).

48 Peter J. Katzenstein, *Corporatism and Change: Austria, Switzerland and the Politics of Industry* (Cornell University Press, Ithaca, 1984).

49 Mancur Olson, *The Logic of Collective Action* (Harvard University Press, Cambridge, Mass., 1965).

50 Ivor Crewe and Bo Särlvik, *Decade of Dealignment* (Cambridge University Press, Cambridge, 1983).

51 Norman St John Stevas, 'Government by discussion', in J. R. Nethercote (ed.), *Parliament and Bureaucracy* (Hale & Iremonger, Sydney, 1982).

52 *The Times*, 7 February 1984, reports Labour plans to repeal Tory legislation concerned with rate capping, abolition of the GLC and privatization of British Aerospace; also 1979 Education Act; 1981 British Nationality Act; 1984 Trades Union Bill.

53 *The Economist*, 21 February 1984, reports a meeting 'to plan Mrs. Thatcher's third term' between working groups from the Centre for Policy Studies and the Prime Minister. None of these concern the political structure.

54 Evidence of P. Mountfield, Budgetary Reform, H.C. 137 of 1981–2.

55 See for example, speeches by Messrs du Cann, Higgins, Bray and Beaumont-Dark in the debate on the Report of the Select Committee on Procedure (Finance), H.C. Debates, 6 December 1983, cols 246–93.

56 At time of writing (early 1985) the Select Committees have not exhibited any reluctance to tackle politically controversial issues. Bipartisan committees have issued trenchant reports criticizing the government's decision to ban unions from GCHQ, increase electricity prices and cut steel capacity further. The Treasury Committee staged an inquiry in Autumn 1984 into the government's Public Expenditure White Paper. It issued a report critical of the government's failure to meet its commitments to reduce public expenditure. It issued a further report on the presentation of financial information to the Commons. ('The Structure and Form of Financial Documents Presented to Parliament', H.C. 110 of 1983–4). Use of Estimates Days Procedures will be a guide to parliamentary support for extension of committee powers.

57 Ian Bradley, 'The strange rebirth of liberal England', *New University Quarterly*, summer 1981, 267–79. Dan Usher, *The Economic Prerequisites for Democracy* (Basil Blackwell, Oxford, 1981).

The Economist, 21 April 1984, reports papers from the Adam Smith Institute and the Institute of Economic Affairs strongly critical of the failure of the Thatcher government to live up to its neo-liberal rhetoric on trade policy and public expenditure.

58 J. S. Mill, *On Liberty* (Library of Liberal Arts edn, Indianapolis, 1980). In reviewing *Democracy in America* Mill comments, 'Commercial people will be mean and slavish wherever public spirit is not cultivated by an extensive participation of the people in the business of government in detail.' But Mill's romanticism – at least in the former work – is itself critically assessed in Gertrude Himmelfarb, *On Liberty and Liberalism* (Alfred A. Knopf, New York, 1974).

59 For a discussion of recent voter volatility and party decomposition in Britain see: Ivor Crewe, 'The electorate: partisan dealignment ten years on', *West European Politics*, VI, 1983, 183–215; also 'Why Labour lost the British election', *Public Opinion*, 6 (3), July 1983; also Ivor Crewe and Bo Särlvik, *Decade of Dealignment* (Cambridge University Press, Cambridge, 1983). Samuel H. Beer, 'Politics without precedent', *Times Literary Supplement*, 3 June 1983, 563. Mark W. Franklin, 'How the decline of class voting opened the way to radical change in British politics', *British Journal of Political Science*, 14, 1984, 483–508.

Bibliography

Amery, L. S., *Thoughts on the Constitution*, Oxford University Press, London, 1964.

Ashford, Douglas, *Policy and Politics in Britain: The Limits of Consensus*, Basil Blackwell, Oxford, 1981.

Atkinson, A. B., 'Taxation and social security: reflections on advising a House of Commons select committee', *Policy and Politics*, 12 (2), 1984, 107–18.

Bagehot, Walter, *The English Constitution*, Dolphin Books edn, Doubleday, New York.

—— 'Parliamentary reform', in the *Collected Works of Walter Bagehot*, ed. Norman St John Stevas, *The Economist*, London, 1974.

Barnett, Joel, *Inside the Treasury*, André Deutsch, London, 1982.

Beer, Samuel H., *Britain Against Itself*, W. W. Norton, New York, 1982.

—— *British Politics in the Collectivist Age*, Vintage Books, New York, 1969.

—— 'British pressure groups revisited: pluralistic stagnation from the 50s to the 70s', *Public Administration Bulletin* (32), April 1980, 13.

—— 'Politics without precedent', *Times Literary Supplement*, 3 June 1983, 563.

—— 'Votes of confidence in Britain', *George Washington Law Review*, 43 (2), 1975, 365–71.

Benn, Tony, 'The nine lives of a Cabinet Minister', *The Guardian*, 11 February 1978.

Berger, Suzanne (ed.), *Organising Interests in Western Europe*, Cambridge University Press, Cambridge, 1981.

Berrill, Sir Kenneth, 'The role of the Central Policy Review Staff', *Management Service in Government*, 32 (3), 1977, 121–6.

Berry, Jeffrey M., *The Interest Group Society*, Little, Brown & Co., Boston, 1984.

Biffen, John, 'The government view', in Dermot Englefield (ed.), *The Commons Select Committees: Catalysts for Progress?* (Longman, Harlow, 1984).

Birch, Anthony, 'Overload, ungovernability and delegitimation: the theories and the British case', *British Journal of Political Science*, 14, 1984, 135–60.

Birch, Martin, 'Mrs. Thatcher's approach to leadership in government: 1979–June 1983', *Parliamentary Affairs*, 36 (4), 1983, 339–416.

Blowers, Andrew, 'Master of fate or victim of circumstance: the exercise of corporate power in environmental policy making', *Policy and Politics*, 11 (4), 1983, 393–415.

Bogdanor, Vernon, *Multi-Party Politics and the Constitution*, Cambridge University Press, Cambridge, 1983.

Borthwick, R. L., 'The Defence Committee: can it hope to affect policy?', in Dilys M. Hill (ed.), *Parliamentary Select Committees in Action: A Symposium*, Strathclyde Papers on Government and Politics (24), 145.

Boyne, George, 'The privatisation of public housing', *Political Quarterly*, 55 (2), 1984, 180–7.

Bradley, Ian, 'The strange rebirth of liberal England', *New University Quarterly*, summer 1981, 267–79.

Breyer, Stephen, 'Analyzing regulatory failure: mismatches, less restrictive alternatives, and reform', *Harvard Law Review*, 92 (3), January 1979, 605–9.

Briggs, Asa, *Victorian People*, Pelican Books, Middlesex, 1982.

Brittan, Samuel, 'The economic contradictions of democracy', *British Journal of Political Science*, 5, 1975, 129–59.

—— 'The politics and economics of privatisation', *Political Quarterly*, 55 (2), 1984, 109–28.

—— *The Role and Limits of Government*, Maurice Temple Smith, London, 1983.

—— 'The unradical British right', *Australian Financial Review*, 27 November 1984, 13.

Bruce-Gardyne, Jock and Lawson, Nigel, *The Power Game*, Archon Books, Hamden, Connecticut, 1976.

Budget Options in 1984, Institute for Fiscal Studies Report Series No. 7, 1984.

Butler, David, *Governing Without a Majority*, Collins, London, 1983.

Butt, Ronald, 'A thinking centre for government', *The Times*, 26 January 1984.

Campaign Group of Labour MPs, *Parliamentary Democracy and the Labour Movement*.

Cawson, Alan, 'Pluralism, corporatism and the role of the state', *Government and Opposition*, 13 (2), 1978, 178–98.

Churchill, Sir Winston, *Parliamentary Government and the Economic Problem*, Romanes Lectures, Clarendon Press, Oxford, 1930.

Conservative Party (Great Britain), *1979 Tory Manifesto*.

Crewe, Ivor, 'The electorate: partisan dealignment ten years on', *West European Politics*, VI, 1983, 183–215.

—— 'Why Labour lost the British election', *Public Opinion*, 6 (3), July 1983.

—— and Särlvik, Bo, *Decade of Dealignment: The Conservative Victory of 1979 and Electoral Trends in the 1970s*, Cambridge University Press, Cambridge, 1983.

Crick, Bernard, *Reform of Parliament*, Anchor Books, New York, 1965.

—— 'Whither parliamentary reform?', in A. H. Hanson and Bernard Crick (eds), *The Commons in Transition*, Fontana/Collins, London, 1970.

Crossman, R. H. S., *Inside View*, Jonathan Cape, London, 1972.

Crouch, Colin, 'New thinking on pluralism', *Political Quarterly*, 54, 1983, 363–74.

—— 'Pluralism and corporatism: a rejoinder', *Political Studies*, 31, 1983, 452–60.

—— (ed.), *State and Economy in Contemporary Capitalism*, Croom Helm, London, 1979.

Davies, Ann, *Reformed Select Committees: The First Year*, Outer Circle Policy Unit, London, 1980.

Dell, Edmund, 'Some reflections on Cabinet government by a former practitioner', *Public Administration Bulletin* (32), April 1980, 17–33.

Derthick, Martha and Quirk, Paul, *The Politics of Deregulation*, The Brookings Institution, Washington, 1985.

Douglas, James, 'The overloaded crown', *British Journal of Political Science*, 6, 1976, 483–505.

Drewry, Gavin, 'The National Audit Act – half a loaf?' *Public Law*, winter 1983, 532.

—— 'The new select committees – a constitutional non-event?' in Dilys M. Hill (ed.), *Parliamentary Select Committees in Action: A Symposium*, Strathclyde Papers on Government and Politics (24), 1984.

du Cann, Edward, *Parliament and the Purse Strings*, The Conservative Political Centre, May 1977.

—— 'Parliamentary select committees and democracy', *Public Money*, June 1981.

Ellis, Rob, 'Fiscal policy: rhetoric and reality', *Economic Affairs*, April–June 1985.

Else, P. K. and Marshall, G. P., 'The unplanning of public expenditure: recent problems in expenditure planning and the consequences of cash limits', *Public Administration*, 59, autumn 1981, 253–79.

Englefield, Dermot (ed.), *The Commons Select Committees: Catalysts for Progress?* (Longman, Harlow, 1984).

The Federalist Papers, Modern Library College Edition (1961), New York.

Franklin, Mark W., 'How the decline of class voting opened the way to radical change in British politics', *British Journal of Political Science*, 14, 1984, 483–508.

Fry, Geoffrey K., 'The development of the Thatcher Government's "Grand Strategy" for the civil service: a public policy perspective', *Public Administration*, 62, autumn 1984, 322–35.

Garner, M. R., 'The financing of the nationalised industries', *Public Administration*, 59, winter 1981.

Gash, Norman, *Politics in the Age of Peel*, Longman, London, 1953.

Gelb, Joyce, 'Feminism in Britain: the politics of isolation', paper delivered to the 1984 annual meeting of the American Political Science Association.

George, Bruce and Woodward, Michael, 'The Foreign Affairs Committee and the patriation of the Canadian Constitution', in Dilys M. Hill (ed.), *Parliamentary Select Committees in Action: A Symposium*, Strathclyde Papers on Government and Politics (24), 1984.

—— and Evans, Barbara, 'Parliamentary reform – the internal view', in David Judge (ed.), *The Politics of Parliamentary Reform*, Heinemann Educational Books, London, 1983.

Grainger, J. K., *Character and Style in English Politics*, Cambridge University Press, Cambridge, 1979.

Grant, Wyn, 'Insider groups, outsider groups and interest group strategies in Britain', University of Warwick, *Working Paper* (19), May 1978.

—— *The Political Economy of Industrial Policy*, Butterworth, London, 1982.

—— and Wilks, Stephen, 'British industrial policy: structural change, policy inertia', *Journal of Public Policy*, 3 (1), February 1983, 13–28.

Gray, Andrew and Jenkins, Bill, 'Policy analysis in British central government: the experience of PAR', *Public Administration*, 60, winter 1982, 429–50.

Griffith, J. A. G., 'The Constitution and the Commons', in *Parliament and the Executive*, Royal Institute of Public Administration, London, 1982.

Hailsham, Lord, 'Elective dictatorship', *The Listener*, 21 October 1976.

Haywood, Stuart and Hunter, David J., 'Consultative process in health policy in the United Kingdom: a view from the centre', *Public Administration*, 69, summer 1982, 143–62.

Heclo, Hugh, 'Issue networks and the executive establishment' in Anthony King (ed.), *The New American Political System*, American Enterprise Institute, Washington, 1978.

—— and Wildavsky, Aaron, *The Private Government of Public Money*, 2nd edn, Macmillan, London, 1981.

Hill, Andrew and Whichelow, Anthony, *What's Wrong with Parliament?* Penguin Books, London, 1964.

Hill, Dilys (ed.), *Parliamentary Select Committees in Action: A Symposium*, Strathclyde Papers on Government and Politics (24), 1984.

Hills, John, 'A co-operative and constructive relationship? The Treasury response to its Select Committee 1979–82', *Fiscal Studies*, 4 (1), March 1983, 3–9.

Himmelfarb, Gertrude, *On Liberty and Liberalism*, Alfred A. Knopf, New York, 1974.

Hoskyns, Sir John, 'Conservatism is not enough', *Political Quarterly*, 55 (1), 1984, 3–17.

—— 'Whitehall and Westminster: an outsider's view', *Fiscal Studies*, 3 (3), 1932, 162–73.

Hunt, Lord Crowther, 'Whitehall – the balance of power', *The Listener*, 6 January 1977, 10–11.

Huntington, S., *American Politics: The Promise of Disharmony*, Harvard University Press, Cambridge, Mass., 1982.

—— 'The democratic distemper', *Public Interest* (41), 1975, 9–38.

Jenkins, Roy, *British Government and Politics: Some Reflections*, The Royal Institution, London, 24 November 1977.

Jenkins, Simon, 'The "Star Chamber", PESC and the Cabinet', *Political Quarterly*, 56 (2), April 1985, 113–21.

Johnson, Nevil, 'An academic's view', in Dermot Englefield (ed.), *The Commons Select Committees: Catalysts for Progress?* Longman, Harlow, 1984.

Jones, J. Barry, 'Limited power and potential infuence: the Committee on Welsh Affairs and the policy process', in Dilys Hill (ed.), *Parliamentary Select Committees in Action: A Symposium*, Strathclyde Papers on Government and Politics (24), 1984.

Jordan, Grant, 'Iron triangles, woolly corporatism and elastic nets: images of the policy process', *Journal of Public Policy*, 1 (1), 1981, 95–123.

—— 'Parliament under pressure', *Political Quarterly*, 56 (2), April 1985, 174–82.

Judge, David, 'Ministerial responsibility', *The House Magazine*, 26 November 1982, 4–6.

Katzenstein, Peter J., *Corporatism and Change: Austria, Switzerland and the Politics of Industry*, Cornell University Press, Ithaca, 1984.

Kay, John and Sandler, C., 'The taxation of husband and wife: a view of the debate on the Green Paper', *Fiscal Studies*, 3 (3), 1982, 174–5.

Kemp, Peter, 'A civil servant's view', in Dermot Englefield (ed.), *The Commons Select Committees: Catalysts for Progress?* (Longman, Harlow, 1984).

King, Anthony, 'Governmental responses to budget scarcity', *Policy Studies Journal*, 13 (3), March 1985, 476–93.

Klein, Rudolf, *The Politics of the National Health Service*, Longman, Harlow, 1983.

Knight, Frank H., 'The planful act: the possibilities and limitations of collective rationality', in *Freedom and Reform: Essays in Economics and Social Philosophy*, Liberty Press, Indianapolis, 1982.

Laski, Harold, *A Grammar of Politics*, George Allen & Unwin, London, 1948.

Lea, David, 'A trade unionist view', in Dermot Englefield (ed.), *The Commons Select Committees: Catalysts for Progress?* (Longman, Harlow, 1984).

Lehner, Franz and Schubert, Klaus, 'Party government and the political control of public policy', *European Journal of Political Research*, 12, 1984, 131–46.

Likierman, Andrew, 'Management information for ministers: the MINIS system in the Department of the Environment', *Public Administration*, 60 (2), 1982, 127–63.

—— and Vass, Peter, *Structure and Form of Government Expenditure Reports: Proposals for Reform*, Association of Certified Accountants and London Business School, 1984.

Lindblom, Charles E., 'Decision making in taxation and expenditures' in *Public Finances: Needs Sources and Utilisation*, National Bureau of Economic Research Conference Series 12, Princeton University Press, Princeton, 1961.

—— *The Intelligence of Democracy*, The Free Press, New York, 1965.

Loth, Renee, 'Coalition, communication and consensus', *John F. Kennedy School of Government Bulletin*, spring 1984.

Lowe, David, 'Legislative oversight and the House of Commons new committee system', paper delivered to 1981 meeting of the American Political Science Association.

Lowe, Philip and Goyder, Jane, *Environmental Groups in Politics*, George Allen & Unwin, London, 1983.

Maass, Arthur, *Congress and the Common Good*, Basic Books, New York, 1983.

McCarthy, M. A., 'Trade unions, the family lobby and the Callaghan Government – the case of child benefits', *Policy and Politics*, 11 (4), 1983, 461–85.

McDonald, James and Fry, G. K., 'Policy Planning Units – ten years on', *Public Administration*, 58, winter 1980, 421–37.

Mackintosh, John P., *The British Cabinet*, 3rd edn, Stevens & Sons, London, 1977.

Marsh, David (ed.), *Pressure Politics: Interest Groups in Britain*, Junction Books, London, 1983.

—— and Grant, Wyn, 'Tri-partism: reality or myth?', *Government and Opposition*, 12, 1977, 194–211.

Marsh, Ian, 'The assets test: a case study in the politics of expenditure control', *Australian Journal of Public Administration*, 44 (3), September 1985.

—— *An Australian Think Tank?* University of New South Wales Press, Sydney, 1981.

Marshall, Geoffrey, 'What are constitutional conventions?', *Parliamentary Affairs*, 38 (1), winter 1985, 33–9.

Mill, J. S., *On Liberty*, Library of Liberal Arts edn, Indianapolis, 1980.

Moore, Thomas G., 'Airline deregulation in the United States' (unpublished paper), Australian Graduate School of Management Workshop, 24 May 1984.

Moran, Michael, *The Politics of Industrial Relations: The Origins, Life and Death of the 1971 Industrial Relations Act*, Macmillan, London, 1977.

Mosley, P., 'The Treasury Committee and the making of economic policy', *Political Quarterly*, 52 (3), July–September 1981, 348–55.

Neild, R. R. and Ward, T., *The Measurement and Reform of the Budgetary Process*, Institute for Fiscal Studies, Heinemann Educational Books, London, 1978.

Norton, Philip, *The Constitution in Flux*, Martin Robertson, Oxford, 1982.

Offe, Claus, 'Ungovernability: the renaissance of Conservative theories of crisis', in *Contradictions of the Welfare State*, Hutchinson, London, 1984.

O'Higgins, Michael, 'Privatisation and social security', *Political Quarterly*, 55 (2), 1984, 133–5.

Olson, Mancur, *The Logic of Collective Action*, Harvard University Press, Cambridge, Mass., 1965.
—— *The Rise and Decline of Nations*, Yale University Press, New Haven, 1983.
Owen, David, 'Agenda for competition with compassion', *Economic Affairs*, 4 (1), 1984, 26–34.
—— *Face the Future*, Cape, London, 1981.
—— 'We have had enough of conservatism with a small "c"', *Political Quarterly*, 55 (1), 1984, 17–23.
Panitch, Leo, 'The development of corporatism in liberal democracy', in Philippe C. Schmitter and Gerhard Lehmbruch (eds), *Trends Towards Corporatist Intermediation*, Sage Publications, Beverly Hills, 1979.
—— 'Recent theorisations of corporatism: reflections on a growth industry', *British Journal of Sociology*, 31 (2), 1980, 159–84.
Pliatzky, Sir Leo, *Getting and Spending*, Basil Blackwell, Oxford, 1982.
—— 'The Whitehall machine', *Political Quarterly*, 55 (1), 1984, 24–9.
Politics and Industry – The Great Mismatch, Hansard Society, London, 1980.
Pollitt, Christopher, 'The Central Policy Review Staff 1970–1974', *Public Administration*, 52, winter 1974, 375–91.
Powell, Enoch, 'The menu and the bill', *The House Magazine*, 5 March 1982.
Pym, Francis, *The Politics of Consent*, Hamish Hamilton, London, 1984.
'Reshaping Britain, a programme of social and economic reform', *Political and Economic Planning*, 1974.
Richardson, J. J. and Jordan, A. G., *Governing Under Pressure: The Policy Process in a Post-Parliamentary Democracy*, Martin Robertson, Oxford, 1979.
Riddell, Peter, *The Thatcher Government*, Martin Robertson, Oxford, 1983.
Robinson, Ann, 'Monitoring the economy – the work of the Treasury and Civil Service Committee', in Dilys M. Hill (ed.), *Parliamentary Select Committees in Action: A Symposium*, Strathclyde Papers on Government and Politics (24), 1984.
—— 'The myth of central control', *The Listener*, 17 June 1982, 9–10.
—— *Parliament and Public Spending*, Heinemann, London, 1978.
—— and Sandford, Cedric, *Tax Policy Making in the United Kingdom: A Study of Rationality, Ideology and Politics*, Heinemann Educational Books, London, 1983.
—— and Ysander, Bengt-Christer, *Public Budgeting Under Uncertainty: Three Studies*, The Industrial Institute of Economic and Social Research, Stockholm, 1983.
Rothschild, Lord, 'A useful exercise with interest', *The Times*, 2 July 1983.
St John Stevas, Norman, 'Government by discussion', in J. R. Nethercote (ed.), *Parliament and Bureaucracy*, Hale & Iremonger, Sydney, 1982.
Schmitter, Philippe C. and Lehmbruch, Gerhard (eds), *Trends Towards Corporatist Intermediation*, Sage Publications, Beverly Hills, 1979.
—— and —— *Patterns of Corporatist Policy Making*, Sage Publications, Beverly Hills, 1980.
Schumpeter, Joseph A., *Capitalism, Socialism and Democracy*, Harper Colophon Books, New York, 1976.
Schwarz, John E., 'Exploring a new role in policy making: the British House of Commons in the 1970s', *American Political Science Review*, 74 (1), 1980, 23–37.
Sheldon, Robert, 'Public sector auditing and the United Kingdom Committee of Public Accounts in 1984', *The Parliamentarian*, spring 1984, 91–8.

Specialist Committees in the British Parliament: The Experience of a Decade, Political and Economic Planning, June 1976.

Stacey, Frank, *British Government 1966–1975: Years of Reform*, Oxford University Press, Oxford, 1975.

de Tocqueville, A., *Democracy in America*, Anchor Books, New York, 1969.

Usher, Dan, *The Economic Prerequisites for Democracy*, Basil Blackwell, Oxford, 1981.

Walkland, S. A., 'The politics of parliamentary reform', *Parliamentary Affairs*, 29 (2), 1976, 190–210.

—— and Gamble, A. M., *The British Party System and Economic Policy, 1945–1983*, Clarendon Press, Oxford, 1983.

—— and Ryle, Michael, *The Commons in the Seventies*, Fontana, London, 1977.

—— and —— *The Commons Today*, Fontana, London, 1981.

Ward, Terry, 'Cash planning', *Public Administration*, 61 (1), 1983, 85–90.

Wass, Sir Douglas, 'The Civil Service at the Cross Roads', *Political Quarterly*, 56 (3), 1985, 227–42.

—— 'The 1983 Reith Lectures', *The Listener*, 24 November 1983, 19–25; 8 December 1983, 21–7; 15 December 1983, 12–17.

Webb, Sydney and Webb, Beatrice, *A Constitution for the Socialist Commonwealth of Great Britain*, Cambridge University Press, Cambridge, 1975.

Whiteley, P. and Winyard, S., 'Influencing social policy: the effectiveness of the poverty lobby in Britain', *Journal of Social Policy*, 12 (1), 1983, 1–27.

—— and —— 'The origins of the new poverty lobby', *Political Studies*, 32, 1984, 32–54.

Wildavsky, A., *Speaking Truth to Power: The Art and Craft of Policy Analysis*, Little, Brown & Co., Boston, 1979.

Williams, Shirley, *Politics is for People*, Harvard University Press, Cambridge, Mass., 1981.

Wilson, James Q., 'American politics, then and now', *Commentary*, 67 (2), February 1979, 39–46.

——'Policy intellectuals and public policy', *Public Interest*, 64, summer 1981, 31–46.

Winkler, J. T., 'Corporatism', *Archiv European Sociology*, 17, 1976, 100–36.

Young, Hugo and Sloman, Ann, *But Chancellor: An Enquiry into the Treasury*, BBC Publications, London, 1984.

Index